The Information State in England

The Information State in England

The Central Collection of Information on Citizens since 1500

Edward Higgs

First published 2004 by
PALGRAVE MACMILLAN
Houndmills, Basingstoke, Hampshire, England RG21 6XS
175 Fifth Avenue, New York, N.Y. 10010 and
Companies and representatives throughout the world

PALGRAVE MACMILLAN is the global academic imprint of the Palgrave Macmillan division of St. Martin's Press, LLC and of Palgrave Macmillan Ltd. Macmillan® is a registered trademark in the United States, United Kingdom and other countries. Palgrave is a registered trademark in the European Union and other countries.

ISBN 0–333–92069–4 hardback
ISBN 0–333–92070–8 paperback

This book is printed on paper suitable for recycling and made from fully managed and sustained forest sources.

A catalogue record for this book is available from the British Library.

Library of Congress Cataloging-in-Publication Data

A catalog record for this book is available from the Library of Congress.

Higgs, Edward, 1952–
    The information state in England : the central collection of information on citizens since 1500 / Edward Higgs.
        p. cm.
    Includes bibliographical references and index.
    ISBN 0–333–92069–4 (hardback)—ISBN 0–333–92070–8 (pbk.)
        1. Public records – England – History. 2. Government information – England – History. 3. Public records – Wales – History. 4. Government information – Wales – History. I. Title.

JN329.P75.H54 2004
026'.42—dc22   2003061146

10 9 8 7 6 5 4 3 2 1
13 12 11 10 09 08 07 06 05 04

Printed in China

Contents

List of tables

Preface

This short book is an introduction to a very large subject – the story of how and why the central state in England and Wales has become involved in the collection and manipulation of information on private citizens. With the help of such information the modern central state can do things to, and with, the citizen body that would have seemed extraordinary in former periods. Indeed, it has been argued that it is just this capacity that sets modern states apart from all previous political formations. Modern states are 'Information States', and without information on citizens they would cease to function.

When using the term 'Information State' for the modern polity, I am not simply talking about a state that undertakes surveillance of its subjects or citizens. Every state that has ever existed has employed spies and collected intelligence. Instead, I want to examine that generalised and structured collection of information which is so typical of modern administration – the creation of routine administrative records, and of databases, paper and electronic, rather than the ad hoc activities of informers and 'spooks'. It is the ubiquity of contemporary state data gathering, and the way in which it collects information in a standardised form for ease of analysis and retrieval, that is so significant.

Historians, and I include myself here, have been fascinated with individual series of nominal records collected by the central state – tax lists, records of land ownership, population censuses, civil registration data, and social surveys. However, this is usually because we want to use these records as historical sources to study something else – population size, the wealth of the aristocracy, demographic trends, occupational structures, and so on. We have seldom sat back from the records to ask if there is any general pattern to the collection of such material by the state, and what this tells us about the nature of that entity and its changing relationship with society as a whole. This may reflect, in part, the tendency in modern historical scholarship towards chronological and subject specialisation that makes it difficult to see the 'bigger picture'. As I will argue below, the creation of the modern Information State in this country has been a long, complex and discontinuous process. The overall shape of this development can only be shown by taking a long chronological sweep, and juxtaposing some unlikely historical episodes.

Where historians have declined to tread, other disciplines have not been loath to enter, and we now possess a number of sociological works which foreground the development of information gathering on individuals as a key aspect of the growth of 'modernity' and of the modern state. As with much historical sociology, the results are stimulating and provocative but hardly satisfy the historian's desire to get to grips with the complexity of the 'patterned mess' that is the past. Sociologists might reply, of course, that they concentrate on the patterns and are more than happy to leave the mess to the historians. Nevertheless, it will be the contention of the present work that the sociologists who have written on the subject have not only misconstrued important events but have applied inappropriate, or at least incomplete, sociological models to the phenomena under analysis.

Any work that attempts to take a broad historical sweep (half a millennium in the present case), and to draw on differing disciplines, is likely to end up falling between a number of stools. The specialist historian is bound to spot factual blunders, failures to understand the proper context within which events took place, gaps in the literature, or important matters missed altogether. The sociologist will, no doubt, find the exposition of sociological theory somewhat crude. However, it seems worth while to attempt to give the general reader a broad overview of the subject, and to bring together the insights of differing disciplines. A work flawed by its ambitions but which stimulates discussion can be more productive than a perfect but limited study that leads nowhere. Given the period covered, this exercise must be based, to a considerable extent, on secondary sources, although much primary material has been consulted. Bringing together such material from different periods and sub-disciplines to bear on the subject of the Information State is a vital, initial stage in the elucidation of its history. It might also be useful to note at this point that my initial interest in the state's creation of nominal records sprang from work in neither discipline but from my activities as an archivist in the Public Record Office (PRO), the national archives, in London.

I should also emphasise that this is a study of state surveillance in one country, and, indeed, a study of one portion of the United Kingdom – England and Wales. This is not to disparage the history of Scotland and Ireland, merely a recognition that they are separate legal and administrative entities which have their own, distinct histories over the past 500 years. Ireland is important to my story, however, as a source of danger for the English state, and as a testbed for means of surveillance later used on the 'mainland'. A sociologist might complain that it is difficult to create general models of social processes on the basis of one, rather peculiar, state. However, the basis of all generalisations must be a comparison of differing societies, and this study can be taken as providing one element in any such comparative project. Also, sociologists who have written on the subject have tended to posit a connection between industrialisation and the growth of the Information State, and it seems not unreasonable, therefore, to examine this relationship in the case of the 'First Industrial Nation'.

In addition, this book is also concerned in the main with the central state's collection of personal information, that is, by agents directly responsible to the Crown, or to ministers of the Crown. The activities of local government will bulk large in its early sections and will then tend to fade from view. This partly reflects space constraints in a work of this length but also a basic argument that I want to make in this book. Many sociologists have tended to treat the central state as 'the' state, and to ignore the activities of local authorities. The development of surveillance activities in the former has tended to be seen, therefore, as a novel creation out of thin air. I wish to argue, however, that much information gathering went on in the local state in the early modern period, and that what is significant today is the concentration of this information, and the function it supports, in central government. This explains why the present volume has had to cover such a broad chronology.

Nor will this work discuss, except in passing, the burgeoning of commercial databases of information on private individuals, or the creation of vast systems of physical surveillance in prisons, mental hospitals, and via CCTV. Again, this partly reflects space constraints but I also believe that the tendency to roll discussion of central record keeping in with these subjects leads to confusion. The reasons for the creation of centralised databases of information on citizens are not necessarily the same as those for the creation of the 'carceral state', or for the explosion of direct mailing. Indeed, the assumption that they are, and that state information gathering can be explained in terms of the same models, will be one of the main targets at which the present work tilts. The creation of vast information systems relating to credit-worthiness, consumer preferences, expenditure patterns, and so on, are of great importance but the existence of the Information State is, perhaps, of greater moment because personal information gathering can be linked to the state's powers of physical coercion.

A book such as this springs from many sources, and I owe many debts of gratitude. Former mentors and friends at the PRO helped to instil in me an abiding interest in texts and their inter-pretation, although many will find my engagement with theory somewhat frivolous. Long days spent invigilating in the Round Room at the old PRO in Chancery Lane cannot help but make one aware of the extent to which all historical research is based on the patient work of archivists. Academic colleagues at the Wellcome Unit for the History of Medicine at the University of Oxford, and at the Universities of Exeter and Essex, have helped to sharpen my ideas via numerous conversations, as have students taking courses into which some of the ideas presented below have intruded. Nothing helps to focus one's mind on the need to improve an argument more than the blank stares of 30 undergrad-uates, or a penetrating question that leaves one floundering. I should also like to thank Margo Anderson, Bruce Curtis, Graham Mooney, Kevin Schürer, Steve Smith, Simon Szreter, Yoke-Sum Wong, David Vincent and John Walter, who commented on some of my ideas, and saved me from making obvious blunders. Above all I should express my gratitude to Professor Jeremy Black, who commented on a synopsis of this book and encour-aged me to write it. His insights were extremely useful, and his practical guidance invaluable, although I am not sure that he would agree with some of my analysis. As is usual on these occa-sions, it is necessary to aver that the errors and misjudgements in the present work reflect my own failings, rather than the failings of those who have helped me.

Important aspects of the work presented here, especially those relating to medical statistics and public health, were based on research undertaken whilst in receipt of grants from the Leverhulme and Wellcome Trusts, and to them I owe a great debt. The latter body needs especial thanks for facilitating my move from the Civil Service to academic life via a research fellowship and a university award.

Last, but certainly not least, I thank my wife Liz and my son Oliver. The first kept me focused on completing the volume, and the second distracted me just enough to keep a sense of proportion about it.

List of abbreviations

ACPO   Association of Chief Police Officers
CCID   Cabinet Committee of Imperial Defence
CCTV   closed-circuit television
DHSS   Department of Health and Social Security
DVLA   Driver and Vehicle Licensing Agency
EHS   Emergency Hospital Service
GMC   General Medical Council
GRO   General Register Office
GSS   Government Statistical Service
HIPE   Hospital In-Patient Enquiry
JP   Justice of the Peace
LGB   Local Government Board
NCCL   National Council for Civil Liberties
NHS   National Health Service
NHSCR   National Health Service Central Register
NINO   National Insurance Number
OCR   optical character recognition
ONS   Office for National Statistics
OPCS   Office of Population Censuses and Surveys
PAYE   Pay As You Earn
PEP   Personal Equity Plan
PNC   Police National Computer
PRO   Public Record Office
TESSA   Tax Exempt Special Savings Account
UAB   Unemployment Assistance Board
UISC   Unemployment Insurance Statutory Committee

1 Introduction

Surveillance and *Modern Times*

When the gathering of information on citizens by the state is discussed, one thinks inevitably of certain cultural symbols: of the total surveillance societies of Winston Smith and Big Brother in Orwell's *Nineteen Eighty-Four*, or of the glass city in Evergeni Zamiatin's *We*. One of the most engaging portraits in this vein is perhaps the opening section of Charlie Chaplin's film *Modern Times* of 1936. Here Chaplin's famous tramp, the 'little man' of the modern age, lives and works within a great factory, which is itself a vast machine. He, and the other sheep-like masses, turn out endless and meaningless components, the purpose of which is unfathomable. At every turn the little man is watched and monitored by a controlling factory owner and his agents, the foremen and line managers of the factory, and even by his own workmates. Men clock in, their work is measured, and they are continually surveyed by hidden cameras. Chaplin cannot even go to the toilet for a smoke without the whole wall turning into a giant image of his employer, who orders him back to the assembly line. Eventually Chaplin is literally swallowed whole by the machine/factory, and is driven mad. At this point he runs amok and is taken away to an asylum.

For Chaplin the world had become a vast automaton in which human beings were mere cogs watched at every turn by a dominant elite. But is this a true reflection of 'modern times', in both the categorical and the temporal sense – does this say something true about society today, and something about the manner in which it differs from the past? Certainly a comparison between the

1

information-handling powers of the state in England in previous historical periods and those of the present time confirms that the modern state has an infinitely greater capacity for such activities.

At Christmas 1085, for example, William the Conqueror decided that he would create a record of the manors that made up the realm of England that he had conquered nearly 20 years previously. He sent out commissioners to visit each shire and to hold specially enlarged sittings of the county courts. Juries from the hundreds, or wapentakes in former Danish areas, and representatives from each manor, came before them and answered the following questions:

1   What is the name of the manor?
2   Who held it in the time of King Edward (the Confessor)?
3   Who holds it now?
4   How many hides are there?
5   How many teams, in demesne and among the men?
6   How many villeins? How many cottars? How many slaves? How many freemen? How many sokemen?
7   How much wood? How much meadows? How much pasture? How many mills? How many fisheries?
8   How much has been added or taken away?
9   How much was the whole worth? How much is it worth now?
10 How much had or has each freeman or each sokeman? All this to be given in triplicate; that is, in the time of King Edward, when King William gave it, and at the present time.
11 And whether more can be had than is had?[1]

This information was collated by monks at Winchester, and the finished product, Domesday Book, was almost ready when William died in 1087.[2]

Historians have tended in the past to play down the practical usefulness of William's great survey, arguing, for example, that there was no real connection between the resources of the manor and the taxes – the *geld* – it paid.[3] For M. T. Clanchy the purpose of Domesday Book was essentially symbolic. The Normans, he argues, were impressed by the way in which written records, in the form of charters, gave apparent permanence to their individual acts. They assumed, therefore, that a large written survey would give similar durability to their rule of the whole of England. Clanchy goes on to claim that Domesday was hardly used for any practical administrative purposes whatever.[4] More recently, however, quantitative historians have claimed that there is, in fact, a rather good statistical relationship between resources of the manor, at least in some counties, and the taxes paid.[5] Elizabeth Hallam has also argued that the survey allowed William and his heirs to know the value of royal manors to be sold off; to calculate incoming feudal incidents; and levy dues on vacant bishoprics and abbeys. Even when the recorded sums due were no longer useful, the information on ownership of lands, tenants-in-chief, and feudal rights pertaining to the Crown, was of inestimable value. Similarly, the information on administrative units, such as hides and carucates, allowed the levying of the *geld* into the twelfth century.[6]

Domesday Book was thus undoubtedly the single most exhaustive exercise in data collection by the central state in England until the taking of the first population census in 1801. The great veneration in which the record was held by administrators in premodern England, and by modern medieval historians, attests to its unique status. However, the great survey had distinct limitations. It was a one-off exercise that was not repeated on a comprehensive scale, or even kept fully up to date. It was a collation of local oral intelligence at one point in time, and the length of the collection process was considerable, at least by modern standards. It was never a 'live database'. In addition, much to the disappointment of numerous genealogists, Domesday Book was not a census of the population but essentially a record of landholding and landed wealth. As such, it only mentions a few thousand landowners by name, and the rest of the population appear as numbers of anonymous villeins, cottars and slaves, and then in a very incomplete manner.[7] William, probably England's most powerful monarch, had intended the survey as a means of identifying and controlling only that tiny minority of his subjects that held land directly off the Crown. Norman methods of control over the rest of the population were usually somewhat cruder and more violent, as testified by the laying waste of much of the rebellious North of England by William in 1069 and 1070 – 'the harrying of the North'.

Compare this now to some of the activities of the modern central state. Perhaps one of the best sources for gauging the extent of central state information gathering in modern Britain is the 1978 report of the Lindop Committee on Data Protection.[8] This body examined the holdings of personal data on computer in central government as a preliminary to making recommendations that formed the basis of the United Kingdom's 1984 Data Protection Act. Table 1.1, based on this report, gives a breakdown of all government datasets of information on citizens, which contained over one million records in the late 1970s, and a rough functional category for each. Although this does not include all datasets, especially those in non-electronic form, the overall pattern of state information keeping revealed here is probably fairly representative of the situation both then and now.

This vast, ongoing system of data collection enables the modern state to intervene at a minute level in the daily lives of citizens. For example, whereas in Domesday Book the basic unit of assessment for taxation purposes was a whole manor, the modern state routinely collects detailed information on the incomes of all individuals in paid employment, or who receive an income from property. This data is either obtained directly from taxpayers themselves via annual assessments, or provided by their employers through the PAYE (Pay As You Earn) system. Taxation can thus be deducted at source, even before people receive their wages. With a revenue system of such scope and power it is unlikely that King John would have lost the Angevin Empire and been forced to sign Magna Carta, or that Charles I would have been unable to establish his superiority over Parliament in the early seventeenth century. But how has the modern state gained such an apparatus of revenue extraction, when earlier monarchs failed?

In addition, whilst Domesday Book took over 18 months to compile, and exists in splendid isolation, modern technology enables the state to gather and process information at great speed, and to integrate it with a vast array of pre-existing datasets. A single example, relating to the detection of speeding drivers, can give a flavour of the capabilities thus conferred. In May 1999, for example, the Home Office announced the extension of a system known as SPECS. This, based on roadside cameras linked to optical recognition software, flashes up the car number plates of

Table 1.1   Datasets relating to identifiable individuals, containing more than one million records in British government departments, 1 March 1978

Department and task	No. of records	Functional category
HM Customs and Excise		
Value Added Tax	1,083,843	Taxation
Department of Education and Science		
Teachers' records	1,401,300	Employees
Further education students	9,000,000	Welfare
Employment Group		
Training Opportunities Scheme	1,500,000	Welfare
Employment Census	1,000,000	Survey
Department of Health and Social Security		
National Insurance Contribution Record	45,000,000	Taxation
Payment of Retirement Pension, Widow's Benefit and Child Special Allowances	9,000,000	Welfare
Child Benefits	7,100,000	Welfare
Payment of Unemployment and Related Supplementary Benefits	4,000,000	Welfare
Mental Health Records	2,000,000	Welfare
Statistical applications Insured population	3,100,000	Welfare
Sickness, Invalidity and Injury Benefits	1,250,000	Welfare
Retirement Pension, Widow's Benefit	3,750,000	Welfare
Doctors' Prescriptions	1,500,000	Welfare
NHS Staff	1,000,000	Employees
Home Office		
Traffic Fixed Penalties Notices	1,100,000	Crime
Court Appearances/Offenders' Index	5,000,000	Crime
Police National Computer Index of vehicle owners	19,000,000	Crime
Index of convicted persons	3,800,000	Crime
Fingerprints of convicted persons	2,250,000	Crime
Broadcasting Receiving Licensing	21,500,000	Taxation
Board of Inland Revenue		
Pay As You Earn for Scotland	2,400,000	Taxation
Schedule D Income Tax for UK Collection	3,500,000	Taxation

Table 1.1   (Continued)

Department and task	No. of records	Functional category
HM Land Registry		
Index of Land Charges	5,000,000	Taxation
Index of Proprietors' Names	2,500,000	Property rights
Department for National Savings		
National Savings Bank		
Ordinary Accounts	12,865,000	Property rights
Investment Accounts	1,076,000	Property rights
National Savings Stock		
Register	1,342,000	Property rights
Premium Savings Bonds	4,236,000	Property rights
Office of Population Censuses and Surveys		
Census of Population	40,000,000 per census	Survey
Registration of Births, Marriages and Deaths Indexes	1,600,000 p.a.	Identification
Scottish Office		
Scottish Dental Estimates Board	2,315,000	Welfare
Scottish Hospitals In-patient Records	8,500,000	Welfare
Scottish Certificate of Education	1,106,640	Identification
Further Education Student Records	1,200,000	Welfare
Census of Population	5,000,000 per census	Survey
Department of Transport		
Vehicle Registration and Licensing	19,000,000	Crime
Driver Licensing	26,500,000	Crime

Source: Report of the (Lindop) Committee on Data Protection, British Parliamentary Papers 1978–79, V, Appendix 6

speeding vehicles on giant roadside computer screens, along with their speed in miles per hour, and an instruction to their drivers to slow down. SPECS also downloads the registration information of the vehicles to storage devices contained in cabinets by the side of the road to act as evidence in the event of prosecution. The system also relays the information to the Driver and Vehicle Licensing Agency (DVLA) in Swansea, which maintains and constantly updates databases containing information on the millions of drivers and their cars, so that offenders can be identified.

Records on drivers and their vehicles have been compiled continuously for a century, and have been centralised on computer since the early 1970s. Newspaper reports also indicate that SPECS provides information that is used to track stolen vehicles, so the data collected by the system is presumably relayed to the Police National Computer, which supports a database of stolen cars.[9]

This example of the ability of the modern state to enforce its will (and such examples could be multiplied endlessly), shows the vastly increased 'infrastructural power'[10] of the latter compared to pre-modern political formations. Such information gathering allows retribution to be exercised more certainly and with greater discrimination. One can imagine, with a shudder, the use to which an autocrat like William 'the Bastard' would have put such power. Indeed, there is one recent historical example of how information on individuals could be used by a violent, absolutist regime – that of Adolf Hitler in Germany. The Nazis used the data gathered via the German censuses as the basis of estimates of the numbers in particular target groups in defined areas. This information informed the planning of transportation to the concentration camps during the Holocaust, whilst individual-level data was used to select people for elimination. In doing so the Nazis drew upon the most advanced available information technology supplied by IBM. Information gives the modern state the power of life and, ultimately, of death.[11]

Much sociological writing on the subject does in fact assume that all state information gathering is to do with domination and control, and is a threat to civil liberties. Yet, on the other hand, a modern British Home Secretary might well argue that the aim of a system such as SPECS is to help prevent people breaking laws that are designed to protect lives. Dead people do not have civil liberties. There has also been a tradition of social scientists calling for increased state information gathering in order to provide the means of analysing and eliminating social problems.[12] In this sense, state information gathering can be seen as having a utopian potential. As Michel Foucault has pointed out, information gathering is part of the Enlightenment State's attempt to be the 'Good Shepherd' of healthy bodies on earth, thus superseding the pastoral care of souls undertaken by the Church.[13] Foucault hardly looked with favour on such claims but many others have seen the state as having a duty to introduce change that will create a better society. Also, much information gathering by the state is not for the purpose of keeping people under surveillance but is to enable citizens to safeguard their own rights through the recognition that state registration provides. In short, information gathering is *not* always the same as surveillance.

On one level, the present book can be seen as an attempt to tease out the utopian and dystopian strands in this story, and to evaluate their relative importance. However, one person's utopia is another's dystopia, and systems introduced out of the best possible motives can always be turned to dubious ends. Perhaps the best strategy is simply to tell the story of the development of state information gathering in England, and let readers make up their own minds.

Arrangement of the book

The Information State in England follows a broadly chronological arrangement, although this structure is frequently modified to allow the consequences of developments in one period to be traced over time. The next chapter, Chapter 2, is, moreover, a consideration of some existing explanations of the rise of state information gathering put forward by sociologists and historians. The models used therein will act as a counterpoint to much of the subsequent analysis. A central tenet of many of these accounts is that state information gathering is synonymous with surveillance in the interests of elite social control, and is connected with 'modernity' – with those processes of modernisation, industrialisation and nation building that have been part and parcel of the history of the West since the Industrial Revolution. The third chapter looks, therefore, at whether information gathering linked to the state existed in pre-modern England between about 1500 and 1800. It argues that many accounts underestimate, indeed often ignore, the extent of information gathering in the society of that period, mainly because they neglect the essentially decentralised nature of governance. Existing accounts of the 'rise' of the centralised Information State also tend to see such data gathering in terms of the needs of a dominant capitalist class to impose control on a 'society of strangers' created by the Industrial Revolution. The fourth chapter looks, therefore, at the development of those prime examples of early nineteenth-century state information gathering, the census and civil registration, in this light. The light, however, fails to illuminate very much, and some other explanations for their development need to be put forward.

Chapter 5 looks at the period from 1870 to 1914, which sees the groundwork being laid for the modern Information State. This was both a result of the geopolitical needs of the state, and of the need to incorporate the working classes into the political nation. How far such developments can be seen in terms of 'social control' is a matter as complex as it is profound. This period also sees the decline of local forms of governance, and this needs to be considered in some detail as the corollary of the rise of the central state. The following chapter, Chapter 6, deals with the twentieth-century Information State in total war and total welfare in the years from 1914 to the 1960s. Although information gathering expanded rapidly in this period, the British state did not always prove itself to be the sort of rational, Weberian state that some sociologists would have us believe. The contradictory roles of the state as agent both of social control and social empowerment will be considered. Taking these years as a single entity may seem strange but they hang together as a period when the forces unleashed in the pre-First World War world remodelled the British state.

Chapter 7 looks at information gathering in the recent past, and the potential impact of information and communications technology. As noted in the case of SPECS, data can now be handled and combined in ways unimaginable even 40 years ago. But has this changed the nature of the state, or merely allowed it to do its work, for good or ill, more efficiently? This will be the background to a discussion of the development of campaigns for data protection and freedom of information. The final chapter is a summary and conclusion.

2

Some models of state information gathering

Introduction

This chapter is not an exhaustive account of the existing theoretical work of sociologists and historians on the development of the gathering of information on individuals by the state. That would be beyond the scope of a book such as this, and would detract from its empirical aims. Rather it is an attempt to draw out some general assumptions within the existing literature, which will act as counterpoints to the arguments to be developed shortly. These assumptions can be summarised as follows:

1 that information gathering on the citizen is an innovation linked to the Industrial Revolution and the Enlightenment, and the associated genesis of the nation state;
2 that the 'state' undertaking this function is to be seen in terms of the modern central state;
3 that information gathering was instituted for the purposes of social control;
4 that this new system replaced older 'communal' forms of social control which were distinct from the state;
5 that this social control was imposed on the population in the interests of dominant elites;
6 that surveillance and the collection of information on citizens were part of a single process.

Although these various assumptions are implicit, and often explicit, in the publications of the various scholars to be discussed here, some of these same works contain passages that seem to contradict such arguments. These contradictions point, in turn, to a more complex, and interesting, history of information that is waiting to be written.

At the outset a distinction has to be made between the surveillance of individuals and information gathering on the same. The latter implies the bringing together of sets of meanings that refer to people. This can be done via speech, in the form of the interrogation of, or discussions about, individuals. In modern bureaucratic systems, information gathering is in the form of the collection and storage of more permanent symbols – words, fingerprints, DNA profiles, etc. – that tell human beings something about other human beings. Surveillance, on the other hand, has the narrower meaning of watching identifiable individuals to ensure that they do something, or more frequently that they do not do something. Such surveillance can be either physical, or based on information gathering, or a combination of both. But this means that information gathering and surveillance are not the same thing – information gathering can be used for things other than surveillance. Information can be collected to plan beneficial social activities, or be used as a means of ensuring that the state and others recognise one's rights, as in the registration of property rights. Nor, incidentally, is surveillance in the narrow sense necessarily always a bad thing.

For some historians this chapter's theoretical discussions will perhaps appear otiose and unnecessary. They are important, however, in that they explore some models of change with which the subsequent historical account can be compared. Those who are still not convinced can move on to the third, more traditionally empirical, chapter.

Industrialisation and information gathering

Sociology was born in the nineteenth century in the aftermath of the Industrial Revolution, and its classic texts – those of Durkheim, Marx, Spencer, Tönnies and Weber – are meditations on that momentous event in world history, and on its social and institutional impacts. Understanding modernity, in the sense of grasping what makes the modern, industrial world different from societies in the past, is still a fundamental concern of historical sociology. As Michael Mann notes, in the sociological tradition the emergence of industrial capitalism at the end of the eighteenth century is seen as producing the pivotal dichotomies and transitions in modern social theory – from status to contract, from mechanical to organic solidarity, from the sacred to the secular, and so on.[1] It should not be a surprise to discover, therefore, that sociological accounts of state information gathering implicitly regard the late eighteenth and early nineteenth centuries as the key period in its genesis.

For example, Anthony Giddens, at least in his two-volume *Contemporary Critique of Historical Materialism* (first published in the 1980s), sees this period as the transition from absolutist forms of government to the nation state. He further argues that this transition in state structures is associated with, although not reducible to, the rise of industrial capitalism. The state reaches out and penetrates all aspects of social life, just as capitalist production and the market permeate all economic activity.[2] Although Giddens is often rather vague about dates, he sees the development of the systematic collection of official statistics as an index of this process. Amongst such statistical forms he includes the results of the centralised collation of information created in the process of the registration of births, marriages and deaths; and the collection and analysis of data pertaining to residence, ethnic background and occupation. He also includes here the creation of what came to be called 'moral statistics' by Victorian statists, relating to suicide, delinquency, divorce and so on.[3] In the case of England, this process of 'informatisation' in government could be traced back to the taking of the first decennial census in 1801; the establishment of the modern system of civil registration in 1837; and the burgeoning of official reports being laid before Parliament in the early nineteenth century.[4]

Similarly, Christopher Dandeker, in his *Surveillance, Power and Modernity*, links information gathering and surveillance with the rise of the modern bureaucratic state, and of specialist forces of social control such as the uniformed police.[5] The latter were again a new feature of English society in the early to mid-nineteenth century. As will be argued shortly, many sociologists follow Giddens and Dandeker in contrasting the information gathering/surveillance capabilities of the modern state with the supposed absence of such powers in the pre-industrial period.

James Rule, for example, in *Private Lives and Public Surveillance*,
stresses the general lack of state information gathering in the
communities of early modern England, and states that bureaucratic surveillance is the 'product of modern industrial society'.[6]

Those working in other scholarly traditions have also seen the
rise of state information gathering within a similar chronological
framework. Michel Foucault has linked the rise of modern forms
of surveillance and state information gathering to another
eighteenth-century phenomenon – the Enlightenment,[7] whilst
Caplan and Torpey link them to the genesis of the nation state
during the French Revolution.[8] Yet again, David Lyon associates
the rise of modern surveillance with 'modernity' in terms of
nineteenth-century developments such as the growth of military
organisation, industrial towns and cities, government administration, and the capitalist business enterprise within the European
nation state.[9]

Yet Rule also notes that it would be difficult to imagine any
system of mass surveillance based on information gathering
existing in Britain before the turn of the twentieth century.[10]
Similarly, despite his emphasis on the contrast between modern
industrial and pre-industrial states, Dandeker places great emphasis on the requirements of modern, industrialised warfare as the
basis of the rise of the bureaucratic surveillance state in Europe.
However, he notes that England did not feel the same military
pressures towards thorough-going state bureaucratisation until
the twentieth century because until then it lacked a large standing army. If the 'First Industrial Nation' did not have a system of
mass surveillance based on information gathering in the latter
sense for a century after industrialisation, can one establish a
causal link between the two? The chronological disjuncture
between the advent of industrial society in Britain, and the development by the central state of mass information systems for the
active surveillance of the population will be examined in later
chapters of the present work.

Surveillance as social control

State information gathering has often been seen by sociologists
and other scholars in terms of social control. This concept is a

fundamental sociological tool but one that has shifted its meaning over time. Originally, in the work of progressive thinkers of the early twentieth century, such as George Herbert Mead, Robert Park and E. A. Ross, social control was seen as a means of constituting society via persuading people to accept social goals and values. Society was conceptualised as developing out of innate human qualities of consensus, communicability and empathy, rather than as a result of repression, violence, or blind economic forces – hence *social* control.[11] In the post-Second World War period the meaning of the concept bifurcated. On the one hand, systems theorists such as Talcott Parsons saw social control as the repression of deviant acts which undermined social systems based on accepted roles and patterns of behaviour – it safeguarded the structural integrity of systems, rather than the well-being of individuals.[12] On the other, thinkers influenced by Marx, such as C. Wright Mills, came to see the preservation of such social systems via the elimination of deviancy in terms of the interests of the rich and powerful, who benefited from the structures of exploitation and domination inherent in such systems. Social control was conceptualised as essentially coercive. The use of the concept by those interested in institutions of socialisation and resocialisation, such as schools, prisons and asylums, further helped to shift the concept towards theories of coercion, although still retaining the idea of social control as being essentially for the purpose of self-discipline.[13]

In historical accounts that use the concept, social control has been broadened to become a somewhat amorphous tool by which the beliefs of particular social elites are imposed on the rest of society. Corrigan and Sayer, in their seminal work *The Great Arch: English State Formation as Cultural Revolution*, envisage social control by the state as being used by the capitalist classes for the purposes of inculcating various norms of activity which enable the ongoing reproduction of the capitalist economy. Citizens are trained to respect property and their superiors, to work hard and to moderate their demands, so as to maximise the possibilities of capitalist accumulation. This does not simply imply indoctrination but the creation of a 'life world' in which alternative ways of thinking and behaving are excluded.[14] In some Marxist accounts state supervision of the population amounts to the production of standardised, docile human units for use in capitalist production.[15] Surveillance by the state acts here as a useful reinforcement to the activities of capitalists in monitoring and disciplining their own workforces. Some historians, such as A. P. Donajgrodzki in the introduction to his edited volume *Social Control in Nineteenth Century Britain,* may recoil from the over-simplification of such models but still see the state as being used by the upper and middle classes to force morally 'correct' values on the poor.[16]

Dandeker and Giddens admit that the collection of information by the state, and the use of this information to supervise the activities of people within any collectivity, are two separate processes.[17] They argue, however, that these processes are connected, and in practice they often write as if they are inseparable. Surveillance, in terms of the state collection of information on members of the population that enables them to be kept within the sights of the state, is part of that process of 'internal pacification' that Giddens holds as central to the development of a modern industrial society. Such information gathering both enables the detection of those committing acts that threaten the dominant rules of that society, and also the planning of social settings which constrain such deviancy. Giddens is plainly thinking in terms of the use of planning to control or limit how individuals can interact.[18] Dandeker also argues that the collection of information allows the prevention of actions against the established social system. Like Giddens he believes that information gathering allows the organisation of social space, especially in terms of architecture and town planning, which helps to forestall such deviant acts. The state administers 'subject populations'.[19]

The link between information gathering, surveillance and the imposition of norms is perhaps taken to its extreme by Rule in the theoretical introduction to *Private Lives and Public Surveillance,* in which all relationships based on rules of conduct are seen as involving some form of sanction. Even relationships between lovers are conceptualised by Rule as behaviour bounded by what each expects of the other, and by the unpleasant consequences of violating such expectations. Rules of conduct imply sanctions, and sanctions can only be applied if wrongdoing is discovered via surveillance.[20] This is a simple model of social control, although its application to intimate relations between affective couples appears reductionist, if not somewhat perverse. Rule's subsequent analysis of state information collection is then undertaken within this extreme model of surveillance.

Dandeker and Giddens also see state information gathering, surveillance and 'internal pacification' as representing the interests of elites but not in terms of the state as the 'executive committee of the capitalist classes'. For both scholars, state elites, political and administrative, are autonomous in that they have their own agendas – dynastic or national glory in the case of monarchs, and personal advancement in the case of the police, medical professionals and civil servants. In practice, the need for resources to fight wars, or excuses to justify the exercise of professional power, mean that in domestic policy, political and administrative elites seek to foster the efficient running of the capitalist system. Their interests and those of capitalist elites often coincide.[21] Dandeker lays particular emphasis on the needs of the state *qua* state, in that it needs to mobilise its population for the purposes of war.[22] The autonomy of the state has also been stressed by other historical sociologists, such as Theda Skocpol and Michael Mann.[23]

In many of these accounts state information gathering in terms of social control is seen as a direct threat to civil liberties, and 'internal pacification' is always in danger of descending into an Orwellian dystopia.[24] This perception of state information gathering as potentially authoritarian is heightened by the consideration of it in conjunction with physical surveillance in factories, prisons and military formations. Much of Dandeker's account of surveillance is actually about forms of discipline in such settings. But this is not taken as problematic, since, according to Dandeker, 'the techniques of the prison [spread] to the entire social body' in the nineteenth and twentieth centuries. In his account the population become the mere 'objects' of public policy through the continuous administrative penetration of everyday life. In this he is following Foucault's pessimistic assessment, especially in his *Discipline and Punish*, of modern society as a vast, ever-expanding and ever-deepening arena for the exercise of power by economic, professional, political and administrative elites.[25] Dandeker and Rule also place state information gathering and surveillance in the context of Max Weber's theories of bureaucracy. State bureaucrats are goal orientated, using formal, rational means of achieving their ends. In doing so they subject society to an 'iron cage' of rules, regulations and surveillance.[26]

Such a bleak picture of the relationship between society and the state in the modern period is a logical conclusion of applying an extreme model of social control in the interests of ruling groups. This construct has been strongly criticised by historians such as F. M. L. Thompson and Martin Wiener, who object to the reduction of people to passive recipients of such officious moulding. They argue that, at least in the nineteenth century, many middle-class attempts to influence the mores of the working classes were simply ignored, or subverted. When they were relatively successful, as in the case of the inculcation of thrift, this was merely because official morality was congruent with indigenous working-class concepts of respectability and independence. The conceptualisation of the working classes within the context of such social control theory is, they argue, both inaccurate and patronising.[27] Other historians, such as Jane Caplan and John Torpey, see modern state information collection as a means of making people 'visible to the state', but argue that this can both underpin rights and liberties and threaten individual autonomy.[28]

Giddens also believes, in a positive vein, that the population has engaged with the state and capitalism in an active manner. Surveillance, he argues, creates an arena of conflict or contestation out of which emerge the rights of citizens as a means of limiting the power of capitalists and their state allies. Civil rights emerge in opposition to surveillance as policing; political rights as a means of monitoring state administrative power; and what he calls 'economic rights' as a means of limiting surveillance in terms of the 'management' of production in factories by capitalists. Economic rights are thus to be found in the workplace, and the main agency of their achievement were trade unions via their struggles over wages, and over the terms and conditions of employment. Giddens claims that this formulation is a reworking of one put forward originally by T. H. Marshall in his 1949 essay, 'Citizenship and social class'.[29] However, this is an odd, and revealing, misreading of Marshall, since the latter never referred to 'economic' rights but to 'social' rights.[30] Marshall saw the latter in terms of the welfare benefits, education and assured standard of life, both physical and cultural, that the working classes obtained via the state in the nineteenth and twentieth centuries. Similarly, Marshall's civil rights covered the right to own property and to conclude valid contracts, as well as liberty of the person, freedom of speech, thought and faith, and the right to justice.[31] Such rights, as will be discussed below, are often dependent on state information collection, but they cannot be seen simply as limits to the surveillance of potential deviants, or as a direct reaction to the physical constraints of factory production.

This suggests other reasons for the collection of information by the state – that it underpins general rights and liberties within a pluralist society, rather than simply pinpointing individuals for direct control. Information gathering is not necessarily reducible to surveillance in a narrow sense. Giddens is also being inconsistent since he believes that the autonomy of the state is real, and stresses that it can be used by the working classes to forward their own interests. The state comes, therefore, to work within a system of 'polyarchy' or political pluralism, in which the state elites have to balance and accommodate the needs of differing groups, although always bounded by the requirements of capitalist production.[32] This model of 'bounded pluralism' and of the autonomy of the state is also one that has recently been elaborated by Mann in his discussion of the rise of the nation state.[33] In a similar vain, philosophers such as Charles Taylor have argued that identification and recognition are the prerequisite for individual and collective claims against the state.[34]

In practice, writers such as Giddens and Rule recognise that state information gathering cannot be incorporated into any simplistic model of social control, in the sense of identifying and pursuing deviants. Rule, after a detailed analysis of the working of state information gathering in Britain, concludes that the vast majority of citizens feel that they benefit from information-based surveillance which deters crime, or promotes the efficient workings of the benefits system by preventing fraud. Rule-bounded activity can benefit the majority, not just elites. Similarly, Giddens recognises that information gathering is the necessary condition of the administrative power of the state, whatever the ends to which this power is put. Thus, for poor citizens the efficient working of the benefits system can create a source of potential freedom.[35] As Rule argues, 'There can be no question, then, that surveillance mechanisms developed for relatively benign purposes can also serve the needs of repression. But this is hardly to suggest, as some writers would seem to imply, that the availability of potentially repressive tools in itself engenders repression.'[36]

Despite his Foucauldian rhetoric, Dandeker also sees popular demands for citizens' rights as being the driving force for the expansion of surveillance and information gathering in modern, democratic societies.[37]

Many of the studies of information gathering and surveillance discussed here have, therefore, an ambivalence at their core. On the one hand, they see the origins of state information gathering in terms of social control in the interests of elites. On the other, they recognise that the contemporary state may serve non-elite interests. Indeed, for Giddens this has become one of the central tenets of the 'third way' in politics (i.e., one that avoids what he sees as the negative effects of both communism and unconstrained market forces), which he sought to foster in the 1990s.[38] Giddens is rather vague, however, as to exactly when such polyarchy was achieved, and he does not indicate directly how this might affect the role of state information gathering over time. Such questions can only be answered in terms of a detailed historical analysis. That Giddens attempts to shoehorn Marshall's theory of rights into a model of surveillance as social control in the interests of elites, rather than seeing it in terms of the achievement of poly-archy, reveals some of the strains inherent in his account. It also shows the dangers of assimilating information collection directly to the history of physical surveillance, or the pinpointing of individuals via information systems. But, as Corrigan and Sayer suggest, the benefits and freedoms created by such rights have been of a specific form – those consonant with the efficient running of capitalism. The question is perhaps, therefore, how far the system is compatible with independent working-class aspirations and codes of morality.

States and statistics

Arguments imbued with various forms of social control theory can also be found in some recent historical accounts of the development of state statistical production in the modern period. The creation of statistics has, of course, been seen as one of the principal reasons for the collection of nominal data, and as a means by which the state plans social activity. In the relevant historical accounts emphasis has been placed on the role of statistical production in the creation of the power of central government. Statistical representations, it is argued, have created what Benedict Anderson has called the 'imagined community' of the nation.[39] Nation, it should be noted, has almost always trumped class in the European political conflicts of the modern period, and nationalism can thus be seen as a means of defending capitalism.

Thus, historians have regarded the establishment of national statistical bureaux across much of Europe in the early nineteenth century as a means of creating unitary national identities via the production of statistical measures that levelled differences, and suppressed local and ethnic identities.[40] Statistics based on common administrative units, standard measures and a common language were used to create a unitary understanding of the nation as an indivisible entity, in order to dissipate centrifugal tendencies amongst recently consolidated territories, and thus to maintain the stability of state systems. At the same time, national legislators and state statisticians could justify their own authority by using the collection of information on the population as proof that they were consulting the needs of the people, from whom all political authority was, in theory, derived.[41] Michel Foucault has also seen the eighteenth and early nineteenth centuries as a period when statesmen and *savants* began to think in terms of acting upon the population as a whole. The latter became an entity to be measured and manipulated in the interests of the state. Hence, the rise of demography and statistics is linked to 'governmentality'.[42] Bruce Curtis, writing about the Canadian censuses, sees such activities in a similar vein as an attempt 'to tie individuals to places within an administrative grid and then to hold them steady so that they may become objects of knowledge and government'.[43]

The classic example of such strategies was early nineteenth-century France, where various revolutionary, Napoleonic and republican central state bureaux amassed national statistics by which, according to Stuart Woolf,

> 'France one and indivisible' was to be constructed through the very act of cataloguing the innumerable variations bequeathed by environment and history within the national boundaries. Unity was construed as uniformity, to be achieved by identifying and gradually limiting local differences.[44]

Other national elites influenced by revolutionary France responded in similar ways. The Batavian Republic, for example, which was set up in the Netherlands in 1795 to replace the previous federal polity, began gathering national data in an analogous manner to France.[45] Silvana Patriarca has put forward related arguments with respect to the attempts to create an identity for a unified Italy during the nineteenth century.[46]

Such historical accounts have been concerned with the conscious creation of new national identities after revolution or defeat in war. It is a moot point, however, whether such arguments can be applied wholeheartedly to England, since that state did not undergo such a thoroughgoing refoundation in the early nineteenth century. It avoided revolution, and was generally successful in international conflicts. On the other hand, in the nineteenth century England created one of the most impressive bodies of statistical data in the Western world. At the same time, the creation of a statistical apparatus was not used to construct a fully integrated polity in the British Isles as Scotland, Ireland and England all established separate institutions for the collection of census and civil registration data. Indeed, as will be noted below, Victorian official statistics in the British Isles were used to reveal local differences rather than simply to give a unitary picture of the nation. This in turn reflects the centrality of the local state in the nineteenth-century British constitution. In addition, and despite Malthus, population as a conceptual totality was probably less of a political issue in early Victorian England than it was to become at the end of the nineteenth century.

Gemeinschaft and Gesellschaft

Another strain of argument that enters many accounts of the development of information collection is the contrast between local, self-regulating 'communities' in pre-modern society, and modern social control provided by the central state. Lurking here is a classic sociological model of historical change that needs to be delineated in some detail – the contrast between *Gemeinschaft* and *Gesellschaft*.

Many accounts of the development of state information gathering, surveillance and social control in the nineteenth century start from the assumption that industrialising society saw a breakdown in control mechanisms designed for older social forms.

'Traditional communities' are seen as having their own internal means of maintaining order and stability. For Michael Ignatieff (in his work on the development of surveillance in the penitentiary system, *A Just Measure of Pain*), pre-modern societies were based on face-to-face relations which did not require the intervention of the state. Thus, 'The father chastised the lazy son, the master chased and caught the runaway apprentice, the farmer reprimanded and dismissed his labourer.'[47] For Dandeker such societies policed themselves via the system of parish constables, the 'hue and cry', and the discipline of servants by their masters. Rule also stresses that in small-scale rural societies those breaking the rules were unlikely to escape the sanctions of community disapproval since they would be known to their fellows through face-to-face acquaintance. Capitalism, industrialisation and urbanisation are then seen as undermining such traditional means of social control both by the sheer scale of city life, and its anonymity. Similar arguments have been made by Frank Webster in his *Theories of the Information Society*.[48] This, in turn, necessitated the creation of state surveillance and information-gathering mechanisms as a means of reimposing social control in what Dandeker describes as a 'society of strangers'.[49]

The use of this phrase links such arguments to one of the key texts in the development of modern sociology, Ferdinand Tönnies's *Gemeinschaft und Gesellschaft*. This work, originally published in 1887, contrasts the communal life of ancient rural communities (*gemeinschaft*) with forms of contractual association in modern urban settings (*gesellschaft*). In the *gemeinschaft* people toil together and are bound by ties of kinship, tradition and the common working of the soil. The *gemeinschaft* is an 'organic' entity in which feelings of love, habit and duty combine to create harmony. Obedience to established social conventions is maintained by the family and the habitual deference due to friends and neighbours. In the *gesellschaft*, on the other hand, all are strangers to each other, and people are orientated towards the fulfilment of personal goals and profit. In such settings, others become mere tools to personal gain in a market economy. The state, then, acts as a means of keeping individuals from each others' throats, and enforces the rule of capitalists over the discontented working classes.[50]

This model plainly has many intellectual affinities with the modern work of sociologists on the state and information gathering/surveillance, who share, to some extent, in Tönnies's nostalgia for a lost communal life.[51] However, although Tönnies often wrote as if the *gesellschaft* succeeded the *gemeinschaft* in time – the transition from pre-modern to modern society – he actually believed that the two ways of thinking were to be found side by side in the same period. In a typical nineteenth-century manner he saw women, children and the 'common people' as exhibiting the outlook of the *gemeinschaft* in his own society, whilst adults – men and the educated – represented the *gesellschaft*. When he wrote of the *gesellschaft* as a state of warfare of all against all, he was plainly thinking of the seventeenth-century political theorist Thomas Hobbes, some of whose works – *The Elements of Law Natural and Political* and *Behemoth or the Long Parliament* – he was editing at the time. Hobbes believed that an absolute state was necessary in order to create the conditions for peaceful co-existence.[52] This places the *gesellschaft* in a period long preceding the elaboration of modern systems of state information gathering and surveillance.

Tönnies, therefore, did not regard his two social forms as mutually exclusive. As Michael Ignatieff has subsequently argued, in an important revision of his earlier work on the penitentiary, modern industrial society is still permeated by forms of human sociability, in the family and in civil society in general. In contemporary society one still finds numerous relationships conducted according to the norms of co-operation, reciprocity and the 'gift relationship'.[53] Rules do not necessarily depend on state sanctions to function properly. Anthony Giddens has also stressed the importance of fostering such social forms as a means of regenerating communities blighted by crime.[54] The dividing line between traditional and modern societies, as between traditional and modern states, is much messier than one is sometimes led to believe by some students of surveillance.

Centralised and dispersed states

When sociologists talk about state information gathering – indeed, when they talk about 'the state' in general – they are almost invariably referring to the central state. This in turn is defined in terms of the monarch or Parliament, and a centralised administration responsible to one or the other. Such central states vary in these accounts according to the degree that their influence and power penetrates the society over which they have dominion. Anthony Giddens distinguishes between 'traditional' societies, in which the central state's administrative penetration is low, and the modern nation state in which such penetration is very high. Traditional states, either monarchies or city republics, are essentially concerned with warfare in order to conquer new lands or to protect what they possess, and their domestic policies are designed to maintain order and property so that they can extract taxes. Beyond this they are relatively uninterested in what goes on in local communities, which organise themselves internally. In the modern nation state, the central state intervenes at a minute level to mould society, information gathering being one of the means it employs to do so. Indeed, so great is this penetration that the state *becomes* the nation – hence the 'nation state'. James Rule posits a similar model of state formation in his *Private Lives and Public Surveillance*.[55] The history of the state is thus the history of how power expands from a central point.[56] In many ways, this recapitulates many of the dichotomies between *gemeinschaft* and *gesellschaft*.

This stark contrast between traditional and modern states involves a somewhat simplistic typology of historic state formations. In the great sweep of Giddens's *Contemporary Critique of Historical Materialism* one passes from empires based on city states to European absolute monarchy and then on to the nation state.[57] Similarly, in Dandeker's account of the development of information gathering and surveillance in society, one moves from societies such as warrior bands and religious groups based on 'personal administration', to states based on 'bureaucratic dictatorship', as in the case of Stalinist Russia, or 'rational-legal bureaucracy', in modern Western societies. Dandeker hardly mentions any intermediate form of society, apart from a brief discussion of political formations based on patronage, taken from the single example of the workings of the British Royal Navy in the eighteenth century.[58] Given the ambitious scope of the historical accounts being offered in these works, omissions are inevitable but such episodic accounts are somewhat misleading.

Forms of the pre-modern state with which British historians might be familiar are given rather short shrift in these accounts.

Giddens simply declines to discuss the nature of the feudal polity, jumping from the Akkadian Empire of Sargon the Great in the third millennium BC, to the absolutism of Louis XIV in the seventeenth century AD.[59] He gives little extensive consideration to situations where, in respect of the execution of its will and the collection of intelligence, the central state had to depend upon local elites. In the case of pre-modern England, these would include the medieval feudal barons, or the gentry who acted as the justices of the peace in the early modern period. For Dandeker and Rule, such states are, by definition, weak and incapable of mounting effective systems of information gathering and surveillance. Indeed, they are hardly states at all.[60] The whole of what one might call local government is ignored, or seen as merely a limitation on proper state formation. Similarly, the relationship between the Crown and the representatives of local elites in Parliament, and how the latter, at least in England, came to function as the effective central authority, are also not explored. In this, as in many other respects, England may have followed a rather different path to modernity than that traversed by other Western states.

Yet when Dandeker discusses the introduction of the surveillance of the uniformed police in early Victorian England, he claims that this was 'a further concession gained by sectors of the propertied middle class from an aristocratic polity experiencing the unrest associated with the rise of the market'.[61] There is no indication here of when the local elites that formed an obstacle to state formation suddenly became the state in themselves. This points to a weakness at the heart of the model of the state offered in these accounts. Many of the forms of information gathering and surveillance which men and women in England experience, or have experienced in the past, emanate from local government working either as an executive of the central state, or as a delegated power in its own right. Similarly, the social classes that provided the local magistrates who enforced central state policy in early modern England, also helped to make such policy by sitting as members of the House of Commons. Having ignored this intermeshing of local and central authority, many sociological accounts of state information gathering have failed to ask if centralised state information gathering in the nineteenth and twentieth centuries was a new form of activity, or merely an old activity displaced from local to central government. This will be a central theme of the present book.

Michael Mann is equally capable of seeing the aristocracy and gentry as part of the '*old regime* state', whilst claiming that their power is the negation of that of the state.[62] On the other hand, he is much more willing to see the state as power relations stretching out from a centre but incorporating local power elites. This way of looking at the state as a dispersed network of power relations, rather than as a 'thing', has been emphasised in a sociological context by John Hall, as will be discussed in greater detail in the next chapter.[63] An even more radical solution to the issue of local–central polarity is to dispense with the idea of the 'state' as a set of relationships or things altogether, and to think of it as a set of processes whereby power and authority is exercised and reproduced. The actors in these processes can be varied and linked in changing constellations, and the 'state' is merely the term that certain actors call themselves when participating in such activities.[64]

Conclusion

It is to be hoped that enough (perhaps too much) ground has been covered in this chapter to indicate the ambivalence, if not contradictions, found in a number of the existing accounts of the development of state information gathering. On the basis of this discussion one might suggest the following list of counter-theses to those enumerated in the introduction as requiring further analysis:

1 that the gathering of information on the citizen was not an innovation linked solely to the Industrial Revolution, or the Enlightenment, and the associated genesis of the nation state;
2 that the 'state' needs to be seen in terms of processes wider than those undertaken by the central state;
3 that information gathering was not always instituted for the purposes of social control;
4 that state and older, 'communal' forms of social control have reinforced each other in past societies;

5   that this social control was not always imposed on the population in the interests of dominant elites, although the latter may have sought to give the 'interests' of other social groups a particular definition;

6   that surveillance and the collection of information on citizens are not necessarily part of a single process – information collection is not always for the purpose of pinpointing individuals.

Stated in such a bold fashion, these are probably as misleading as the original theses but they contain more than a grain of truth, and will inform much of the subsequent discussion in the present work.

After such a lengthy discussion of sociological and post-modernist theory, however, it might be best to move on to some history proper.

3

State information gathering in early modern England

Conflict within local communities in the early modern period

The picture of early modern England as made up of stable, harmonious communities held together solely by relationships of mutuality and co-operation, and 'traditional' forms of production, has been undermined by modern historical research. Indeed, a scholar such as Alan Macfarlane has gone as far as to claim that there was precious little 'community' in the villages of seventeenth-century England, and that the concept is really just a comforting myth for those living in the modern industrial world.[1]

This is undoubtedly an exaggeration but early modern England was certainly not a stable, 'feudal' society as traditionally defined. Indeed the countryside possessed many of the features of a developing capitalist economy. Following F. W. Maitland, the great Victorian historian of the English law, Macfarlane argues that there had been complete alienability of land by owners since the thirteenth century.[2] This meant that the turnover of property in local communities could be rapid, although rates differed from region to region. Thus, two sixteenth-century rentals of the manor of Earls Colne in Essex show that out of 111 pieces of land listed in 1549 only 31 were in the hands of the same families in the rental of 1589. Hired labour in the form of farm servants also appears to have been a crucial feature of English agriculture from the late Middle Ages onwards.[3] However, Macfarlane's assertion that there was no peasantry in early modern England overlooks the key importance of small landowners in the countryside, and the relations of power between the rich and the poor. It helps, nevertheless, to undermine the picture of static, isolated communities found in some sociological literature.

Population movements in this nascent commercial economy could be as frequent as in modern, industrial society. The population of England was growing in the sixteenth and early seventeenth centuries, and again in the late eighteenth.[4] Between 1524 and 1665, it more than doubled in size from about 2.3 million to perhaps 5.6 million persons, with an especially rapid increase of more than one per cent per annum in the years 1576 to 1586. The rate of expansion varied by community – the agricultural parish of Terling in Essex grew by about 75 per cent from 1524 to 1671, whilst the industrialising Tyneside parish of Whickham experienced a growth of some 150 per cent over the period 1563 to 1620, and of a further 60 per cent between 1620 and 1666.[5] At Honiger in Suffolk, of the 63 family names recorded in the period 1600–34 only two can still be found in the parish register for 1700–24. Similarly, just over half the population of Cogenhoe in Northamptonshire disappeared and were replaced between 1618 and 1628, while at Clayworth in Nottinghamshire the turnover of population between 1676 and 1688 approached two-thirds, only a third of those disappearing being accountable for by death.[6] Such churning of populations has led Macfarlane to claim that, 'Any particular community in England in the past was probably no more isolated than a Chicago suburb or twentieth century Banbury.'[7] This might, of course, be true in terms of migration patterns but would be a gross exaggeration in terms of the daily interaction of its inhabitants.

Such mobility was associated with important social changes related to rising price levels. Landlords faced by inflation resorted to tighter estate management, racking rents and enclosing the common lands. Substantial farmers, especially near towns, created surpluses for the market and so benefited from the price increases. On the other hand, the poor, without access to land, suffered both from the higher cost of living, and from restrictions of access to the resources of the open fields. Such differential fortunes created social strains and increasing polarisation. At the same time, the number of vagrants may have increased by as much as 65 per cent between the early 1570s and the 1630s, with 25,000 persons being arrested for vagrancy between 1631 and 1639.[8]

Although it would be misleading to see the result as a class society, one might agree with Keith Wrightson in seeing it as possessing 'an *incipient* class dimension in its distribution of wealth'. Certainly, by the mid-seventeenth century great inequalities of wealth existed – perhaps 50 per cent of English land was owned by the 2 per cent of the population who belonged to the gentry, whilst a further 15 per cent or more was the property of the peerage.[9] Overall there was an increase in social distance in the later sixteenth and early seventeenth centuries with the expansion of the lesser gentry; the emergence of an urban 'pseudo-gentry'; the diversification of the prosperous 'middling sort'; the whittling away of the husbandmen of fielden England; and the massive growth of the labouring poor. Wrightson discerns a clustering of social groups around a small number of 'social and cultural milieu' – 'the gentleman', 'the quality', the 'best inhabitants', 'the middling sort' 'the people', 'the meaner sort', 'the inferior sort' and 'the poor'.[10]

This increase in social distance led to rumbling conflicts over local resources, enclosure of the common lands, and labour discipline. Increasingly, local elites – minor landowners, craftsmen, the 'respectable' – began to share in the concerns of the gentry, peerage and Crown with regard to the imposition of order on a restless society.[11] To these tensions were added the consequences of the burdens imposed on ratepayers by the imposition of the Poor Law system in the course of the sixteenth and early seventeenth centuries, through which the indigent of the parish were paid a dole raised via a parish rate. The poor now became a legal charge upon the wealth of local elites rather than the object of charity, and this in itself may have hardened attitudes towards them.[12] Thus, measures to control the results of social tensions may only have deepened their root causes by increasing social distance. Such attitudes set the context within which any discussion of the workings of the early modern state needs to be set.

The decentralised nature of the early modern state

A cursory examination of Table 1.1 reveals that the information gathering undertaken by the modern central state can be classified under a fairly small number of headings. The state maintains records on taxpayers, its employees, and those to whom it pays welfare benefits. It also gathers information on those who break its laws, or have the potential to do so, as well as underpins property rights via the registration of ownership. Modern states also undertake general-purpose surveys in order to provide data to inform policy making and intervention in society. The state taxes, employs, provides financial support, maintains 'law and order', protects private property and surveys the nation.

The pre-modern state in England regularly carried out some similar activities. English kings have always taxed their subjects to fight wars from at least the tenth century onwards.[13] Similarly, the Old Poor Law was Tudor state policy enshrined in acts of Parliament.[14] Royal justices itinerant were trying local criminal cases in the twelfth century,[15] and supervising local justices of the peace and parish constables since the later Middle Ages.[16] The registration of baptisms, marriages and burials by the clergy of the Church of England had been introduced in 1538 by Thomas Cromwell, acting as Henry VIII's vicar-general.[17] Royal courts had also been underpinning property rights in land since the reign of Henry II in the twelfth century via collusive court cases producing fictitious 'fines', which were enrolled in the records of the central courts.[18] Michael Clanchy has argued that by the second half of the thirteenth century it was imprudent for anyone to wander far from his or her village without some form of identification in writing.[19] However, such activities did not, as a general rule, create the sorts of centralised, comprehensive and searchable databases that are associated with the modern state. Nor was the central state the prime locus of such activities in pre-modern England. In the main, law was enforced, welfare dispensed and property rights recorded at the local level.[20]

However, it would be misleading to assume, therefore, that early modern England exhibited those features of the *gemeinschaft* found in the sociological model associated with Tönnies. Social control was not simply a matter of what went on within biological families, master and servant relations, and the voluntary associations of neighbours. Such relationships were, of course, of crucial importance for socialising the young and facilitating order, as they still are today. However, they were supplemented by a whole range of formal institutions and officials linked ultimately to the central state, such as local and central, lay and ecclesiastical courts, justices of the peace, and overseers of the poor. Indeed, in some ways, public surveillance in early modern England was more intense and wide-ranging than anything experienced in Western societies today.

It could be argued that such institutional arrangements actually reveal the impotence of the early modern state since it had to share power with the localities that provided the unpaid officers of local government. This is, however, to take too narrow a view of the state. The early modern state was not simply a set of central institutions that claimed power or a monopoly of violence over a particular territory. Rather, it was a series of processes through which authority was exercised, which in turn created routines of interaction across society as a whole. Authority can be understood here as the issuing of commands with the expectation that they will be obeyed, either out of fear, or, more typically, because the right to issue such commands is accepted by those being commanded. As such, the state was not a pre-existing thing which subsequently did things, it was an 'emergent property' of these processes of interaction.[21] The state permeated society in the early modern period, and its differentiation out of civil society in the modern period was an historical process of change, not a creation *ex nihilo*. The modern central state is merely a particular form of polity, not the ideal type.

As much of the recent historiography on early modern England has argued, the state was distinct from the locality not by being central but by being more extensive than the locality – it was constituted by the active linkage of elements in the localities for the purposes of exercising authority. As Steve Hindle puts it, one should 'think less of *government* as an institution or as an event, than of *governance* as a process, a series of multilateral initiatives to be negotiated across space and through the social order'.[22] The state formed a national community of those in every locality who were willing and able to involve themselves in the exercise of authority. Michael Braddick has gone as far as to claim that the period saw rule *through* rather than *by* the monarch, as local elites took advantage of royal authority to pursue their own agendas.[23] The state as such was a composite affair, with differing components having different orientations but with enough common interests to bind it together for most of the time. Mark Goldie has dubbed this composite state a 'monarchical republic'.[24] Whether the 'chief inhabitants' of the parish who undertook some of the functions of government at the micro-level had an understanding of the larger state is, of course, doubtful.[25] Such decentralised governance by local office-holders can be seen as stretching back into the medieval period.[26] This was not a Weberian central state, as modern sociologists understand it, but one that was still recognisable as a state, with officers wielding authority claimed as legitimate over defined territorial units.[27]

England's decentralised polity could fall apart at the centre, as it did in the seventeenth century when King and Parliament became rivals for supreme power. The English Civil Wars of the 1640s reflected, in part, the belief amongst local elites that Charles I wanted to rule without the need to co-operate with their representatives in Parliament. Similarly, James II was ejected in 1688 when he proceeded with an extensive remodelling of borough charters, and the wholesale replacement of Anglican magistrates.[28] However, this did not necessarily lead to a disintegration of all order but to rival claims of authority and legitimacy that were fought out at the local level.

This understanding of the state in the contemporary historiography is similar to the arguments put forward by the sociologist John Hall, who sees England in the early modern period as having an organic, rather than a 'capstone', state. That is, unlike the late Roman or Chinese empires, the state was not powerful enough to impose its own structures on society as a consequence of its military might. In medieval Europe the state evolved slowly and doggedly in the midst of a pre-existent civil society. The monarch's best means of gaining resources was to co-operate with his subjects. Perhaps the most important mechanism in this process was the king's decision to make money by providing a certain infrastructure to society, as clearly seen in the provision of justice. But this was not a zero-sum game: local communities gained but so did the state.[29] This is in marked contrast to the fate of Imperial Rome, which collapsed in the end because local elites preferred to see the state wither away rather than support it – there was little to choose between the predations of the barbarians and of the Imperial tax collectors.[30] This is an interesting formulation but may take the absolutist ideology of an empire like China at face value, rather than looking at what actually happened on the ground.[31]

Local elites and the 'middling sort' entered into this pact with the centre because the monarch provided them with services, prestige and useful support in achieving the preservation of their own property and authority. According to Gerald Harriss (referring to late medieval England), 'as political society grew, so it needed the monarchy more, not less: to distribute patronage and power, to regulate and harmonise its tensions, to provide a sense of direction and identity'.[32] Wealth and lineage counted for much in being able to claim gentry status but selection for county office was the true test.[33] This might be contrasted with Scotland, where the relative weakness of the central state prevented the creation of such organs of local government as the parish Poor Law system and the justices of the peace.[34]

The social legislation emanating from Parliament in the sixteenth and seventeenth centuries reflected local concerns about poverty and order, and generalised creative experiments carried out in the counties. The state was responding to the fears of the 'middling sort', and consolidating local action, as well as ensuring that local disorder did not get out of hand to threaten the stability of the realm as a whole. This was especially the case with local misdemeanours relating to the activities of the poor, or those which encouraged their concentration in any one spot, such as hedge-breaking for fuel, sheltering vagabonds, allowing sub-tenanting, and so on.[35] According to Marjorie McIntosh,

> as early as 1460s–70s and increasingly across the sixteenth century some jurors were prepared to present and punish their neighbours for committing customary acts of charity. These leaders presumably felt that they had to take action to preserve the stability, good order, and economic well-being of their community against the multiple challenges imposed by the presence of a rising number of poor people, especially when they were outsiders. The approach relied on a *de facto* distinction between those poor who warranted sympathy and perhaps charitable assistance because they were unable to labor for their own support, and able-bodied idlers who were to be treated more severely.[36]

In other words, the principles of the Elizabethan Poor Laws grew out of, and codified, developments in the localities. Rather than an imposition, local communities could look upon the state as a resource upon which they could draw.[37]

What is interesting about the early modern state in England is not the narrowness but the breadth of its claims, covering everything from the power to tax to the right to control religious beliefs. That this was done via alliances with local elites certainly reflects certain infrastructural limits to the central state. But that local elites were willing to co-operate with the monarch in exercising authority and implementing what were often sweeping social, religious and political changes also shows the great strength of this decentralised form of power. The Tudors may have lacked a paid bureaucracy in the provinces but they were able to overthrow a set of religious institutions that had dominated English life for a millennium, and to defend themselves from the world empire of Spain. Similarly, the eighteenth-century English state was not an absolutist monarchy like France, depending as it did upon local elites for the collection of crucial forms of taxation. Yet the self-same subjects of this decentralised state were willing to pay almost three times as much in taxation per head as their French rivals in the 1780s. Local gentry may have ensured that they usually avoided the heaviest burdens but at times of crisis, as in the 1690s and at the end of the eighteenth century, they were willing to vote and pay more progressive taxes.[38] It was the ability of the English state to mobilise its resources in this manner that allowed it to defeat its arch-enemy throughout most of the century. As Alexis de Tocqueville put it in the early nineteenth century:

> The English aristocracy voluntarily shouldered the heaviest public burdens so as to be allowed to retain its authority; in France the nobles clung to their exemptions from taxation to the very end to console themselves for having lost the right to rule.[39]

What is important for the present argument is to show that information-based surveillance linked to this state formation long preceded the Industrial Revolution. However, since what surveillance of the population took place (and there was a lot of it in early modern England), took place at the level of the locality, it was here that records of that activity are to be found. These mostly found their way into the parish chest, local diocesan record offices, and latterly local county record offices, rather than into the archives of the central courts and departments of state.[40] Moreover, such records were usually written minutes of face-to-face, oral proceedings in courts, or of quasi-judicial gatherings, rather than the structured, standardised nominal records found in modern computer databases. Extracting information about individuals from such unstructured material was, and is, a difficult business.

Period specialists will, no doubt, bridle at the idea of attempting to delineate the period 1500 to 1800 in terms of a homogeneous state. The England of George III was very different from that of Henry VII – much power had shifted from the Crown to Parliament; central oversight of the localities had increased; certain forms of surveillance, especially the religious, had declined; and there had been the rise of a professional, administrative class. But there is, on the whole, enough continuity in how the central and local state interacted, and how this impacted upon forms of surveillance in society, to allow some very general comments to be made. Certainly, there is much more in the way of discontinuities between governance under William Pitt and that under Tony Blair, than in the earlier period. In the eighteenth century governance was still essentially in local hands but by the late twentieth century Britain was probably the most centralised country in the European Union.

The decentralised state in action in early modern England

Rather than seeing the early modern state as a set of institutions based in London, it might be more appropriate to see it as a series of overlapping networks exercising authority at all levels of society, from the nation as a whole down to the parish. At the smallest level were the officers of the parish – the constable, the overseers of the poor and of the highways, and the members of the vestry court. These were usually appointed from amongst the 'respectable' members of the local community but charged with enforcing the law of the land. Boroughs had a similar range of officers – mayor, aldermen, constables, clerks, watchmen, and the like – which could, over time, include a considerable portion of the male, adult population of such communities.[41] At the highest level – the whole realm – stood the Crown in Parliament, the latter itself made up of representatives of the local gentry, borough elites and peerage. At this level general laws were made which were enforced at other levels of the political system. There was a general intermingling of government and disciplinary powers – men who sat in Parliament might also be local officials wielding authority.

In the middle, and at the level of the county, sat the justices of the peace (JPs), appointed by the Crown from amongst the local gentry but performing their duties without payment for the prestige attached to the post. On one hand, the justices, either singly or in groups in the quarter sessions, enforced statutes concerning the peace of the realm. On the other, they were charged with administrative duties such as overseeing the work of the parish overseers and constables.[42] By the end of the reign of Elizabeth I no fewer than 309 statutes had imposed responsibilities on JPs of either a judicial or administrative nature.[43] The lot of the JP was not always a happy one, caught as he was between the needs the Crown, and the needs of the local parish elites upon which he depended for carrying out his duties. JPs were watched over by the Privy Council, by whom they were exhorted, encouraged, ordered and rebuked. They were inspected and reported upon by regional councils, lords lieutenant, bishops and above all by the assize judges, who visited the counties twice every year and brought back their reports to Westminster. In accordance with such reports, county commissions of the peace were periodically reshuffled, unsatisfactory magistrates being removed and deserving individuals included.[44] Since prosecution depended upon members of the community bringing prosecutions, and local temporary officers, such as the constable, acting against criminals, the JPs also had to depend upon the co-operation of the local population. The art of being a JP lay in balancing these forces, acting when, as often was the case, centre and locality sought the same ends, and temporising when a too harsh application of the law might cause problems on the ground. As a result, laws and administrative arrangements were interpreted differently in differing areas, and sometimes ignored altogether.[45]

This series of overlapping networks created a great chain in which local business could be dealt with at many levels, some of them highly formal. This can be seen most clearly in the legal and judicial field. At the top of the hierarchy of courts for criminal cases stood King's Bench, which was able to remove cases from inferior courts – quarter sessions, assizes, and even manorial leets and minor borough courts.[46] Similarly, if parties to local civil cases had enough resources, they could have them lodged in central equity courts, such as those forming part of Chancery and Exchequer, or in Star Chamber and Common Pleas. Thus, litigation between

Lord Berkeley and Sir Thomas Throckmorton in 1580–81 resulted in 13 Star Chamber bills, 12 in King's Bench and Common Pleas, and almost numberless suits at assizes and quarter sessions.[47] England in the early modern period was in many ways a much more litigious society than it is today.

In addition to such lay structures, there was also a hierarchy of ecclesiastical courts, stretching from the High Court of Delegates, Court of Arches and Prerogative Courts of Canterbury and York, down to local bishops' and archidiaconal courts. Since the head of the Church of England was the monarch, such courts enforced parliamentary statutes and royal proclamations, as well as canon law, laying down a uniformity of religious beliefs and practices. Within limits imposed by statute, they could bring prosecutions for apostasy, idolatry and heresy; Catholic recusancy, sectarianism and related offences; the abuse of ministers or ecclesiastical officers, and misbehaviour in church or churchyard; wilful absence from church, failure to receive the communion, and neglect of baptism, churching or catechism; the profanation of Sundays and holy days by working, playing games or drinking in service time; and the practising of witchcraft and sorcery.[48] The existence of people who denied the authority of the Crown in such matters, either because they recognised a higher external authority (Roman Catholics), or only that of their own conscience (some Protestant dissenters), was a direct threat to central government power. The imposition of religious uniformity may have failed[49] but the attempt to regulate such beliefs is certainly not something that the modern Western state would contemplate today. One might feel uneasy about seeing the Church as part of the state, and the clergy certainly felt that their authority was derived from a higher source,[50] but early modern monarchs behaved as if they controlled both the beliefs and personnel of the Church of England.

Equally problematic in the modern context would be some aspects of the jurisdiction of ecclesiastical courts over moral and social issues, including scolding, talebearing and defamation; usury; drunkenness; and a wide variety of sexual offences. Finally, the courts had an extensive jurisdiction in matrimonial matters – they adjudicated disputes over marriage contracts, issued marriage licences, heard petitions for separation and annulment, and brought prosecutions for irregular marriage, unlawful separation and similar offences.[51] Ecclesiastical courts also handled matters relating to wills and probate, upon which many property rights depended. They were able to impose the penalty of excommunication, and could hand over those found guilty to the secular powers for still more severe punishment. The most common form of punishment, however, was to do penance. Those who were unable to prove their innocence by getting others to speak in their favour might have to appear barefooted and dressed in a sheet in the local church, or the market-place. Penitents would declare why they were doing penance, or carry an explanatory placard or symbol.[52]

This paraphernalia of administrative and legal bureaucracy could be irksome but it was also useful for local elites who sought to impose order and decorum. Given the centrality of marriage, family and neighbourliness to social and economic life, the regulation of these institutions via the ecclesiastical courts was taken for granted for much of the time. Prosecutions for bastard-bearing and other notorious forms of sexual immorality, and lawsuits over sexual slander, all meshed to a greater or lesser degree with pressing local concerns. The great majority of correctional proceedings originated in presentments made in visitations by the lay representatives of the parishes, the churchwardens and the 'questmen', 'sworn men' or 'enquirers', whose particular responsibility it was to report prosecutable offences. These were chosen in most parishes by respectable parishioners and the incumbent clergy. By choosing what cases to present, local elites could create their own disciplinary regimes. By associating themselves with their 'betters', and the workings of justice system, they once more gained prestige and authority.[53] But, as with the JPs, the ecclesiastical authorities had to be careful that too rigorous a policing of religion and morals, as in the case of the repression of Nonconformity, did not disrupt local patterns of co-operation.

A similar mixture of central and local concerns may explain the institution of parochial registration in the early sixteenth century. Thomas Cromwell saw it as a useful means, 'for the avoiding of sundry strifes, processes and contentions rising from age, lineal descent, title of inheritance, legitimation of bastardy, and for knowledge whether any person is our subject or no'.[54] In an age so concerned with legal rights to land and other property, such an institution must have been of great importance. It has also been suggested that the registration of baptisms, burials and marriages would help decide who had a 'settlement' in any given parish, and so prevented false claims to poor relief. Parish registers may also have subsequently helped to identify local Dissenters.[55]

Forms of local surveillance

This complex of overlapping networks and modes of authority created what was at times a vast and intense system of information gathering for the purpose of surveillance. A solitary JP, for example, was empowered to conduct the preliminary examination of suspects and witnesses to a felony, take cognizances, and on the basis of such investigations to commit suspected felons to prison, and bind over the unruly to be of good behaviour. He was to enquire into apprenticeship disputes; seek out and suppress vagabonds, rogues, nightwalkers, nocturnal prowlers in masks, and players of unlawful games. He bound over soldiers who were discovered to have sold their arms or horses to appear at the sessions, or imprisoned them; and he dealt in a similar way with those spreading false rumours. He searched wax manufactories for illicitly made candles; examined and bound over recusants; enquired into poaching cases; and in times of dearth he could look into and supervise the sale of corn and malt.[56]

As already noted, many villagers were willing to keep a close watch over the moral failings of their fellow parishioners, and to present them to the ecclesiastical authorities. It was through such actions that the 'common fame' that so often led to presentment arose, and examples of such surveillance are common in court records. In the case of illegitimate children, women could even be interrogated during labour by the midwives and their assistants to discover the child's paternity. Once the father's identity was established, the ecclesiastical court could order him to meet the expenses of confinement and purification, to support the child, and to provide the woman with a dowry.[57] In parts of the country such as Devon, the ecclesiastical courts were still hearing cases based on presentment concerning bastardy, ante-nuptual fornication and unlawful cohabitation into the middle of the eighteenth century.[58]

The workings of the old Poor Law generated some of the most rigorous forms of information-based surveillance in early modern

England. Given that the English system was almost unique in Europe, the extent of the surveillance it entailed was also remarkable. The establishment of a Poor Law system itself created a justification for information gathering since it helped to categorise individuals as differing types of social problem. Given that the amount raised locally as the poor rate rivalled the amounts collected as central taxes, there was a strong incentive to act.[59] The deserving and undeserving could be distinguished by their behaviour and moral worth, and while the former were to be relieved by the poor rate, the latter could be whipped without compunction, sent back to their home parishes and compelled to work there. All that was required was the close local examination of those who were needy, and the identity of the true, worthy poor would be revealed.[60] On one level this created a social right to communal support, the removal of which in the nineteenth century was vigorously opposed,[61] but it also created a system of surveillance to weed out the 'unworthy'.

Under the 1572 Vagabonds Act, money raised by the poor rates was only to be given to 'impotent persons' after careful examination of their credentials. JPs were to take surveys of the poor in their county divisions and then to 'tax and assess' all inhabitants to provide for them. Overseers were to be appointed in each parish, and were to conduct monthly inspections to ensure that strangers were excluded from the dole. The need for local information on the numbers and nature of the poor for Poor Law purposes led to the taking of local censuses of the poor, some of which have survived. That for Norwich in 1570, for example, covers 2,359 people in 790 households, or 22 per cent of the population, although this may have been a high figure for the numbers of people in towns falling under the gaze of the authorities. However, this system of surveillance typically covered a large proportion of the population – in towns in the sixteenth century, five to seven per cent were pensioners, with perhaps the same again receiving occasional relief.[62]

A close watch was also to be kept on migrants, who might potentially become a charge on the parish.[63] The system of surveillance thus established by statute led to examinations of people on the move. Under the 1531 Vagabonds Act, those shown to be vagabonds were to be whipped, and then returned to the place where they were born, or where they last lived for at least three years. The qualification for settlement was reduced to one year in 1598, but otherwise this remained the usual treatment of vagrants throughout the Tudor and Stuart periods. The 1572 Vagabonds Act went still further – vagabonds were to be whipped and bored through the ear by order of the quarter sessions for the first offence, unless masters could be found to take them on. For a second offence they could be hung as felons, unless taken into service for two years. In practice, only a small minority of migrants were whipped and sent back to their parish of birth or last residence; other kinds of settlement regulation were invoked against obviously respectable travellers. Sometimes they were allowed to remain in town after giving sureties, or were expelled without punishment. Other strangers were legally distinguished from vagrants because they could show that they had obtained employment, or had recently rented accommodation in a town.[64]

Legislation in 1388 and 1495 had already distinguished between the able and impotent beggars; and badges had been issued to some of the latter in Gloucester in 1504 and in other towns, including London, in the 1520s. The Vagabonds Act of 1531 extended this, in theory, to the whole kingdom.[65] Under an Act of 1697 all those in receipt of poor relief were also supposed to have the letter P and the initial of the parish sewn on their clothes. Many parishes did not insist on this humiliation but the practice of badging was not abolished in law until 1782.[66] The 1531 Act also introduced a second procedure: the local licensing of approved beggars. All beggars were to be punished unless licensed by justices of the peace. This system of 'internal passports' bred attempts to circumvent it, and there was a wholesale trade in counterfeit passports of the sort prescribed by the Statute of Artificers for people travelling in search of work. Forged certificates claiming losses by fire, or allowing travel as maimed soldiers, were even more useful.[67]

Relationships within poor families were also watched by the authorities. According to the Poor-Relief Act of 1601, grandparents, parents and children were, in theory, obliged to support one another. Consequently, there are cases of grandparents being compelled to take in grandchildren; and of children being forced to contribute weekly pensions to their aged parents. In practice, however, the needs of the nuclear family normally took precedence.[68] At the same time the Poor Law authorities were equally concerned to avoid new burdens on the parish, which encouraged them to keep an eye on people who housed impoverished relations coming from elsewhere.[69] This also applied to women bearing bastard children, who might be treated with scant consideration. Edward Ward (1667–1731) described the parish overseers of the poor gathering 'information' from such a poor unfortunate in a poem of 1705:

> Who the kind unwelcome news [of the illegitimate birth] no sooner heard,
> But the stern lobcocks in a gang appeared,
> And, with their awful frowns and woeful threats,
> Frighted the female sinner into fits:
> Who, coming to her foolish self again,
> Declares the father, where 'twas got, and when,
> How many times she'd sinned, and what he said
> To coax her to resign her maidenhead;
> Whether the gem upon a bed was lost,
> Or standing with her rump against a post;
> Whether her kind consent was fairly won,
> Or if the pleasing job by force was done;
> Whether fair promises her heart ensnared,
> Or money gained admission to her beard;
> What she first thought on't, how she liked the sport;
> Whether it pleased her well, or if it hurt;
> Whether she cried, or had a greater will,
> When once engaged to struggle or lie still;
> And whether, when attacked in love's surprise,
> She opened not her legs, but shut her eyes.
> Thus each old bawdy sot, with ruby face,
> In gold-twine buttons, and a band of lace,
> Would take his turn th' offender to torment
> With questions fulsome and impertinent:
> Thus listen with a lank, lascivious ear
> To bawdy secrets told them out of fear,
> Shameful to own and scandalous to hear.[70]

This is plainly a satire but that such scenes could be conceived indicates the ill reputation of such confrontations.

One should be careful not to exaggerate the intensity and scope of surveillance of this sort, and the information gathering upon which it was based. The ambitions of the early modern state far exceeded its powers, and the enforcement of draconian laws could be patchy in time and space. However, a world in which people felt justified in spying on their neighbours and denouncing them before the courts; in which immorality could be punished by public humiliation; in which internal passports could be necessary for the poor to move freely from place to place; and in which those receiving poor relief or begging might be required to wear distinguishing marks of shame, might appear eerily reminiscent of some of the excesses of twentieth-century totalitarian regimes. This was, perhaps, one of the analogies that Arthur Miller was drawing in his play *The Crucible*, set in the English colony of Massachusetts in 1692, and drawing on the witch-hunt trials of the period.

Central state surveillance: war and taxation

If the enforcement of law and order, and the provision of welfare, were essentially local activities, the question arises as to what exactly was the role of the centre. Certainly, the monarchy, and the legal and military authority it could wield, acted as a guarantor of the peace and stability of the realm. But, on the whole, the monarch's principle interests were in 'high' politics and foreign policy. Most of the money raised in central taxation in England until the late nineteenth century was spent on warfare and foreign affairs,[71] and English monarchs preserved their dominant role in the direction of such matters long after much of the decision making respecting domestic affairs had passed to Parliament. This division of responsibility was taken over and formalised by the English colonists in North America when they set up the United States at the end of the eighteenth century, with the powers of the President in foreign policy being similar to those of George III. Much central information collection was, therefore, designed to prosecute war.

The foreign policy undertaken by the Crown in this period was not simply a function of capitalist expansion, as some have implied. According to Michael Mann it was 'functional' for four main sections of society – the monarchy itself, the royal administration, the military aristocracy and gentry, and the merchant/capitalist classes. For the Crown, warfare was pursued for dynastic advantage, whilst it provided its immediate officers with opportunities for exercising power and prestige. Merchants and capitalists might hope to gain access to markets and favourable trading conditions, and the Crown needed a thriving economy to provide the resources to pursue an active foreign policy. For the aristocracy and gentry warfare largely meant plunder and glory.[72] One of the principal reasons officers went to sea in the Royal Navy in the eighteenth century was the hope of gaining a fortune in prize money,[73] as in the case of Captain Wentworth, the hero of Jane Austen's *Persuasion*, who gained a fortune of £20,000 from captured ships. Even such an illustrious commander as Horatio Nelson saw a victory at sea partly in terms of the prize money he might gain, and fell on the deck of the *Victory* at Trafalgar in the blood shed by his prize secretary, John Scott.[74] In these practices such officers were merely continuing the traditions of their medieval forebears, for whom the ransom obtainable from prisoners was an important inducement to support the monarch in his military campaigns. Given this confluence of interests in pursuing an active and successful foreign policy, it was not surprising that pacific or defeated monarchs often found themselves in trouble at home. Hence, in part, the sorry stories of King John, Henry VI and Charles I.

One must also remember, however, that English foreign policy in the early modern period was intimately bound up with issues of religion and political ideology. An active foreign policy against Spain, and later France, implied a defence of the Protestant religion against Catholicism. This was also a defence of an important element of the wealth and prestige of the English gentry and aristocracy, in the form of the landed property of the Catholic Church, which had passed into their hands at the time of the Reformation. In turn, this could be seen as the protection of the English form of decentralised state, based on co-operation between the Crown and local propertied elites, against the sort of absolute state found in France. In the minds of Englishmen, Catholicism and absolutism were insolubly linked. Such prejudices were not without some foundation, as can be seen from the secret Treaty of Dover between Charles II and Louis XIV of France of 1670. In this Charles agreed to eventually announce his conversion to the Catholic faith in return for an average pension of £123,664 a year in order to make himself independent of parliamentary taxation.[75] After the Glorious Revolution of 1688, when the Catholic James II was replaced by the Protestant monarchs William III and his wife Mary, the French monarchy supported the Catholic Stuarts' claim to the English throne. This meant that the dynastic interests of the Crown and the propertied interests of local elites were further cemented in support of a decentralised polity.[76]

Thus, English monarchs had numerous pressing reasons for undertaking warfare in the pre-modern period. During the 'long' eighteenth century, 1688 to 1815, the British army and navy trebled in size and fought six major wars – the Nine Years' War (1688–97), the War of Spanish Succession (1702–13), the Wars of Jenkins's Ear and Austrian Succession (1739–48), the Seven Years War (1756–63), the American War of Independence (1775–83), and the French Republican and Napoleonic War (1793–1815).[77] The average number of men under arms grew enormously, reaching about 200,000 during the American War of Independence, and nearly 400,000 at the height of the Napoleonic War, with an additional 500,000 militia responsible for home defence.[78] Total tax revenues as a share of conjectural national income during peacetime rose markedly from about one or two per cent in 1500 to about 10 per cent in 1700. By the latter date England was perhaps the most heavily taxed nation in Europe after the United Provinces, spending nearly £2 per head on the War of Spanish Succession in the financial year 1709–10, compared to £0.79 per head by France in 1711.[79] Much of the increase in state expenditure across Europe was driven by the increasing size, specialisation, and permanency of navies and standing armies.[80] An expanding fiscal-military state also led to an increase in the number of government employees, who roughly trebled between 1660 and 1714. By the mid-1720s there were over 12,000 central state servants, of whom over half were involved in tax collection.[81]

From the medieval period onwards, the constant requirement for taxation led to the creation of vast and extensive central records of taxpayers and their contributions to the state purse. In the course of the long eighteenth century assessed taxes came to cover a multiplicity of items, including land, houses, windows, male servants, horses, dogs, carriages, hair powder, armorial bearings and, to the horror of contemporaries, even incomes. The surviving records of such payments, now held in the Public Record Office in London in record class E 179, comprise about 30,000 rolls, files and pouches. Even medieval records of this type can give a vast amount of information about named individuals.[82] The poll tax of 1377, for example, was supposed to be levied at a flat rate of 4d on all lay men and women aged 14 and upwards who did not regularly beg for a living. Plainly there must have been much evasion but the tax still produced 4,100 documents, with those for London recording no fewer than 23,314 taxpayers.[83]

Impressive though this sounds, one must not exaggerate the power that this form of information keeping conferred on the central state. Such records were not intended primarily to facilitate the direct extraction of resources from individual taxpayers but were intended to monitor the local administration of an essentially dispersed form of taxation. The workings of the early modern decentralised state penetrated even this most crucial prerequisite for the functioning of central government. Various lay taxes were voted in Parliament by the representatives of local elites, and then assessed and collected locally by the same. English gentlemen expected to have a say in the levying and collection of such state revenues as a means of keeping the power of the Crown in check. The denial of this right to one group of the subjects of the British Crown in the 1770s was to have momentous consequences. When American colonists poured cargoes of tea into the sea in 1773 during the Boston Tea Party, and raised the cry of 'no taxation without representation', they were merely claiming the same rights as those enjoyed by their cousins in England.

The administration of the Land Tax voted in 1693 gives an idea of the typical form in which this decentralised system worked. The local machinery of the tax was set out in the Act of Parliament authorising its collection. Local commissioners, who were to supervise the assessments and local collection of the tax, were also established by Parliament. In the boroughs, the mayor, aldermen and common council were usually nominated to serve on the commission by virtue of office. In the counties, the commissioners were drawn mostly from the local gentry, headed by a few peers and supplemented by the addition of a number of merchants, doctors and barristers. The great bulk of the commissioners nominated in 1693 had served before, and participation in the administration of the tax was a mark of local prestige rather than of subordination to the Crown.[84]

The commissioners were to hold general meetings in each county on 15 February 1693 and then divide into groups, each acting for a hundred or some similar division. The commissioners appointed assessors and collectors, usually in pairs, for each parish, and a clerk to record their business. These officers served under the penalty of a fine, and had to take oaths of personal allegiance to the Crown. Assessments were revised by the commissioners, who had absolute authority to settle disputes. One copy of the tax assessment was given to the collectors and another to the receiver-general for the county. An abstract of the sums charged in the various taxation districts within the area was sent to the King's Remembrancer in the Exchequer, which was in turn to transmit duplicates to the Auditors of the Land Revenue.[85]

Once the tax had been assessed and collected in the hundreds and boroughs, the money was brought together for forwarding to London from the county by the receiver-general. Whilst the commissioners who managed the work in the localities were appointed by Parliament in the Act, the receivers were appointed by the Treasury. Before appointment as receiver each candidate had to submit sureties for Treasury approval, and these were examined every year. Large sums, ranging from £125,000 from the receiver for London, Westminster and Middlesex, to £4,950 from the receiver for Westmoreland and Cumberland, were demanded, which were probably based on an estimate of the largest sum the receiver would handle at one time. Bonds for these sums were annually taken in by the King's Remembrancer, and were delivered out again when the receiver's accounts for the year had been agreed.[86]

If there was a shortfall in the money collected and forwarded to the Treasury as compared to those sums indicated in the assessments, the Exchequer (acting in its legal guise) could issue a writ to the sheriff of the county giving him power to seize the goods of the defaulting collector or receiver. The Exchequer thus had a legal guarantee that it would receive the money due. In this sense the nominal lists in the Exchequer acted as a check on the work of local tax officials, rather than upon individual taxpayers. However, collectors and receivers could shift the blame for default by declaring that they could not satisfy the debt they owed to the Crown because they themselves were owed money by taxpayers. In these circumstances the Exchequer could help the collector to recover such debts in order to be able to claim the money owing to the Crown. Thus, the Exchequer could force individuals to meet the sum due from them but only in an indirect manner.[87]

Even this system provided the Crown with only a formal means of control. Local officials usually acted together to ensure that the sums assessed on individuals were equitable and could be paid. Indeed, this ability to tailor assessments to the resources of taxpayers gave local taxing officers considerable local patronage, authority and prestige, and was part of the reason they undertook the task in the first place. Local officials could be endlessly obstructive if pursued by the Exchequer, through failing to make adequate returns, or only providing total tax assessments for hundreds rather than for individual taxpayers. Usually the role of the central state was in arbitrating disputes between communities and local officials over customary rights and exemptions, rather than pursuing individuals.[88] Rather than attempting to take the administration of assessed taxes into its own hands, the Crown sought to overcome declining tax income by establishing quotas on counties. These were set sums each county had to pay, with local arrangements for collecting the necessary amount being left up to the local taxing authorities.[89] The Crown also shifted taxation towards the Excise, which was a levy on commodities paid by producers and distributors who passed the duty on to consumers in the form of higher prices. The Excise was collected in the eighteenth century by a central Excise Office, and by local state officials, the hated 'Excise men'.[90] However, the tax did not produce the sorts of nominal records that some assessed tax officials forwarded to the Exchequer.

An exception to this decentralised system of revenue collection, and it is a revealing one, was the Crown's extraction of dues from its feudal tenants-in-chief. On the death of the latter, the 'escheator' of the district summoned a local jury to inquire upon oath as to the lands and other property of the tenant, and the name and age of the next heir. Reports of these investigations, *inquisitions post mortem*, were sent to the royal Chancery and Exchequer for scrutiny, and can still be found amongst the state archives. If the heirs were adults, possession of the tenants-in-chiefs' land was granted to them on their appearance in court and performance of homage to the King, and on payment of a reasonable fine or relief. If, however, they were minors, they and their land remained in wardship until they reached full age. This meant that the Crown received the revenues of the estate and could marry off the heir – a valuable form of income.[91] Such arrangements related only to the most prestigious families, and reflected the ancient feudal powers of the Crown stretching back to the Norman Conquest. They hardly represented the genesis of a centralised system of taxation in the modern sense. Indeed, the attempts of the early Stuarts to turn the system into a means of circumventing the need to recourse to Parliament for taxation, was one of the causes of the English Civil Wars of the seventeenth century. Charles II eventually returned from his 'travels' in 1660 but Parliament was careful to abolish the Crown's right to such dues.[92]

Central state surveillance: war and military manpower

If one is seeking the origins of systematic central state record keeping, a much better place to start looking is in the archives relating to military manpower. To undertake military activities European monarchs required money but they also needed men. Prior to the seventeenth century, the English state mostly relied on militias set up locally by the lords lieutenant of the county, or the local commissioners of array, for its defence from external attack. Numerous muster rolls recording those so raised can be found in the records of several departments of state.[93] However, such records hardly gave the central state much control over this decentralised, amateur army.[94]

But the military and fiscal revolutions of the Civil War period created the basis of skilled, professional armed forces for the projection of military power outwards.[95] This was especially the case with the English state's naval forces. The eighteenth-century Royal Navy was a vast employer of men. According to a statement received by the House of Commons in 1763, it had raised no fewer than 184,893 men during the course of the Seven Years War. Even as late as 1896 nearly one-fifth of all government expenditure went on the Navy, and a quarter of a million people worked for the Service, or in industries directly dependent upon it.[96] Much has been made of the press-gang as a means of providing men for naval vessels in the early modern period but despite its brutality it was not as indiscriminate an institution as one might imagine. Naval vessels were complex and potentially dangerous machines, and required experienced and reliable crews to control them. These were not to be obtained simply from kidnapping farm hands, and the main targets of the press-gang were experienced merchant seamen in ports.[97]

But once on board ship, the Royal Navy was keen to maintain its credit with seamen as a good employer in order to ensure their allegiance and fighting spirit. This meant that sailors needed to be paid fully and promptly, and arrangements made so that money could be sent to relatives on land. Such considerations also lay behind the development of systems for paying pensions to officers, and later other ranks, and their widows. This in turn led to the generation of a vast system of pay-books and ship's musters for naval vessels. The latter were instituted to record the service of every person on board ship in order to determine their wages. They also recorded their consumption of victuals and other articles chargeable to their wages, for the purpose of compiling the accounts of the ship's purser.[98] Central supervision of these processes from the seventeenth century onwards led to the deposit by 1832 of over 8,000 ship's pay-books in the archives of the Admiralty, and by the end of the nineteenth century of over 40,000 musters.[99] In the early nineteenth century the Navy also began to keep formal service records for officers. After the peace of 1815, the Navy had ten times as many officers as it needed and no way of retiring them, and so needed to develop means to select good men and follow their careers.[100] The whole Admiralty system represented a collection of nominal data by the central state on an unprecedented scale.

From a very early date the requirements of naval operations impelled the central state towards setting up a register of all seamen. This was intended to provide a reliable pool of sailors upon which the Navy could draw in time of war. Reliability was to be ensured in terms of the rewards attached to the register rather than via the use of overt surveillance backed up by force. The first attempt to establish such a system was as early as 1696. This was a voluntary arrangement in which the prospective benefits of admission as a pensioner to the newly established Greenwich Hospital were held out as an attraction. There was also to be a bounty of 40 shillings per annum, which led to a large number of non-seamen entering themselves on the register in the hope of receiving the bounty. As a consequence, the system proved abortive.[101]

More comprehensive, but equally unsatisfactory, systems of registration were introduced in the nineteenth century, and can be rehearsed here to round out the picture of state military formation. Horatio Nelson resurrected the idea of a register in a

memo submitted to the Admiralty in 1803. He suggested that a
seaman who had served in the Navy during war 'and by his certificates never been concerned in mutinies, nor deserted', should
be granted a bounty according to his length of service. These certificates would be registered and thus induce seamen 'to be fond,
and even desirous of serving in the Navy, in preference to the
Merchant Service...'[102] Registration was eventually revived by
the 1835 Merchant Seaman Act that established the General
Register Office of Merchant Seamen, under Admiralty control,
in the London Customs House. Registers of seamen were to be
compiled from the crew lists, which were to be sent to the Registrar
of Seamen by masters of foreign-going ships at the end of every
voyage, and by masters in the home trade twice yearly. The register
was intended to allow the Admiralty to select those men it needed
in time of war, rather than depending upon the press-gang. Ships of
over 80 tons were also required to carry a quota of apprentices
(a requirement repealed in 1849), whose indentures were to be
registered by the Register Office. By 1841 the names of 213,322
seamen and 26,439 apprentices had been recorded, 82,457 of
whom were liable for impressment into the Royal Navy.[103]

Direct registration was introduced by the Merchant Seamen
Act of 1844, which made it compulsory for every British seaman
to obtain a Register Ticket, issued by customs officers at ports,
before proceeding to sea. Masters were liable to penalty if they
took seamen without tickets and were supposed to enter the
ticket number onto their crew lists. To prevent improper use of
the tickets, they included a description of the holder, and each
customs house held a list of cancelled tickets. By 1851 half a
million register tickets had been issued but they proved unpopular
and many were burnt during the seamen's strike of that year.
In 1857 the registration of seamen was abandoned, as being too
expensive and no longer necessary. The development of a professional Navy, the introduction of continuous service for ratings
after 1853, and the formation of a Royal Naval Reserve after
1859 meant that the Admiralty no longer required a separate
register of merchant seamen, although the Registrar-General did
co-ordinate the enrolment and payment of training allowances to
reservists.[104]

The need to raise and maintain land-based forces also created
a whole array of central records, although not on the scale, or as

methodically, as those relating to naval forces. In 1681 Charles II set up the Royal Hospital at Chelsea, from which soldiers who had left the regular Army with a disabling injury, or as invalids, were entitled to a pension, or institutional care. From the mid-eighteenth century, attestation and discharge documents began to be kept at the War Office for pension purposes. Manuscript lists of commissioned officers in the regular army also began to be maintained centrally from the beginning of the eighteenth century, and a published *Army List* first appeared in 1754.[105] The military needs of the state and central information keeping thus marched hand in hand.

Central state surveillance: monitoring allegiance to the Crown

Much information was also collected to maintain the position of the Crown in the centre of the web of relationships that formed the decentralised state. Curtis C. Breight, drawing on Giddens's arguments about the centrality of information gathering to the state (but not on Giddens's chronology for the development of this function) has claimed that in Elizabethan England the 'very structure of government was built upon human surveillance'. He points here to the prevalence of paid informers, the collection of intelligence, the continuous searches for Catholic priests, and other related activities dedicated to the protection of royal power.[106] Polonius behind the arras spying on Hamlet and Ophelia was a symbol of a much broader activity. Nor was such information gathering confined to the sixteenth century – in the reign of Queen Anne, Daniel Defoe was employed by the government to travel around the country on horseback gathering news about the character and voting intentions of JPs, clergymen and leading citizens.[107] Similarly, in the early nineteenth century the government was hiring paid informers, such as 'Oliver the Spy', to infiltrate radical political groups. But as E. P. Thompson noted, this

> was an ancient part of British Statecraft as well as of police practice. It goes back long before the time at which Christopher Marlowe was caught up in its toils; and espionage and counter-espionage against the Catholics, the Commonwealth and the Jacobites takes us well into the eighteenth century.[108]

But these were relatively ad hoc and unsystematic forms of information gathering. They certainly did not lead to the creation of standardised listings of nominal information, the precursors of modern systematic databases. The documents containing the intelligence gathered by such means poured into the hands of the monarch's secretaries of state in London, to be acted on immediately, or not, as was necessary. They were subsequently stored in coffers in considerable confusion, some being retained centrally and others taken away by the secretaries as their personal property. There appears to have been no officially constituted State Paper Office until the early years of the seventeenth century, when Sir Thomas Wilson became Keeper of the Papers and set about reducing the correspondence 'to a set form of library'. However, few attempts were made to provide digests, calendars and indexes to the State Papers, until the appointment of the first of a series of parliamentary commissioners in 1764. Nevertheless, it was not until 1852, when the State Papers were transferred to the safe keeping of the Public Record Office, that comprehensive finding-aids began to be created. The early modern central state was well aware of the need for information, but not for information systems in the modern sense.[109]

The general lack of bureaucratic systems of surveillance may explain why Tudor and early Stuart monarchs, as their medieval forebears before them, had to spend so much time on endless peregrinations of the provinces to order to keep in touch with local elites. In 1561, a typical year, Elizabeth I was on the road from 10 July to 22 September visiting four counties – Essex, Suffolk, Hertfordshire and Middlesex. In 1593, at the age of 60, she progressed through eight counties, moving up the Thames valley from Surrey and Middlesex, through Buckinghamshire and Berkshire, and on to Wiltshire, Gloucestershire and, finally, Oxford. Some 35 private hosts provided hospitality, as well as the University of Oxford.[110] The number of beds in which it is claimed 'Good Queen Bess' slept may well be exaggerated but such legends have their origins in an important facet of early modern statecraft. Much time was, of course, given over to junketing and the inevitable hunting but such visitations also helped the monarch keep in touch with local elites and their affairs. Indeed, if one defines the central state as a set of institutions in London,[111] then for much of the time the early modern monarch and the royal household were not part of the central state.

This form of immediate physical surveillance, as opposed to the creation of standardised information systems, was perfected in the France of Louis XIV. According to Louis:

> The art of governing is not at all difficult or unpleasant. It consists quite simply in knowing the real thoughts of all the princes in Europe, knowing everything that people try to conceal from us, their secrets, and keeping close watch over them.[112]

In order to facilitate this Louis gathered all the aristocracy of France together at Versailles, and had a set of servants wandering the corridors at night to overhear conversations. Early modern state surveillance of this type led to the creation of a carceral, rather than an information, state.[113] In England after the mid-seventeenth century the monarch also settled more in the capital and the aristocracy were attracted to the court but this process was never taken to its logical conclusion as in France of the *ancien régime*.

A more systematic form of surveillance for the purposes of defending the Crown's position in the decentralised state can be found in the scrutiny of local office-holders, and the compilation of the oaths of allegiance they had to swear. Mention has already been made of the careful central scrutiny of lists of justices of the peace, the bedrock of local administration. Much effort was also put into ensuring that only those who had sworn allegiance to the Crown could hold local positions of authority. Such oaths originated in feudal oaths of homage but were used by the Tudors and Stuarts to ensure that office-holders affirmed their allegiance to the Crown. Office-holders swore oaths of supremacy to Henry VIII in 1536 in the aftermath of his split with Rome, and to his daughter, Elizabeth, in 1559. Another oath was required of everyone over 18 in 1606 in the aftermath of the Gunpowder Plot. Parliamentarians swore oaths and demanded them from citizens during the 1640s and 1650s in defence of their understanding of the Constitution.[114]

After the Restoration in 1660 attempts were made to enforce the allegiance of office-holders to the Church of England. Under the 1661 Corporation Act no person could be legally elected to any office relating to the government of any city or corporation unless they had received the sacrament of the Lord's Supper according to the rites of the Church of England. At the same time they were directed to take the oath of allegiance and supremacy to the Crown. Under the Test Act of 1672, all officers, both civil and military, and persons having places of trust under the King, were ordered to take the oath and make a declaration against transubstantiation. Within the six months after their admission to office they had to receive the sacrament in church, and to send into the court a certificate signed by the local minister and churchwardens confirming this. Such oaths were subsequently enrolled in Chancery.[115] Dissenters could get round these restrictions by occasional conformity but the Test and Corporation Acts were only finally repealed in the 1820s, as part of a general movement to remove the disabilities placed on Nonconformists. Rather than state surveillance expanding unilaterally during the Industrial Revolution, here it was undergoing a marked contraction.

Ironically, Charles II had Roman Catholic sympathies and his brother, James II, was an open convert to Rome. This brought allegiance to the monarch and to the Protestant settlement into conflict, leading to the Glorious Revolution on 1688 in which James was replaced by William of Orange, his son-in-law. William III's own position was to be protected by a 'Solemn Association' entered into by Parliament to defend the King's person and government against all plots and conspiracies and to which all persons bearing office were to subscribe. This covered all members of the House of Commons, the freemen of all city companies, the military and civil officers of the Crown, and the clergy and gentry throughout England and Wales. The returns, comprising nearly 500 rolls, were again kept in the Chancery in Whitehall for reference. Information-based surveillance and the position of the monarch in the decentralised state were thus intimately related.[116]

The early modern state and political arithmetic

Plainly, the early modern English state could collect information on its subjects when required. Modern states use this material to create statistical representations of states of affairs for the purposes of planning. The extent to which government in England in the pre-modern period did the same is a matter of debate.

In the early sixteenth century, Henry VIII's first minister, Thomas Cromwell, had realised how useful a census of the population would be for taxation purposes but had not attempted to carry out such a survey. The period also saw attempts to gain information on enclosures and the extent of rural depopulation.[117] It was the late seventeenth and early eighteenth centuries, however, that saw the first concerted effort to apply 'political arithmetic' to the workings of the state.

In his *Treatise of Taxes and Contributions* of 1662, Sir William Petty attempted to break down the main heads of state expenditure, and made various proposals, including using state expenditure to alleviate unemployment. He also called for the establishment of a general register of vital events to collate parish registers, and thus help to reveal the numbers married, the age structure of the population, the occupational and religious distribution, and the wealth of any area. Petty's friend, John Graunt, suggested in his *Natural and Political Observations*, published in 1661, that 'Government may be made more certain, and regular', if it was known how many people there were of each 'sex, state, age, religion, trade, rank, or degree, etc.'. But neither Petty or Graunt were state officials, and their suggestions do not appear to have greatly influenced state policy.[118]

At the end of the century, Gregory King produced his own *Natural and Political Observations*, which he forwarded to the government. This contained tables based on taxation returns, showing the number and social status of the families which made up the population; calculations of the wealth and produce of the country; and the yield from various taxes. He compared the situation in 1688 with 1695, during which period England was at war with France, and concluded that the subsequent decline in wealth made the war unsustainable. The conflict with Louis XIV also appears to have lain behind calculations undertaken by King's contemporary Charles Davenant, also in 1695, on the yields of various taxes in his *Essay on the Ways and Means of Supplying the War*.[119]

Which taxation records King used (poll taxes, hearth taxes, window tax, duties on baptisms, marriages and burials, and so on), and the care with which he examined them is much debated. D. V. Glass is generally positive in his estimation of King's work, placing his calculations in what he sees as a seventeenth- and eighteenth-century tradition of the state 'collection of... statistics which were and still are, to some extent, used for estimating population size and trend'.[120] Peter Laslett goes still further and suggests that King was consciously creating a semi-official 'state paper' and that his calculations, suitably updated by the Treasury, were to be used throughout the eighteenth century to calculate what a tax would yield before it was imposed.[121] Geoffrey Holmes, on the other hand, claims that King had relatively little access to the taxation returns, and took liberties with the information he did have. He argues that the whole exercise was an attempt by King, a 'divine right' Tory, to persuade the state to abandon a war against the French king, who was supporting the exiled James II.[122]

It is difficult to be certain where the truth lies here. Certainly King's attempts to interest the government in his abilities bore fruit, in that he subsequently became secretary to the Commissioners for Public Accounts and to the Comptroller of the Army Accounts.[123] On the other hand, Glass's claim that taxation returns were 'statistics' collected by the state for demographic research appears to reflect a misunderstanding as to their purpose. Nor can Laslett provide any documentary proof that King's calculations were used in the manner he claims, or ever updated in the eighteenth century. As already noted, the eighteenth-century state had comparatively limited control over the yield of assessed taxes, and moved towards setting counties quotas and dependence on the Excise, rather than using King's work to tailor taxes to the ability of citizens to pay. If such statistics were central to the work of tax officials it would seem odd that the Board of Inland Revenue did not appoint its first official statistician until as late as 1893.[124] In general terms, the early modern state probably had some broad rules of thumb about the expected yields of taxes but the claim that it had detailed tables of population numbers, social stratification and wealth, based on taxation returns, is unproved. Given the rather ad hoc nature of government expedients to raise taxation in the period, such a capacity on the part of the state seems questionable.

The scope of the surviving records

Given the scale of state involvement in local communities in early modern England it is not surprising that abundant material relating to Englishmen and -women survives from the period. This is despite the destruction of documents over the succeeding centuries, and the fact that so many forms of information gathering were oral rather than based on writing. What documentary material on individuals does survive from the period is not in the form of modern databases but is usually found in the procedural records of courts of law, or the minutes of meetings. This material is also dispersed in numerous archives and archival record classes. An appreciation of the riches of personal records that do survive, and the difficulty in bringing them together, can be gained from the Records of Earls Colne project led by Alan Macfarlane at the University of Cambridge.[125] This grew out of Macfarlane's work on documents relating to witchcraft in the Essex Record Office in the early 1960s. Excited by the amount of material he discovered, Macfarlane and a group of researchers decided to input the historical data on the people and land of a number of English villages on computer. They discovered very rapidly that the material involved was so vast that they had to restrict their project to the records relating to the manor of Earls Colne in Essex over the period 1375 to 1750. None of the original team realised that the whole project would take 27 years to complete, and would lead to the creation of a database containing 3,200,000 words of text that is now available on-line.

Much of the material input came from the records of the manor itself, relating to the internal workings of that feudal entity. Many of the records, however, were the archival residues of the state activities described above. These included the records of numerous central equity and common law courts; taxation records in the Exchequer; references in the various state papers domestic; the records of the commissions of the peace, quarter sessions and assizes; Poor Law records; and those of the Church of England acting as a place of registry, a licensing authority, and as a legal jurisdiction. This material was spread over numerous public places of deposit, including the Public Record Office in London, the Essex Record Office in Chelmsford, the Church of England Records Office at Lambeth Palace, the records of the Bishop of London's Commissary at the Guildhall Library, and the Greater London Record Office at County Hall. Some details of the coverage of this database gives an idea of the range and depth of the resource created. For one year, Earls Colne in 1695, one has, for example, baptism, marriage and burial registers; land tax records; bundles of documents and rolls from the quarter sessions; Assize indictments; records of an archdeaconary visitation; and those of apprenticeship indentures generated by the Poor Law administration. The amount and dispersal of this material explains the time required to assemble the final database.

Such material can allow historians to reconstruct the lives of individuals.[126] Take, for example, the case of Edward Osborn, a yeoman. According to the parish registers Osborn was born on 7 April 1663, and was christened on 28 September of that year. In 1683 he was left 20 shillings and a bedstead in her will by Anne Crow, his grandmother. In 1688 he was a witness to the will of John Garrett, and in April 1692 his son Thomas, born in 1690, was christened. Osborn was already an important member of the local elite, because in 1696 he signed the association oath roll at the Essex quarter sessions. The oath was to associate the signatories to the rule of William III in the face of 'a horrid and detestable conspiracy formed and carried on by papists and other wicked and traitorous persons for assassinating his majesty's royal person in order to encourage an invasion from France to subvert our religion laws and liberty...' His position in the local community was underlined by his father's will in that year, by which he became the heir to the landed property of the family. His father died in 1701, since probate act books show Osborn performing the role of executor of his will. In the same year the local baptism registers show him christening four children born at various dates between 1692 and 1701. There was to be another multiple baptism of three children in 1708, and another child was christened in June 1710. But the end of 1701 also saw the trial of a number of men for breaking into his yards and shooting his chickens.

By the second decade of the eighteenth century Osborn was involved in the local administration of the Poor Law. In March 1710 he was a junior overseer of the poor involved in the making of an apprenticeship indenture, and over the next 23 years Osborn is recorded as paying the poor rate on 23 occasions. By 1730 he was 67, and was plainly thinking of his death, since in that year he made his last will and testament. This was not before time because the local parish registers record him as having been 'buried in wool' on Thursday 22 March 1733. This was in conformity to the laws enforcing burial in woollen shrouds to support the woollen industry in England. In April 1733 his will was proved, with his son John acting as executor, and Edward Osborn then disappears from the official record.

Osborn was, of course, an important figure in Earls Colne's local society, and one would expect him to figure in the written record. However, other, less influential, men and women also appear. Take, for example, Margery Manners née Hayward, who married William Manners, husbandman, in April 1582. She survived her husband, who had bequeathed her his cottage 'called Wenders' with his moveable goods in a will of July 1604. Archdeaconry Act Books of 1611 show her acting as administrator of the will after William's death. She made her own will on 12 July 1623, five days before the burial registers record her as being laid to rest in the parish. Yet again, take the case of Osborn's contemporary Deborah Mann, spinster, who was indicted before the Assizes in March 1701 for refusing to work. The same year she appears in the quarter session rolls as a witness in the case of Thomas Kettle of Colchester, who fraudulently delivered wool cards and packs of wool to the wrong person. Deborah must have been well known to the local enforcers of the law because in October 1704 she appeared again before the bench accused with others of being involved in the assault and battery of two labourers. These examples could be multiplied, and historians' knowledge of the lives of such people would be deepened and broadened if the work of the Earls Colne project team were extended to neighbouring parishes, manors and counties. Only then would it be possible to follow people as they migrated through the countryside.

These examples show that people before 1800 were not necessarily anonymous; they were caught up in the meshes of the official administration of the realm. Many of the surviving records reveal such information collection as part of state surveillance but also the creation of rights to property through the official recording of vital events and the will of testators. However, the creation of the Records of Earls Colne database also shows the essentially dispersed nature of the early modern English state.

Conclusion

The picture drawn here of the early modern state, and of society in general, is rather different to that given in the published works on the sociology of information gathering. Local communities were not *gemeinschaft*, insulated from a distant central state, and carrying out their own social control based solely on kinship, neighbourliness and the relations between master and servant. On the contrary, the processes which made up the state were decentralised down to the parish level, and the authority of the central state was a resource that local elites could call upon to protect their own interests, which seemed increasingly threatened by social and economic change. The term 'state' refers, therefore, to a broad constellation of groups – local elites, royal administrators, judges and members of the military – who undertook to carry out the policies of the Crown in Parliament. This was not only for the prestige they gained thereby, but because this served their own material interests. The term will continue to be used in this composite sense throughout the present work, although the groups that compose the state have tended to vary over time. In a certain sense the local 'community' can even be conceived as a by-product of this process of governance – the civil 'parish' was an administrative space defined by the remit of such officers as the overseers of the poor, and its 'chief inhabitants' were those who held such offices, as well as having superior wealth and residential longevity.

Within this decentralised state, information gathering and surveillance were localised and variable but could be as intense and draconian as anything attempted by most modern states. This created rights in some senses but also restrictions on actions and thought. As Bruce Curtis has noted, in a critique of Foucault's concept of 'governmentality', the English state had been attempting to manipulate the population long before the eighteenth and early nineteenth centuries.[127] But this was a localised state that collected information locally, and attempted to pin individuals down to those localities. The central state was also capable of collecting information on its subjects when necessary. However, the Crown's main interests lay in warfare and foreign policy, and central information gathering served these ends, in terms of maintaining the monarch's position within the decentralised network of the state; ensuring that decentralised tax collection worked properly; securing the loyalty of military personnel; and maintaining the good order of the realm to facilitate resource extraction and the loyalty of local elites. The main question that needs to be answered, therefore, is not why state information gathering and surveillance suddenly appeared in the nineteenth century but why such state functions came to be concentrated at the centre. This will be the subject of subsequent chapters of the present work.

4

State information gathering in the classic Liberal State

The constitution of the classic Liberal State, 1830–80

As already noted in Chapter 2, many scholars see the late eighteenth and early nineteenth centuries as marking the genesis of the modern information state. This is, or so it is argued, the period when the central state began to collect information for the control of deviants, and for the planning of urban life. This is certainly a key phase in the process of state formation, although the picture of a centralised, disciplinary state has been overdrawn, and is perhaps a misconception.

The early to mid-Victorian period in England presents a conundrum to modern eyes. On one hand it is seen, for good or ill, as an age of unconstrained capitalist activity, dominated by the 'Victorian values' of private enterprise and personal philanthropy. The modern political right and left look back to it as a period of minimalist state intervention in society with either envy or horror. In this reading of nineteenth-century England both groups are accepting a central argument made by A. V. Dicey in his *Lectures on the Relation between Law and Public Opinion in England during the Nineteenth century*, published in 1905. For Dicey the changing nature of the English state over the nineteenth century could be explained in terms of three organising principles which underlay successive periods of state formation: 'Old Toryism' prior to 1830; *'laissez-faire'* in the period 1830 to 1870; and the age of 'collectivism' thereafter.[1] The political watchwords of the years 1830 to 1870, the period with which the present chapter is mainly concerned, were certainly 'free trade' in economics, and 'retrenchment' in government – classic components of the concept of *laissez-faire*.[2] After the expansion of state activity during the

Napoleonic Wars, this period saw central government expenditure decline from about 12 per cent of the gross national product to six per cent.[3] At the same time, the size of the Civil Service hardly expanded at all between 1821 and 1861, whilst the population of England and Wales swelled by three-quarters.[4]

However, the years 1830 to 1870 also saw the passage of numerous pieces of national legislation that sought to regulate society. One might include here the 1834 Poor Law Amendment Act, which set up the New Poor Law; the 1848 Public Health Act, which began the process of sanitary reform in the cities; the 1829 Metropolitan and 1856 County and Borough Police Acts, which spread the new uniformed police across the country; and the 1870 Education Act, which introduced the concept of education for all children. For Corrigan and Sayer this represented nothing less than a capitalist 'cultural revolution', aimed at transforming class relations during a period of heightened social conflict.[5] Similarly, Philip Harling sees this in terms of the 'social disciplinarian' role of the Victorian state.[6]

The period also saw the rise of powerful civil servants who pushed for the creation of central institutions and legislation to tackle the problems of society. An obvious example of such a bureaucrat was Sir Edwin Chadwick, whose influence lay behind both the New Poor Law and public health reform. Chadwick can be seen as a member of what Theda Skocpol and Dietrich Rueschemeyer have described as the 'knowledge-bearing elites', who were extending their grip on the state in this period.[7] For Harold Perkin, such individuals were not simply servants of the capitalist classes but representatives of a new class and social ideal – that of the 'expert' – that came to dominate society in the course of the modern period. It was they who provided solutions to problems thrown up by capitalist industrialisation, usually to facilitate its workings. But rather than outright oppression, their preferred strategy was the amelioration of conflicts via the creation of consensus and corporate structures, which institutionalised a bounded pluralism.[8] Within the latter there was room for class compromise and individual rights, as long as the basic tenets of capitalism and parliamentary democracy were accepted. Such a strategy helped to persuade radicals that the political elite was not as utterly corrupt and self-interested as they had believed.[9]

In addition, as historians such as Oliver MacDonagh have argued, the mid-nineteenth century also saw a revolution in methods of government predicated upon the discovery and treatment of 'social evils'. In MacDonagh's model there was a first stage in which an 'intolerable situation' was revealed, often by a disaster or 'outrage'. In response, Parliament usually passed initial, permissive or enabling legislation to remove the causes of the problem, but without adequate means of enforcement. This typically led to the appointment of inspectors, or other 'experts', to enforce the legislation. Their involvement with social problems led, in turn, to internal pressure for compulsory legislation, and to a central supervising body to enforce it. In this manner the central state gradually expanded its sphere of operation and its penetration into society.[10] Why situations suddenly became 'intolerable' is left somewhat vague in MacDonagh's work but this pattern of state intervention was plainly marked in the period.

State formation in the mid-nineteenth century only presents such a contradictory appearance – minimalist yet expansive – if one thinks solely in terms of the central state. What was happening, it can be argued, was a gradual shift in the relationships between central and local governance. Almost all the great pieces of social legislation of the Victorian period were designed to expand the activities of local rather than central government. This was, however, to be a local government reformed and monitored by central institutions to ensure that its activities conformed to centrally agreed guidelines. By extending and regularising the local franchise in the towns, the 1835 Municipal Corporations Act began a process whereby local government could be made a fit instrument for carrying out central social policy. Councillors were to be elected by all those liable to pay poor rates, and would normally hold office for three years. As such, members of local authorities were now to be held accountable to a 'public opinion', but one that could be formed nationally rather than locally.[11] It was to be the new incorporations which received powers under MacDonagh's permissive legislation, and which needed to be compelled to undertake action by later compulsory legislation, and by the monitoring of inspectors. Such corporations became the New Poor Law, public health, police and education authorities. Local government expenditure as a proportion of total government spending rose from 21 per cent in 1840 to perhaps 41 per cent in 1890.[12]

The primacy of local activity was perhaps inevitable given the lack of a national political culture. Early Victorians were still mobilised at a local or regional level, whether in the county and urban associations of the middle classes, or the small-scale trade unionism of the working classes.[13] The new industrial town of the early nineteenth century was not in fact a 'society of strangers'. Relationships might be more fluid and instrumental than in the past, and more divided upon class lines, but reciprocity between kin and neighbours was still necessary to meet the crises of life.[14] This was especially so given the cyclical nature of employment in the early capitalist system. Economic and social conflicts were fought out on a local terrain between small-scale manufacturers with roots in the community and their employees.[15] National political parties, or working-class movements, were phenomena that only temporarily overlay intense localised activity.

Attempts to direct local political and social life too closely from Whitehall were likely to end in failure. Thus, the Civil Service career of Chadwick ended abruptly in 1854 when he was ousted from the General Board of Health, on account of his 'over-centralising' tendencies.[16] From then on, government departments responsible for local government affairs, such as the Local Government Board, were careful to respect the constitutional position of the local authorities – they might need to be reminded of their duties, or supported financially, but it was still their responsibility to act.[17] Sir John Bowring explained to Alexis de Tocqueville, when he met the French *savant* in 1833 that, 'England is the country of decentralisation. We have got a government, but we have not got a central administration,' and similar views might have been expressed by many Englishmen in the 1870s.[18]

What was being centralised in the mid-Victorian period was not action but the making and policing of standards. The developing relationship between local and central government, in terms of the setting and monitoring of local norms of behaviour, led to central information gathering.[19] The centre had to measure, and thus understand, local conditions before it could prescribe practical norms, and gauge their implementation. As John Stuart Mill put it in his 'Considerations on Representative Government':

> The authority which is most conversant with principles should be supreme over principles, while that which is most competent in details should have the details left to it. The principal business of the central authority should be to give instruction, of the local authority to apply it. Power may be

localized, but knowledge, to be most useful, must be centralized ... [Central government] ought to keep open a perpetual communication with the localities: informing itself by their experience, and them by its own; giving advice freely when asked, volunteering it when seen to be required; compelling publicity and recordation of proceedings, and enforcing obedience to every general law which the legislature has laid down on the subject of local management.[20]

'Knowledge', of course, increasingly implied statistical knowledge. Such information gathering was limited, in general, to establishing states of affairs prior to legislation, and to monitoring the performance of local government charged with carrying it out. This placed limitations on the sort of data compiled.[21] In part, Mill's emphasis on the importance of maintaining face-to-face relationships in local political communities reflected his attachment to the ideals of classical Greek democracy.[22] However, it also reflected the practical constraints of early Victorian political life. There might, of course, be a considerable difference between the intention behind this system of central control and local practice. Even the New Poor Law was not applied locally in exactly the manner intended by Edwin Chadwick. However, the centre did obtain some influence where none had existed before, and information gathering was used to expand that influence, if in a faltering manner.[23]

A central feature of social policy in this period was also its moralism – it was designed to foster active self-discipline, and personal activity.[24] Men and women were to be taught to be self-sufficient, hard working and moral. The New Poor Law, for example, was intended to inculcate thrift via restricting relief to those prepared to enter the workhouse. For Chadwick, public health provision would reduce the mortality and morbidity that created poverty, and the despair that undermined moral action and independence.[25] Similarly, the new uniformed police patrols were designed to improve the moral tone of public places, whilst prison reform sought to create enclosed environments for 'grinding men good'.[26] This is not to say that previous systems of welfare, policing and criminal justice were not concerned with morality and a certain form of social order. But the new middle-class reformers of the early nineteenth century were far more confident in their ability to apply general rules of good government based on theoretical precepts from the centre.

Such moralism plainly had religious and ethical roots but it was also suited to the creation of a workforce attuned to the needs of the capitalist market-place. Workers had to become rational, economic agents.[27] However, one must guard against seeing the working classes as formless clay upon which such a morality was impressed, since this assumes that they did not also believe in the virtues of independence. This is belied by the long-established demographic practice whereby English men and women appear to have adjusted their age at marriage according to prevailing levels of prosperity so as to build up resources before embarking on the business of married life.[28] The development of working-class institutions of self-help in the eighteenth and nineteenth centuries – friendly societies, trade unions and co-operation – also point in the same direction.[29] Plainly, independence could mean very different things to differing social classes, and it was perhaps the great achievement of nineteenth-century ruling elites to generalise their own definition of the concept amongst other groups in society.

Whatever the reasons for the moralism of social policy in this period, it should be noted that it was not necessarily intended as a means of increasing the power of the state in terms of its penetration into society. The whole intent of the New Poor Law, for example, was to force the population away from dependence on the local state, and in this it was remarkably successful. Thus, there were 6.3 paupers per 100 population receiving some form of poor relief in England and Wales in 1849, but this had declined to 2.5 per 100 in 1900.[30] Similarly, sanitary and public health reforms were designed to remove the working classes still further from dependence on poor relief. Reducing state support may have improved the disciplinary hold that employers had on their employees but this was a rather different strategy to the creation of a disciplinary state.

Both these aspects of English state formation in the early to mid-Victorian period – its localism and its emphasis on moral independence – need to be borne in mind when considering the development of central state information gathering in this period.

The early censuses and the control of deviancy

As already noted, 1801 can be seen as a key date in the genesis of the Information State in England, since it was then that the first decennial census of England and Wales was taken. For the first time in history an attempt was made to take a complete enumeration of the country's entire population. The 1801 census was planned and executed by a clerk of the House of Commons, John Rickman, as were all the censuses up to, and including, that of 1831. As such, the census was plainly a central government project. However, it is only with difficulty that the nineteenth-century censuses can be conceptualised in terms of social control via the identification of individuals, or the central planning of social interaction, as Anthony Giddens appears to argue.

Rather than a response to industrialisation, or looking forward to modern forms of central state intervention in society, the first census appears to have been a reaction to warfare, and a commentary on the past. The year 1800, when the first Census Act was passed, was a time of international conflict, Napoleonic blockade, bad harvests and food shortages. Large numbers of agricultural workers were serving in the militia and so were unable to work on the land. The 1801 census sought, therefore, to get a total for the population of each parish, and subtotals therein for the numbers in three economic categories: those working in agriculture; those in trade, manufactures and handicrafts; and those in other employments. At the same time a separate agricultural survey, showing the number of acres in parishes devoted to differing crops, was also instituted.[31] In this respect, the intent behind early census taking was similar to that which had underlain the work of Gregory King over a century before. Moreover, the 1800 Census Act, like all the decennial Census Acts prior to that of 1840, was entitled, 'An Act for taking an Account of the Population of Great Britain, and the Increase or Diminution thereof'. The population census was also associated with a request sent by Rickman to the parish clergy to provide information on baptisms, marriages and burials from their registers over the previous 100 years. Similar, although more limited, surveys of demographic events were carried out at each of the enumerations from 1811 to 1841.[32] This appears to place these censuses in the context of an earlier population debate that had arisen in the 1750s, as to whether or not the population had increased since the Glorious Revolution of 1688. Conservative defenders of the agricultural interest believed that the population of England had declined under the dominance of a Whig aristocracy and the rising commercial classes. Commerce and political jobbery were seen as having caused a general moral and sexual debauchment that had led to population decline. Others defended the rise of commerce and claimed that the population had increased since 1688. Much of this debate revolved around population estimates based upon taxation records and the evidence of the ecclesiastical registers. This specifically English debate echoed a similar controversy in eighteenth-century France, consequent upon the Baron de Montesquieu's claims that despotic governments caused a decline in the number of their subjects.[33] A new twist was given to the population debate by the publication in 1798 of Thomas Malthus's *Essay on the Principle of Population*.[34]

Similarly pessimistic views to those held by Tory critics of the Whig ascendancy were put forward by radicals such as William Cobbett. As late as the 1820s, despite the evidence of rapid expansion shown by the censuses, Cobbett was convinced that the population was falling. He based his arguments for this on the evidence of the discrepancy between the large size of a number of ancient rural churches and their tiny modern congregations. In his usual blunt manner he insisted in his *Rural Rides* that men who believed the results of the censuses must have been 'brutified' by the prevailing corrupt political system, and that, 'A man that can suck that [population growth] in will believe, literally believe, that the *moon is made of green cheese*.'[35] Cobbett's views reflect the outlook of a man formed almost wholly within the agricultural world of the south of England, where population was indeed declining, or at least stagnant. It was, of course, the cities, the 'wens' that Cobbett avoided at all costs, that saw the great explosion of numbers during the ongoing Industrial Revolution.

The belief that population growth was a mark of good government, and legitimated the rule of political elites, places early English censuses in the broader context of Foucault's arguments respecting the replacement of the 'pastoral power' of the Church by that of the State. However, as already noted, such ideas could be found in sixteenth- and seventeenth-century England, and did not necessarily have their origins in the classical Enlightenment, as Foucault believed. What was perhaps significant in the early nineteenth century was the need to publicise the vitality of the nation as part of a campaign to win support for the state at a time of political unrest.

Certain other aspects of the pre-Victorian censuses point in this direction. In 1831, for example, a detailed question on occupations was introduced in order, in part, to gather information to discredit the subversive use of economic theories such as the labour theory of value.[36] The early state census can be seen in these terms as a larger example of the private surveys being carried out at the same time. The early nineteenth century saw the formation of numerous local statistical societies by middle-class employers and professionals in order to gather statistical information on the conditions of the lower orders. If the 'truth' of social conditions was revealed, it was reasoned, then this would allay popular discontent.[37] But, as will be discussed shortly, such data collection, whether by the state or private individuals, was not seen as a precursor to central control but to local activity.

Nor could the official censuses of the early nineteenth century be used for direct physical surveillance of the population. Rickman's surveys were headcounts, rather than nominal censuses. Overseers of the poor had merely to enter the numbers of persons, or families, in various categories on the printed schedules. However, some local overseers of the poor calculated the totals required in the official returns after collecting the names and details of the members of the households in their parishes, and subsequently used this material for local Poor Law purposes. Some of these parish listings, especially in London, were even collected via the use of locally printed forms.[38] If these early censuses were used for surveillance, then this reflected a continuation of local forms of state control, rather than the creation of new central mechanisms.

Names were first sent to London in the census of 1841, when the administration of the decennial enumerations was taken over by the newly established General Register Office (GRO). The GRO had taken over the task of administering the census at short notice when Rickman died suddenly in 1840. The Registrar-General, Thomas Lister, wanted to ask a broader range of questions than Rickman, and discovered that the cost of having these made by enumerators gathering information by door-to-door enquiry would be prohibitive. Following a suggestion put forward by the Statistical Society of London (the future Royal Statistical Society), the GRO instituted the practice of instructing enumerators to hand out schedules to household heads for them to supply details of the members of their households on Census Night.[39] In the mid-Victorian period, information was collected on the age, sex, marital status, relationship to household head, occupation, birthplaces, and certain medical disabilities of each individual. The household schedules were then to be collected by the census enumerators, copied by them into standardised books, and forwarded to the GRO in London for analysis. The inclusion of names facilitated the work of analysis, and provided a check on the enumerators who, it was feared, might 'sit at home and make marks, and no examiner could detect this error'.[40] As with early modern taxation records, the main targets of such surveillance were the agents of the state, rather than private citizens.

There is no evidence that the census returns were used systematically by the state for tracing individuals in the nineteenth century. The census enumeration books were organised via place and street, and it would have been necessary to know where people lived before the voluminous returns could be consulted. Given the speed with which people changed their place of abode, especially in the cities, the census would soon have ceased to have much practical use as a means of individual surveillance. As any genealogist knows, finding people in the enumerators' books is a difficult, and frequently fruitless, activity. The Victorian censuses were never turned into an ongoing population register, as in other European countries at this date, by the imposition of a duty to report changes of address to the authorities.[41] The GRO was indeed at pains to turn down the numerous requests from foreign governments for information on the whereabouts of their citizens resident in England and Wales. Not only were the mid-Victorian census returns not used for the purposes of individual surveillance but most were effectively lost by the GRO, only turning up by chance in the roof of the Palace of Westminster in the early twentieth century.[42]

In the absence of any means of automating information retrieval, searching the manuscript census enumerators' returns in the nineteenth century was a purely manual operation. Every act of analysis required staff to work their way methodically through the enumerators' books, noting the occurrence of people with particular characteristics on large coding sheets.[43] The tedium of information processing in the Victorian GRO was such that it was not unknown for clerks to be 'seized by mania', and to have to be hurriedly removed to the insane asylum at Bedlam.[44] The possibility, and severe limitations, of using the census as a means of individual surveillance is revealed by the only nineteenth-century occasion when this was actually attempted. In 1871, under instructions from the Home Secretary, the GRO broke its pledge of confidentiality with respect to the recently collected census returns, and provided the London School Board with the names and addresses of all children aged between three and 13 years, their exact ages, and the names and occupations of their parents. This was to facilitate the provision of education under the 1870 Education Act. But this single act of surveillance tied up the GRO's clerical resources at a crucial stage in the analysis of the census returns, and the Office had to ask the Treasury for the huge sum of £2,000, as a contingency, to cover the clerical work involved. This was at a time when the central processing of the entire Scottish census of 1871 cost only £6,339.[45] With Victorian methods of data retrieval, the population censuses were hardly a viable means of individual surveillance.

Civil registration, property and civil rights

But if the census was not a means of direct surveillance, what of that other system of information collection with which the GRO was tasked – civil registration? Although public office-holders linked to the state, that is, the parish clergy of the Church of England, had been collecting information on baptisms, marriages and burials for centuries, the passing of the 1836 Registration Act established a new, centralised form of civil registration. Local registration districts were established based on Poor Law unions, and local registrars of births, marriages and deaths appointed for each. These officers, numbering 2,193 in 1839, were to be responsible for registering such events in their districts, and for-warding copies of the certificates of births, marriages and deaths to the GRO in London. The latter was to be responsible for the overall administration of the system, and the maintenance of a central database of the certificates.[46]

Civil registration certainly came to be implicated in a whole system for regulating the life-courses of individuals. By 1891, the Factory Acts had established a minimum working age of 11 years in factories, and allowed 11- to 14-year-olds to work no more than half time. Education Acts from the 1870s onwards came to mandate the compulsory education of children in certain age groups. In the twentieth century, numerous other aspects of life came to be regulated according to age – driving vehicles, buying alcohol and cigarettes, placing bets, watching 'adult' films, and so on. Citizens had to be a certain age to vote, join the armed forces or retire.[47] Proof of age in many of these situations meant the production of a birth certificate, and, indeed, under various acts of parliament the GRO provided such certificates at a cut price when they needed to be presented in such circumstances.[48]

This use of registration is plainly one of social control but it is difficult to see it simply in terms of the interests of ruling elites. It is certainly true that working-class families in the nineteenth century often resented the imposition of restrictions on the ability of their children to contribute to the family income.[49] Compulsory education could also be seen as a means of educating the proletariat in the virtues of capitalism. However, the Factory Acts also set limits on the freedom of capitalists to use 'human capital' as they saw fit, and was deeply resented by many of them at the time of their introduction. Indeed, employers and working-class families often colluded to get round the legislation.[50] Moreover, many of these aspects of the state regulation of life-stages appear to represent a mediation between the generations, as much as between social classes. One might conceivably see this in terms of an attempt to co-opt sections of the working classes by increasing the power and authority of parents, especially fathers, although this was not always how parents saw it at the time. This increased state regulation could, however, enable some new forms of social survey to be undertaken. When Charles Booth, the pioneer sociologist, began a house-by-house survey of London in the 1890s, he turned to school attendance officers for information on the circumstances of households.[51]

There was, moreover, one use of the registration of births that reveals an attempt by the Victorian state, and the medical experts that had colonised it, to penetrate into the very bodies of its subjects – the manner in which it underpinned compulsory vaccination for smallpox. This brought the Victorian state and the registration service into conflict with important sections of civil society. An Act of Parliament of 1840 had banned inoculation for smallpox whilst making vaccination for the same more freely available. In 1853, however, the Vaccination Extension Act took the unprecedented step of making infant vaccination compulsory. The imposition of an unpleasant and dangerous invasion into the bodies of helpless infants was bitterly contested throughout the nineteenth century by organisations such as the Anti-Vaccination League, which drew support from all social classes.[52] This was an example of the popular opposition to state compulsion that can also be seen in campaigns against the Contagious Diseases Act, and in related conflicts. The 1864 Contagious Diseases Act, and subsequent legislation, provided for the compulsory examination by a naval or military surgeon of any woman deemed by the police to be a 'common prostitute'. Initially the Act was to be enforced in garrison towns in the south of England. If a woman was diagnosed as having venereal disease, she became liable to detention in a locked ward. The Acts were seen by many as legalised rape, and led to the creation of a vociferous movement for their repeal.[53]

The registration system was fully implicated in the vaccination system since, under the 1853 Act, medical practitioners were to transmit duplicate certificates of vaccination to the local registrars, who were to keep them in searchable registers. The central GRO was to provide the necessary books and forms for this purpose. Under the 1867 Vaccination Act, the registrar was to deliver a notice of vaccination to parents registering a birth that required them to vaccinate the child. Medical practitioners or parents were also to transmit certificates of vaccination to the local registrar as before. But the latter was now to notify the local Poor Law guardians if he had not received the appropriate certificate during the preceding half year so that the guardians could look into the matter. Finally, under the 1871 Vaccination Act (1867) Amendment Act, every registrar was to transmit a return of all births and deaths of children under 12 months to the local vaccination officer at least once a month.

Conflicts over vaccination appear to have played a key role in the passing of the 1874 Births and Deaths Registration Act. This piece of legislation made two key changes to the registration system. First, it enforced the certification of causes of death by a qualified medical practitioner, and, secondly, it introduced fines on householders, or next of kin, for failing to register births and deaths within a set period. Historians have implied that both innovations were introduced to improve the quality of medical and demographic statistics, and this was certainly the spirit in which they were suggested by the Royal Sanitary Commission in its report of 1871.[54] However, the debates in Parliament reveal that there was increasing concern respecting 'baby farming' and infanticide in the 1860s and early 1870s. The activities of the Anti-Vaccination League in inducing parents to conceal births in order to prevent vaccination were also crucial in the passing of the Act.[55]

However, it should be noted that the opposition to compulsory vaccination eventually led to the introduction of a 'conscience clause' in the 1898 Vaccination Act, via which the compulsory aspects of the system began to be removed.[56] This was at the same time as countries such as Germany were moving towards legal penalties for non-vaccination.[57] In a similar manner, the Contagious Diseases Acts had already been repealed in 1886.[58] Thus, there were limits to what the Victorian state in England could impose upon its subjects via the use of systems of surveillance. English men and women refused to be simply 'objects' upon which the state worked, and the state, if reluctantly, had to recognise this.

But if the social-control functions of registration were limited in the Victorian period, what was its purpose? The establishment of the system has been seen in terms of the need to release Nonconformists from the requirement to register with the clergy of the Established Church, and the desire of medical professionals for accurate information on mortality. Nonconformists were concerned that their own ceremonies were not recognised in courts of law, and that they were forced, therefore, to submit to baptism, marriage and burial in the parish church. At a time when there was a gradual loosening of the disabilities on Dissenters, such a monopoly on the part of the Church of England was seen as intolerable.[59] Certainly, Dissenters were active in pushing for the new system in Parliament, and the new death certificates met the needs of doctors by carrying a question on cause of death. However, it is surely odd that a purely religious issue should be resolved by the establishment of a vast secular system of centralised surveillance, rather than via the simple expedient of declaring Nonconformist registers legal records. Similarly, despite the interest shown in death registration by the medical community, their requirements were hardly mentioned in the parliamentary debates leading to the passing of the 1836 Act.[60]

The crucial issue that lay behind the establishment of the new system of civil registration was, in fact, the need to protect property rights via the accurate recording of lines of descent. In an increasingly complex capitalist economy, and one in which property descended by entail, primogeniture or wills, there was a need to protect title to property by recording who was related to whom, who was the first born, and who was legitimate. Members of the aristocracy could produce such proof of title via their muniment rooms, pedigrees and the hiring of heralds and genealogists. The middle classes, however, did not have such resources at their disposal. For them, the dispersal of parochial registers across the country in parish chests and diocesan offices, allied to the poor physical preservation of, and lack of finding aids to, such records, created considerable problems. Fortunes might be lost through the inability to prove in court that property rightly belonged to a particular individual, or to the persons from whom it had been purchased. Proving title in such a dispersed system was also expensive, since it might require visits to a number of differing places of record. The expansion of Nonconformity, and the inherent difficulties in working back from date of baptism to date of birth, further undermined confidence in the quality of the parochial records of the Established Church.[61] In terms of its comprehensiveness and organisation, ecclesiastical registration in England and Wales was far inferior to that in countries such as Norway, where there were no comparable dissenters and the state had applied legal sanctions to those who failed to register deaths since the eighteenth century.[62]

In the aftermath of the 1832 Reform Act, which increased the responsiveness of Parliament to middle-class interests, a concerted effort was made to rectify such deficiencies by the creation of the centralised system of civil registration. This would explain why the new GRO was housed in Somerset House in London, close to the Inns of Court where lawyers resided, and to the future Supreme Court of Judicature in the Strand. The new institution's main clients were members of the legal profession, and most of its staff were employed on creating the vast registers of births, marriages and deaths, and indexes to them, which the former wished to consult. In his *Annual Report* for 1859, the then Registrar-General noted that in that year 4,133 successful searches had been made in the registers at the GRO, the 'greater number' being undertaken by solicitors. There were, of course, a considerable number of searches that were unsuccessful.[63] As can be seen from Table 4.1, the numbers of searches in the central GRO grew by leaps and bounds.

This centralisation of registration data was associated with a fundamental reform of the English legal system. There was widespread discontent with the complexities, arcane trappings and delays of the central courts of law, which Jeremy Bentham excoriated in so many of his writings,[64] and which Charles Dickens satirised in his portrait of the case of *Jarndyce* v. *Jarndyce* in *Bleak House*. According to John Stuart Mill, every time the client of a lawyer settled his estate he had to pay the latter richly for interpreting the 'cabinet of historical curiosities' that was the body of English law formed by centuries of accretions of judgments.[65] These concerns led to an extensive process of legal reform, associated with lawyers such as Brougham and Mansfield, which in the course of the Victorian period saw such developments as the elaboration of the classical theories of contract and limited liability; new laws relating to trade unions, divorce and women's property rights; the amalgamation of the higher courts into the Supreme Court of Judicature; and the establishment of the county court system.[66]

Table 4.1   Numbers of searches in the registers at the central GRO, 1845–95

Year	Average annual searches
1845–49	952
1850–54	1,669
1855–59	3,485
1860–64	7,025
1865–69	11,309
1870–74	18,292
1875	25,407
1885	36,450
1895	53,289

Sources: *38th Annual Report of the Registrar General for 1875* (London: HMSO, 1877), p. liii; *59th Annual Report of the Registrar General for 1896* (London: HMSO, 1897), p. xxxvi.

In order to make the civil register a complete record of lines of descent, it was necessary to ensure that it covered all classes of society. It was impossible to say that members of the lowest classes in society would not become property owners in time, or were not the descendants of members of 'decayed' landed families, as in the case of the Durbeyfields in Thomas Hardy's *Tess of the d'Urbervilles*. It was assumed, therefore, that all classes in society would see the practical advantage of maintaining their civil rights, in T. H. Marshall's conception of the term. As Lord John Russell, the Home Secretary, explained in Parliament, he was 'quite sure that when the plan was established, the advantages attending it would be so obvious, and would soon be felt by all classes of persons, they would so soon perceive the benefit of having their children's names inserted in the general register, that it would not be long before everyone would be willing to concur in carrying out the plan'.[67] Indeed, civil registration coverage seems to have been fairly complete within a comparatively short period of time.[68] This was despite the lack of any means of compelling registration – it was the registrar who was fined for non-registration of births, marriages and deaths, not members of the public. In this way, an institution for the preservation of the civil rights of one class helped to generalise those rights, if in a formal sense, to all social classes. This was part of that creation of a generalised public sphere in which all, in theory, can participate, which is such a marked feature of modern Western societies.[69]

The GRO was, in fact, only one of a number of places for recording the property rights of named individuals being created at this time. Amongst one of the earliest of these bodies was perhaps the Public Record Office (PRO), the modern national archives, established in 1838. Although the Public Records Commissions of the early nineteenth century had noted the importance of public records to historians, the legal uses of this material were also emphasised.[70] The decisions of courts of law, royal grants of rights and property enrolled in Chancery, *inquisitions post mortem*, and the series of deeds and other instruments in the possession of the state, were plainly of crucial importance to property holders. The Public Record Office Act of 1838, in fact, only related to the records of the courts of law, and it was not until 1852 that an order in Council brought the records of the executive departments of state into the PRO's ambit.[71] A new PRO repository for housing the central legal records began to be erected in Chancery Lane in central London in the 1850s, close to the GRO in Somerset House, and surrounded by the law courts and the Inns of Court. This incorporated the old Rolls Chapel, under whose seats the records of the Court of Chancery had been kept for many years. Until quite recently one of the main public reading rooms in the Chancery Lane building was known as the Legal Search Room, to distinguish it from historical research carried out in the Literary Search Room. It was only in 1996 that the national archives finally decamped from legal London to the relative obscurity of Kew in the suburbs of the metropolis.

The area of London around the GRO and PRO rapidly became the location for the establishment of numerous other places of record. The Patent Office, set up under the Patent Law Amendment Act of 1852, also moved into Chancery Lane, and spawned a Trade Marks Registry there by 1875.[72] A Land Registry was created round the corner at 34 Lincoln's Inn Fields under the provisions of the 1862 Land Registry Act.[73] This was next door to the Design Registry, which had been set up in 1839 by the Board of Trade to protect title to property in textile and other manufactured designs.[74] In addition, a Principal Probate Registry for holding testamentary documents was attached to the new Court of Probate. The latter had been established in 1857 to replace the various ecclesiastical courts that had dealt so inefficiently with wills and administrations until that date.[75] The wills repository was originally sited in Great Knightrider Street next to Doctors Commons, where lawyers specialising in probate cases resided, but moved to Somerset House by 1875. Here it lodged cheek by jowl with the GRO.[76] The creation of this complex of places of record should not be seen in terms of the middle classes using the state to impose social control on the rest of society. As with civil registration, it represented the creation of those generalised civil rights that helped to create civil society itself, although a civil society bounded by the institution of private property. Such systems of data gathering might help to identify the deviant but usually in order to protect individual rights, if of a specific kind, rather than to enable ruling elites to suppress dissent.

The creation of this centralised state system of identification of the individual's right to property, indeed of the individual as a property-owning citizen, sits uneasily with a conception of England as an essentially backward nation state. One often thinks of modern

France as the classic centralised state, yet when this was born in the upheavals of the French Revolution, the identification of *citoyen* via civil registration was still decentralised in the municipalities, leading to endless confusion.[77] The Victorians in England were far more advanced in creating national systems of identification – but for the purposes of consolidating civil society rather than the nation state. This may help to explain why in England, unlike France, it was perfectly legal to change one's name, or indeed to use another name, as long as this was not for criminal purposes.[78] In England the identification of citizens was to help individuals themselves as property holders, rather than to increase the power of the state.

In the course of the nineteenth century, the registration system also helped to protect, or create, other forms of individual rights. Registration can be seen as helping to maintain legally sanctioned monopolies by which professional groups were guaranteed an income stream. The 1858 Medical Act, which set up a General Medical Council (GMC) for the purpose, amongst others, of maintaining a register of suitably qualified medical practitioners, can be seen in this light. Those not suitably qualified, in the sense of not having recognised medical qualifications, were excluded from the register, and had certain legal disabilities placed upon them. Under the Act, local registrars of births and deaths were to send notices of the demise of doctors in their districts to the GMC to enable the medical register to be kept up to date.

The establishment and maintenance of the register has been seen by scholars such as Ivan Waddington as the first tentative step towards the gradual closure of the medical profession to those practising 'unorthodox' medicine, which helped maintain the incomes of those medical practitioners within the magic circle.[79] Irvine Loudon, however, claims that the 1858 Act failed to create a professional monopoly since it did not outlaw 'unorthodox' medicine.[80] Similarly, Anne Digby calculates that doctors' incomes were falling in the late Victorian period, although one could argue that they might have fallen further without some ring-fencing.[81] Whatever the precise effect of the strategy of professional closure, the use of civil registration to maintain the medical register appeared so successful to contemporaries that similar provisions were extended by law to other groups such as pharmacists, dentists and veterinary surgeons.[82] In a sense this was social control in the benefit of a series of elites, since 'deviant' practitioners were excluded from business, and thus prices were held higher than they might have been.

The work of the GRO also helped underpin that other facet of Marshall's model of developing rights – participation in political activity via the vote. The population totals in the censuses helped in the process of maintaining equitable electoral boundaries. This became increasingly important as the franchise widened in the course of the nineteenth century. In addition, under the 1878 Parliamentary and Municipal Registration Act, local civil registrars were to send overseers of the poor the names, ages and addresses of all males dying within their districts, to enable the overseers to maintain the local voters' register. By 1920 there was an Electoral Division within the GRO concerned solely with the workings of the 1918 Representation of the People Act, and with 'numerous other statutes dealing with franchise law (Parliamentary or local), electoral registration and the conduct of elections'. This included responsibility for supervising the preparation of registers of electors by local registration officials.[83] In this the GRO was undertaking a function found elsewhere in Western states – in the USA, for example, the census had been used from 1790 as a means of apportioning state representation in Congress.[84]

With the exception of vaccination, civil registration, as in the case of Victorian census taking, was not conceived as a means to enable the state to keep watch on potential deviants. Recording where and when people were born, married and died is hardly the best means of facilitating social control in this sense. Indeed, one might argue that civil registration helped abolish the whole concept of religious deviancy by making it possible for Nonconformists to prove their legal rights without recourse to the clergy of the Church of England. Rather, Somerset House was to be seen as a resource that individuals could draw upon in their daily lives, although it was assumed that this would be for the purpose of substantiating rights to private property.

Statistics, personal responsibility and the local state

Despite its initial creation as a place of record, the Victorian GRO rapidly gained a reputation for the generation of statistics. These included the vast series of statistical reports based on returns collected after each census, and a series of *Annual Reports of the Registrar General*, and associated publications, giving details of vital events and the state of public health.[85] In modern Britain one would tend to view the generation of such statistics as a preliminary to central intervention in society but this was not necessarily the case in the period under discussion here.

The statistics derived from the census returns by the GRO can certainly be placed in a much broader movement to create a picture of the nature and relative strength of the concert of European nation states. As early as the 1850s, European official statisticians began meeting in International Statistical Congresses to plan for the collection of information across the Continent on a uniform basis.[86] Such men were fired by the belief, ably propagated by the great Belgian statist Adolphe Quetelet, that if enough data could be collected on a common basis it would reveal patterns of human behaviour that could be reduced to laws, as in the physical sciences. This would then give states the means of effectively intervening in society.[87] In Foucault's terms, this represented the reification of 'population' as an entity whose characteristics could be discovered and manipulated.

William Farr, the GRO's statistical superintendent, was the British representative to the first such meeting in Belgium in 1853, and returned with a proposal for a state statistical apparatus to undertake a comprehensive series of surveys on a uniform European pattern, covering:

1   state revenue and expenditure 'well classified';
2   civil and military establishments, and the expense of local and municipal government;
3   the census of population taken at the same, and at equal or at least corresponding intervals of time, across Europe;
4   the registration of marriages, births and deaths, and causes of deaths;
5   the emigration and immigration of population;
6   churches, scientific societies, schools, public institutions of various kinds, connected with the 'moral and intellectual progress of the people';
7   friendly societies, savings banks, insurance societies, institutions for the relief of the poor, charities and social institutions of various kinds;

8   crimes and punishments;
9   surveys, maps, descriptions and measurements of the territory; 'indications of the superficial and subterraneous contents of the land'; observations on the temperatures, rain and other elements of climate;
10   statistics of agriculture;
11   statistics of industry;
12   statistics of commerce.[88]

This can be seen as representing an attempt by a pan-European class of 'experts' to create data to underpin the creation of administrative structures and homogenous representations that would consolidate the nation state. In this the experts were perhaps looking to their own self-interest, as the employees of the state, rather than simply to the needs of capitalism. Certainly, well-read men and women in England in the 1850s would not have based their understanding of the nation on incomplete, personal experience, as William Cobbett had in the 1820s. However, the full implementation of Farr's vision took a century to complete, and his grandiose proposal, contained in his report on the Belgian congress, was quietly filed away by the Treasury, which had paid for his trip. The introduction of the various components of this project depended on the creation of a perceived need on the part of the political and administrative classes, and this was absent in the mid-Victorian period. In addition, the administrative structures for statistical production in the United Kingdom in the Victorian period did not lend themselves to the creation of a unitary picture of the state. As already noted, each of the separate kingdoms – England, Scotland and Ireland – eventually had their own General Register Office, which analysed and presented data in differing, and sometimes incompatible, ways. Statistics emphasised the disunity of the UK, rather than homogenised it.

It is also difficult to see how much of this data could be used for central intervention in society when there was no administrative or legal machinery for such intervention. Thus, the Victorian GRO was well aware of the military uses to which accurate population totals could be put. William Farr, for example, wrote a piece entitled 'The Great Powers' in the *Annual Report of the Registrar General* for 1853, based on international census and registration data. Farr's essay was an unabashed exercise in weighing the relative military might of the Great Powers, for, as he noted, 'The aggressive and defensive powers of states are made up of many elements: the number of men available for war is, next to the martial character of the people, one of the most important.' He went on to calculate the population of an age to bear arms and the numbers actually in the armies of England, France, Turkey, Austria, Prussia and Russia.[89] Farr appears to have envisaged the comparative demography of nations in almost Darwinian terms: 'There is a relationship betwixt death and national primacy: numbers turn the tide in the struggle of populations and the most mortal die out.'[90] These considerations might help to explain the timing of the first appearance of tables on the population and demography of particular nations in the *Annual Reports*. Thus, in the aftermath of the French expulsion of the Austrians from parts of Italy in 1859, the GRO began publishing a comparison of vital rates in England, France, Austria and Italy.[91] Similarly, tables on Prussia began to appear on a regular basis in the aftermath of the Franco-Prussian War.[92] However, England did not possess any state machinery for conscription that could have made use of such information.[93] The country did not need such administrative structures in the aftermath of the Napoleonic Wars since its defence depended on a highly professional navy. In this England stood in marked contrast to many Continental powers, which introduced military conscription in the course of the nineteenth century. In states such as Russia the taking of the census was intimately connected with supporting this system.[94]

Similarly, much of the analysis of civil registration data was in fact for medical purposes, as was that found in the *Census Reports*. In the *1861 Census Report*, for example, the largest section of the commentary, nearly a third of the whole report, was given over to an analysis of the contents of the column in the returns devoted to medical disabilities. This was despite the universal recognition that the information gathered on blindness and the deaf and dumb was unreliable and incomplete. Between 1851 and 1891 the only major innovation introduced into the census schedule was the addition to this column of questions relating to the imbecility, idiocy or lunacy of household members; an enquiry that was hardly likely to produce very accurate data.[95] Yet there was no provision of health care by the central state until the establishment of the National Health Service in the 1940s.

In addition, the vast statistical outpourings of the Victorian GRO did not always appear in a form suitable for central intervention. Much of the mortality data in the *Annual Reports* related to local, rather than national, conditions, often in what appears today to be tedious detail. The information contained in the *Census Reports* had a similar local bias, enumerating age and sex ratios, marital status, occupational structures, and details of birthplaces, down to the level of counties and boroughs. Nor did the detailed conventions used in arranging much of this material lend themselves to intervention in social or economic life. Occupational data in the mid-Victorian *Census Reports*, for example, included employers and employees, the retired and the unemployed, under the same occupational headings. A term such as 'Cotton manufacture' in the occupational tables included the owners of cotton mills, their employees who span and wove the thread, and the clerks who worked in their offices.[96] Such were the problems with using the census for economic analysis that in 1888 Charles Booth, the social investigator, and the economist Alfred Marshall, led a deputation of social scientists to the Chancellor of the Exchequer and the President of the Local Government Board, demanding revisions to the occupational classification systems and the establishment of a new Census Office.[97]

But these apparent inadequacies in the GRO's statistical work become explicable if one examines its work in terms of the constitution of the classic liberal state outlined above. Statistics were not intended primarily to facilitate central intervention so much as personal and local responsibility. It does not appear, for example, to have been medical science, or the central provision of health care, that lay behind the initial introduction of cause of death into death certificates and the creation of a statistical arm within the GRO. Rather, it was the need to provide data for actuarial tables, and to inform the public about the healthiness, or otherwise, of various localities and occupations. This reflected the concerns of followers of Jeremy Bentham, such as Edwin Chadwick, to underpin what they took to be rights and obligations within the working-class family via a two-pronged strategy. On the one hand, working men and women were to be encouraged to fulfil their duty to maintain their families via the threat of the workhouse under the New Poor Law. On the other, they were to be encouraged to act 'rationally' by the provision of information on the risks associated with certain unhealthy jobs or places of residence; and by the security of knowing that the friendly societies and insurance schemes in which they invested their money were actuarially sound. Thus, a considerable proportion of the *Annual Reports of the Registrar General* in the 1840s and early 1850s was given over to publishing life tables for insurance purposes. The actuarial work of the GRO gradually faded away thereafter because the national life tables created by Farr were of limited use to insurance companies and friendly societies that insured specific social or occupational groups. Such bodies could also generate life tables from their own extensive data, or, in the case of friendly societies, via the pooling of the life experience of their members by the Registry of Friendly Societies.[98]

As the actuarial work of the GRO declined, so its medical work expanded under Farr's direction. Farr was a mathematically minded medical man who subsequently used the information collected on cause of death and mortality to forward medical and sanitary science through the publication of general, local and cause-specific mortality rates, and his investigations into how diseases spread (epidemiology). His development of medical classifications of diseases (nosologies) led eventually to the modern International Classification of Diseases.[99] Farr also used local mortality rates to compare differing districts, and invented a 'Healthy Places Mortality Rate', based on rural communities, in order to estimate 'preventable' mortality in the cities. This was used to shame unhealthy districts into sanitary reform, or at least to provide ammunition for local sanitary reformers to press for change.[100] This use of statistical data was part of Mill's strategy of deploying centralised information to stimulate local activity.

Farr coupled his presentation of local statistical data with a commentary in an accusatory style that gained publicity via the wide circulation of his reports as Parliamentary Papers. A flavour of his rhetoric can be obtained from the following extract from the quarterly returns in the *Annual Report* for 1853 relating to Newcastle upon Tyne:

> What no sceptical philosopher would have dared to propose as an experiment, what no haughty conqueror ever condemned the inhabitants of a subjugated city to endure – this fine English town on the Tyne – the centre of the coal trade – of intelligence of every kind – and of engineering

knowledge – has done and suffered. All the excreta, which are thrown into the streets or water closets, are washed down the acclivities of the streets into the river; the fermenting mass is driven up and down by the tides, and has thence since July been pumped by the engine at Elswick all over the town through the water pipes for domestic uses: it has been used for ablution, it has been washed over the floors, it has been drunk as a beverage by many of the children and the wives, as well as large numbers of the higher and middle as well as the working men of the town. This sad fact in the history of Newcastle will be remembered when the loss of 1,500 lives [from cholera], by which it was followed, is forgotten.[101]

For the GRO, the census also fed into its broader project of personal empowerment, and local medical and sanitary reform. Population totals for named administrative districts were required in order to work out local mortality rates, expressed in so many deaths per thousand population. Local sex and age ratios had also to be established to allow death rates to be corrected so as to enable differing places to be properly compared. Information on occupations was required to enable occupational life tables to be calculated. Hence, occupational categories in the *Census Reports* had to include all men and women, whether employed, out of work or retired, in order to allow the calculation of life expectancies at all ages. Understanding the occupational categories in the mid-Victorian censuses in terms of a survey of health also explains why they were arranged according to the material being worked up, and why employers, hands and clerical workers were all lumped together. Farr assumed that the materials people worked with, or which were in the atmosphere where they worked, affected their health.[102]

In still broader terms, Farr believed that the key to understanding differential death rates between the countryside and the town, and between various areas within towns, was population density. The higher this was, the greater the problems associated with removing human effluent, which was in turn the prime source of the 'zymots' that led to disease. 'Zymots' was Farr's term for hypothetical chemical pathogens, which were supposed to have poisoned the blood. Thus, the cause of cholera was taken to be an unknown chemical, dubbed 'cholerine', in the surroundings of the deceased. Indeed, the whole structure of the mid-Victorian censuses can be seen in terms of a survey of the factors contributing to the growth of population density, and thus to the health of the people. Hence questions on the numbers of houses and people in defined areas; on the determinants of family formation and reproduction, such as the age, sex and marital status of the population; and patterns of migration.[103]

These public health activities of the GRO need to be seen in terms of social rights and obligations at the level of the locality, since the whole public health movement of the Victorian period was predicated upon the assertion that local authorities had sanitary duties towards the members of their communities, and that members of the public had rights to health. The former concept was enshrined in the 1848 Public Health Act, which contained a provision that local authorities could be compelled to establish health boards to implement local sanitary reform if their annual mortality rates were found to be above 23 per thousand, as measured by the GRO. Conceiving of the responsibilities of the state, both local and central, and the legitimate claims of the citizen in these terms, was something that would have appeared wildly revolutionary 50 years earlier.

It could be argued, however, that these early statistical activities of the GRO helped to narrow what a right to health could mean in practice. As Christopher Hamlin has recently claimed, the eighteenth century conceived of ill health and death as reflecting the effect on individual, unique constitutions of a multiplicity of environmental factors – heat, cold, damp, aridity, diet, bodily movement or inactivity – known as the 'non-naturals'. This model of health could be used by early nineteenth-century radicals, such as the Chartists, to claim rights to decent diets, housing and working conditions. By narrowing the concept of disease to that of the effect of monocausal pathogens derived from human effluent on the body, Edwin Chadwick, Hamlin argues, reconceptualised social medicine as public health – the right to health became the right to proper sanitation. Rights could be delivered administratively, rather than in terms of social and economic change.[104]

The early medical classifications of William Farr, with their insistence on the naming of a single 'primary' cause of death, rather than attributing deaths to general environmental factors, fits into this Chadwickian project. Rather than diseases being caused by general social conditions, Farr saw them in terms of his individual chemical pathogens. The only exception to this was his early belief that 'starvation' was a possible cause of death, for which he was roundly criticised by Chadwick.[105] But like Chadwick, Farr saw decent sanitary arrangements, rather than far-reaching changes in social organisation, as the solution to the problems of ill health. Again, as so often with state information gathering in this period, what was important was not the suppression of deviancy, or the central control of the physical environment, but the provision of rights, if in the circumscribed form appropriate to preserving the basis of a capitalist society. But sanitary reform, involving restrictions on how houses could be built and rented, how businesses could be run, and increasing the local rates, also placed restrictions on the freedom of the well-to-do to use their property as they wished. Property carried responsibilities as well as rights.[106] Even Chadwick eventually came to the view that, '*laissez faire* means letting mischief work and evils go on that do not affect ourselves'.[107] The creed of the sanitary 'expert' thus helped to modify the concept of absolute private property.

Thus, although the analysis of 'population' through statistics may have been the key to understanding society, this did not mean that the mid-Victorian central state acted upon this entity directly. Rather it sought to change the behaviour of individuals via the provision of information and the creation of rights and obligations. To this end statistical data in parliamentary reports was disseminated widely to such bodies as mechanics' institutes.[108] Population 'thinking' did not lead to centralised population policies. This would explain why the scale and range of information collection by the GRO in the period was also quite modest, as were its resources. Throughout the Victorian period the permanent staffing of the GRO did not exceed 90 clerks, and its Statistical Department never comprised more than 19.[109] This is perhaps understandable, given the quite narrow sanitary project of the GRO and its role as an agent of propaganda rather than of central planning.

State surveillance of the deviant in mid-Victorian England

This discussion of official information gathering should not be taken to imply that the Victorian state was not concerned with the surveillance of those regarded as deviant. The early nineteenth century saw, after all, the formation of uniformed police forces throughout the country. But these were mostly local manifestations of state authority, and the surveillance they provided was mainly physical rather than based on information gathering.

Many modern scholars see the creation of the first modern police force, that of the Metropolitan Police in 1829, and the subsequent expansion of the uniformed police into the provinces, in terms of social control in the interests of elites. It is undoubtedly true that members of the working classes were prepared to call upon the new police to protect their life and property but those who had most property plainly benefited disproportionately. In addition, politicians of the day, such as the Duke of Wellington and Sir Robert Peel, saw the new police as a means of defeating radical movements without recourse to inefficient and heavy-handed formations such as the militia, yeomanry and regular army. The provincial police were supervised by local police authorities but the Metropolitan Police were responsible directly to the Home Secretary, and can be seen, therefore, as an arm of central government. The police in London were also a pool of disciplined agents to send against large-scale disturbances outside the capital, especially riots against the New Poor Law and Chartist 'disturbances'.[110] The timing of the establishment of provincial forces often reflected local conflicts, as in the case of the Staffordshire force, set up in 1842 after a miners' strike.[111] As Roger Geary has stressed, the police have always been on hand to police industrial disputes, and have usually been seen by working-class communities as taking the side of the employer.[112]

In the early nineteenth century, there were numerous suggestions for facilitating such policing via the collection of information on criminals and the working classes. From 1805 onwards, court clerks were instructed by the Home Secretary to make annual returns of the numbers committed for trial on certain identifiable offences. This system was broadened, and made more comprehensive, by the publication of new *Criminal Statistics* from 1857 onwards, showing prosecutions and 'indictable crimes known to the police'.[113] Middle-class reformers such as Patrick Colquhoun and Edwin Chadwick saw a need to combine the Poor Law and police systems to control the poor via a systematic tabulation and classification of the entire labouring population.[114] In addition, the Metropolitan Police regularly circulated information on offences and offenders, within both London and the provinces, via the *Police Gazette*. This had originally been set up in 1773 by

Sir John Fielding as the *Hue and Cry*, and disseminated from the office of the Bow Street court, where he acted as magistrate.[115]

However, in practice, systematic information collection played comparatively little part in early and mid-Victorian policing. As already noted, despite Chadwick and Colquhoun, there was no attempt to introduce a systematic population register to identify where people lived. Britain did not possess a system of internal passports, as had been the case in Russia from 1719, Revolutionary and Napoleonic France, and many other European countries in the nineteenth century.[116] The much-vaunted crime statistics may have been largely meaningless, because according to one recent account the police and civil servants in the Treasury effectively rationed the amount of money available for prosecutions – hence their remarkable stability at about 50,000 prosecutions per annum, and 90,000 indictable crimes known to the police, throughout the period from 1857 to 1925.[117] Similarly, the *Hue and Cry* had been replaced by the *Police Gazette* in 1827 because the Home Office regarded it as 'useless' as a means of disseminating information. Yet in 1882, after consulting with his colleagues, the Director of Criminal Investigations at Scotland Yard believed that the *Police Gazette* was 'not read by the police, and is all but valueless as a means of communication'. Ill-digested lists of crimes and criminals circulated to police forces weeks after the event did not provide a convenient and reliable means of accessing information.[118]

The early uniformed police were simply not equipped to undertake the comprehensive information gathering some middle-class reformers desired. In part, this reflected the inefficiency of the early forces, renowned as they were for indiscipline, drunkenness, and a massive turnover of constables.[119] Traditional policing revolved, in the main, around pounding the beat, inspecting property and controlling the public space, rather than collecting information about criminals. Beats were carefully planned and measured to facilitate the physical surveillance of property. In London in the second half of the nineteenth century, the average beat during the day was seven and a half miles, whilst the average equivalent at night was only two miles. Such districts were walked by uniformed officers at a steady rate of two and a half miles per hour. During the day constables patrolled the outside of the pavement, whilst at night they walked on the inner side from where they could more easily check bolts and fastenings – 'shaking hands with doorknobs', as it was known. On the much bigger rural beats a country constable's patrols were usually varied from day to day to ensure that he visited his entire district at least once or twice a week. Much patrolling was done by night, hardly the best time to collect information but useful for spotting attacks on property in the empty roads.[120]

In addition, early police reformers such as Peel were keen to distance the new forces from the French model of police as a system of espionage.[121] Hence, the emphasis on the *uniformed* policeman, visibly performing his duty *in public* on the streets, precisely in order to allay fears over personal freedom and privacy. The distinctive, but deliberately non-military, blue tail-coat, blue trousers (white in summer) and black glazed top hat of the Metropolitan Police meant that there was no doubt where, and who, the policeman was. Plain-clothes investigation was, on the whole, avoided. Thus, even London did not have a very extensive detective force. A detective branch had been set up in the Metropolitan Police in 1842 but it comprised only two inspectors and six sergeants. Twenty-five years later it still had only 16 members. Sergeant Cuff, the sagacious detective in Wilkie Collins's *The Moonstone*, was a wholly atypical policeman in the mid-Victorian period. The emphasis of the early police was on deterring crime, mostly petty street offences, by their conspicuous presence, rather than solving crimes once they had happened.[122] In many ways what was important was not the surveillance of the public by the police but the surveillance of the police by the public.

Even when the police were involved in the surveillance of political movements, their activities were often remarkably open. It is true that in 1833 a select committee of the House of Commons heard that William Popay, a plain-clothes London policeman, had attended meetings of the National Political Union of the Working Classes and sent in reports, and that the police could also count upon the activities of informers. However, when in April 1840 two officers attended a Chartist committee meeting in plain clothes, they left the meeting rather than give false names and addresses, and returned later in uniform requesting permission to be present. Similarly, in the aftermath of the suppression of the Paris Commune in 1871 many Communards fled to Britain, and came under police surveillance. A detective-sergeant who tried to infiltrate a refugee meeting in Islington in May 1872 was thrown out and warned that he would have his head broken if he returned. He reported that he did not return, 'in order that no breach of the peace should take place'. The Home Office then hit upon the happy idea of writing a letter to Karl Marx for information. Marx, as a sober citizen, replied sending details of the International Workingmen's Association.[123]

It was not until the 1870s that the first, rather ineffectual, attempts were made to create a central database of information on criminals. The ending of transportation to North America, and the opposition of the Australian colonies to continued transportation there, had led in 1853 to its substitution by penal servitude in England, much to the British government's regret. A ticket-of-leave system, whereby convicts were released early on good behaviour, was originally used in Australia to reward such conduct. This system was introduced into England at the time of the cessation of transportation to 'keep faith' with several thousand transportees serving sentences in government prisons, who had the expectation of ultimate release on licence in the colonies. The sudden cessation of prisoners' hoped-for release was seen as creating a real grievance, and presenting a threat to prison discipline. But the ex-convict now came to be seen as a member of the 'dangerous classes' in the midst of English society, rather than as a group expelled to the outer reaches of the Empire.[124]

'Moral panics' in the 1860s, such as the London 'garrotting panic' of 1862, and general concern over the ticket-of-leave system, led to the passing of the Habitual Criminals Act in 1869. This set up an Habitual Criminals Register at Scotland Yard, later transferred to the Home Office, to record all persons convicted of crime in England. This was so that if they reoffended they could be placed under police supervision for seven years, in addition to any other sentence passed on them. Following Michel Foucault, this could be seen as part of that process by which the concept of a criminal 'class' was elaborated in order to justify the creation of a whole system of repression, in the interests of economic and professional disciplinary elites.[125] On the other hand, as Wiener has noted, this system served to draw a line between the criminal, to be subjected to strict state surveillance, and a supposedly law-abiding majority, who had a right to privacy.[126]

However, despite the publication of alphabetical registers of habitual criminals, giving names, 'distinctive marks' and descriptions, the Registry was hardly ever used by the police. This was

because it could not be accessed very easily. One needed a name
to use it properly, which rather negated its use as a means of identification. The published registers were only for prisoners released
in one year and did not, therefore, contain all habitual criminals;
few marks were really distinctive; and the registers were published
up to 20 months after a convict's release – the period when he or
she was most likely to re-offend.[127] Under the 1871 Prevention
of Crimes Act, photographs of convicts were also sent to the
Registry, which held 34,000 portraits by 1888. But sepia photographs could not easily be classified and indexed, especially by
colour of eyes or hair, and the whole collection might have to be
searched by eye to find a particular individual. In addition, people could look alike, easily disguise their appearance, or change as
they grew older.[128] The use of photography was developing in
French and German policing at about the same date, and proved
equally problematic.[129] The local knowledge in the heads of
policemen on the beat was thus still the principal means by which
criminals were caught after a crime had been committed.

Some local forces began keeping their own records of criminals. At Birmingham there was a register that showed, by means
of coloured drawings, the tattoo marks with which so many criminals ornamented their bodies; whilst at Liverpool, special registers were kept of the maiden names of the wives and mothers of
criminals, because it was believed that in a large proportion of
cases an offender, when he changed his name, took either his
wife's or his mother's. But these were not attempts to maintain
such an elaborately classified register of descriptions as at
Scotland Yard. Where offenders were to be traced by an index of
personal descriptions, it was, in Liverpool at least, the Habitual
Criminals Register that was used for the purpose.[130]

The need to supervise habitual criminals in London led to the
creation of a separate Convict Supervision Office by the
Metropolitan Police in 1880, with which the Habitual Criminals
Register is often confused. Visiting officers verified the addresses
and workplaces of those being supervised, and by 1886 its records
covered 32,000 supervisees. The Office acted as a deterrent to
re-offending but was also seen as leading to the 'reformation, or
restoration to honest labour, of old offenders, thereby preventing
fresh crime'. To this end the dissemination of any information to
employers, or other acquaintances of the person under supervision,

was frowned upon without the authority of the commissioner of police. Rather than a simple means of repression, it almost appears as a forerunner of the probation system in its attempts to 'build character' through the law. This bureau gradually expanded its remit as the movement of criminals into and out of London led to the compilation of records on ex-convicts from across the whole country.[131]

The Supervision Office also compiled books of distinctive marks and descriptions of convicts, and kept albums of photographs, but its small permanent staff – one chief inspector, one inspector, four sergeants and four constables in 1887 – could not keep pace with the work required. Nor was the speed of data retrieval very great. A parliamentary committee of 1893 discovered that in March of that year, when 21 officers searched the Mark Registers at Scotland Yard for 27 prisoners, the total time spent doing so equalled 57 and a half hours, and yet they made only seven identifications. This was an average of more than two hours for each prisoner, and more than eight hours for each identification.[132] This may explain why the Office failed to become the centre of criminal investigation in the Metropolitan area.

What is striking here is that long after the creation of an industrial society, policing in England was based very little on information gathering. Surveillance was haphazard and unbureaucratic rather than the routine and systematic activity one might imagine from some sociological accounts of the rise of the Information State. Instead of collecting information on deviants, the main strategy of the early and mid-Victorian state was to create carceral institutions, such as prisons and mental asylums, to facilitate physical containment and observation.

Conclusion

On the whole, it is difficult to see the gathering of information by the English state in the early to mid-nineteenth century simply in terms of the control of deviants, or as central planning to limit social interaction, in the interests of elites. Some middle-class reformers and Civil Service experts may have envisaged using the state to establish an extensive system of individual surveillance, and to help create a homogenised national identity.

However, in practice, there was comparatively little attempt to use the census or civil registration for tracking individuals, and much emphasis was placed on revealing local, as opposed to national, conditions. Such patterns of behaviour are explicable in terms of the absence of effective data retrieval technologies, and the liberal constitution of the state.

The emphasis in this period was on the central collection of information to facilitate personal initiative, or the mobilisation of local 'public opinion'. Rather than repression, the census and civil registration helped to underpin civil, political and social rights. Where state information gathering was used in attempts to implement direct control of individuals, as in the case of vaccination, the directing of life courses or policing, such activities tended to be limited, ineffectual, or as redolent of class compromise as of class domination. The rights and obligations created in this process were, of course, generally consistent with the workings of capitalism but within this constraint there was room for a mediation of interests.

5

The New Liberal State and information gathering

The crisis of classic liberalism in England, 1880–1914

The classic Liberal State of the mid-Victorian period, based as it was on localism and moralism, was in crisis in the last decades of the nineteenth century, and in the years immediately before the Great War. Belief in the value of a decentralised polity, and in the importance of personal, moral responsibility, came to be challenged by both internal and external forces. Increasingly the central state was seen as the answer to the problems of society and Empire. The central state was under pressure either to regulate local government more effectively, or to impose new responsibilities on the decentralised authorities, or to carry out their functions itself. This led over time to an increase in the scope and scale of information gathering in Whitehall. These changes represented an incipient shift in the nature of state processes, although its impact should not be exaggerated in this period. However, if one looks at the later consequences of some of the institutional changes inaugurated in these years, their importance becomes plain.

In the late nineteenth century Britain found its global economic and political hegemony threatened by the rise of foreign competitors. The rapid industrialisation of Germany and other countries made it increasingly problematic for Britain to maintain its superiority in naval power. The 'First Industrial Nation' was being surpassed economically – in 1870 Britain's overseas trade still exceeded that of France, Germany and Italy combined. In the period 1883–1913, however, the share of world trade in British hands dropped from 37 to 25 per cent, whilst Germany's rose from 17 to 23 per cent, and the USA's from three to 11 per cent. In the course of the 1890s Britain's steel output was surpassed by that of both the USA and Germany.[1] This relative economic decline was associated with that reduction in rates of economic growth, and continuing low yields on domestic investment, known as the Great Depression. Per capita growth in the British economy may have been negative in the last decade before the Great War.[2] These problems were compounded by deficiencies in terms of crude manpower – when Germany was first fully unified in 1871 its population, at 41 million, was already 10 million more than that of the UK. By 1914 this gap had doubled. At the same date the USA was a nation of 100 million people, and still expanding rapidly. Britain, on the other hand, had one of the lowest population growth rates in Europe. There appeared to be insufficient men to defend the Empire on land, whilst Germany was using its new industrial power to construct a fleet to rival the Royal Navy.[3]

British self-confidence was especially undermined by the disasters of the Second Boer War (1899–1902), when some 400,000 troops under British command managed only with great difficulty to defeat a much smaller Boer army. This imperial débâcle can be explained in terms of the disorganisation and poor leadership of the imperial forces but the military and other contemporaries blamed the poor physical condition of the troops enlisting in the army. General Sir John Frederick Maurice estimated that out of every five men who wished to enlist, there were only two remaining in the army as effective soldiers after two years' service.[4] In Manchester during the war, 8,000 out of 11,000 volunteers for the army had to be turned away, and, of the remainder, 2,000 were declared fit only for the militia. This led to the creation in 1904 of an Interdepartmental Committee on Physical Deterioration, which took evidence on the subject.[5] By the end of Victoria's reign, the effortless military and imperial superiority assumed by the mid-Victorians had evaporated.

A general belief in the deterioration of the fighting qualities of the male population was given added weight by the poverty surveys carried out by Charles Booth and Seebohm Rowntree from the 1890s onwards. Booth believed, on the basis of his survey of the working population of London, that 8.4 per cent of the metropolitan population lived in abject poverty, whilst 22.3 per cent were 'in want' – they lacked 'comfort', although they were not ill clothed or fed.[6] Rowntree found that nearly ten per cent of the population of York at the turn of the century were in what he called 'primary poverty' – they did not have a high enough income to purchase the necessaries to maintain 'physical efficiency'. He also believed that 18 per cent of the population lived in 'secondary poverty' – they had an income sufficient to maintain physical efficiency but managed their affairs in such a manner that they fell short of this target.[7] The revelation of the extent of poverty and want throughout the country led to a questioning of the efficacy of local welfare systems, and to the establishment of a Royal Commission on the Poor Laws in 1905. The belief in the ability of the poor to extricate themselves from poverty via the benign encouragement of the New Poor Law was seriously undermined.[8]

This general perception of crisis manifested itself in numerous ways that often transcended the boundaries of political parties. According to Searle these included: admiration for the German and Japanese cult of efficiency ('thorough') and of state policy; a concern for the improvement of the national physique and health via state intervention; calls for reform of the machinery of government, and improvements in education; the cult of the expert; the emphasis on 'science' in government and society; the veneration of the business man in politics; general arguments for the conscious application of the technocratic state to the advancement of the nation; and so on.[9] Such strategies were summed up in the call for 'national efficiency', and many looked to the central state, rather than to decentralised, local, government for action. Indeed, the existence of Britain's somewhat ramshackle and dispersed polity was seen as the root cause of many of the problems. It is perhaps ironic that such statist approaches to national mobilisation had originally been adopted by many European countries in the mid to late Victorian period in an attempt to challenge Britain's economic and imperial hegemony. This statism was, it has been suggested, now feeding back into British government policy making.[10]

Just as the United Kingdom's position in the world seemed under threat, so there were challenges to its internal cohesion. In the late nineteenth century a rising tide of discontent swept Ireland, focusing on demands for access to land and Home Rule. This was given added weight in the UK Parliament in London by the presence of Charles Stewart Parnell's Irish nationalists, who came to hold the balance between the Liberal and Conservative Parties. William Gladstone twice attempted to bring in Irish Home Rule but was defeated by the Lords and dissensions in his own party. At the same time, various Irish revolutionary groups, such as the Fenians, carried out terrorist attacks within both Ireland and England. Modern transport systems, and the financial and moral support of Irish Americans, meant that it was increasingly difficult for the British government to confine the Irish Question to Ireland.[11]

The propertied and masculine basis of the state was also being challenged. The early modern and classic liberal states had been systems by which central and local elites, who were predominantly male, deployed their power and authority, even when it was claimed that this was for the benefit of all. Propertied qualifications, and the concept of the household suffrage, meant that the franchise was limited to such elites, as was the execution of policy decided locally and centrally on the basis of that franchise. Increasingly in the late nineteenth century, however, organised labour and women's movements came to challenge this system of authority.

Historians are divided as to whether the late Victorian labour movement should be seen in terms of a threat to property itself, or more narrowly to the propertied basis of the state. On one hand, it has been argued that the sustained decline of commodity prices and profit margins during the Great Depression, and increasing competition from the USA and Germany, led to attempts by businesses to reduce wage costs, and to rationalise or mechanise labour. Technical innovation and labour dilution threatened the position of the independent, 'respectable' working class that the Liberal State had so long attempted to foster. A militant trade unionism had also emerged amongst the semi- and unskilled labour force, which appeared to reject the mid-nineteenth century social and political consensus.[12]

The upper and middle classes feared, or so it is argued, that the 'respectable' working classes might throw in their lot with the 'submerged' underemployed and semi-criminal groups, if poverty and unemployment were not tackled. The fear of revolution is said to have been highlighted by the emergence of socialist political parties such as the Social Democratic Federation, the Independent Labour Party and the future Labour Party, and by riots of the unemployed in London in 1886 and 1887.[13] This in turn, it can be argued, led to the introduction by the Liberal government of old age pensions in 1908, and of health and unemployment insurance under the 1911 National Insurance Act, as a means of undermining calls for fundamental change in society, via creating a contented and more efficient workforce.[14] Importantly for the present argument, the welfare reforms of 'New Liberalism' involved disbursements from central funds, rather than from local rates. They thus represented an attempt to reform welfare provision without having to solve the intractable problems of the local Poor Law system.

Other historians have argued, however, that the fear of revolution has been overdone. Middle-class commentators did not see the rioting in London as a working-class uprising but as the work of the 'bandits of civilisation', and were careful to distinguish between this 'residuum' and the 'real' working classes. This view was one shared by contemporary Marxists such as Friedrich Engels.[15] Arguably, the real issue was not revolution or no, but on what terms the working classes, or rather working men, were to be incorporated into the political nation, and which of the existing political parties would benefit from this. Although Chartism had failed in the 1830s and 1840s to obtain universal manhood suffrage, the Reform Acts of 1867 and 1885 had enfranchised some working men who owned modest property. Both the Conservative and Liberal Parties in the late Victorian period were attempting to outbid each other to co-opt this new electorate. They were also attempting to draw a distinction between the 'respectable' working man, and the disreputable and profligate. The citizen was to be constructed as a hard-working, law-abiding provider for his family, who participated in the political nation via the judicious use of the ballot box in support of one or other of the established political parties.[16] The presence in the 1906 Parliament of 53 Labour MPs also presented a challenge to the Liberals' assumption that they could maintain an alliance between the radical middle classes and the aspiring 'aristocracy of labour'.

Whilst the Conservatives wished to pay for increased welfare provision via tariffs on foreign imports, the Liberals hoped to do this through direct taxation. The latter were as much concerned with the threat of tariff reform to the principles of free trade, as of the possible defection of the working classes to the Tories.[17] There was also a belief on the part of politicians and Treasury officials that if working-class voters were joining the political nation then they needed to be brought into the taxation net – that there should be no representation without taxation.[18] However, if this was the Liberal Party's election strategy in the Edwardian period then it was an abject failure – the working population tended to vote either Labour or Conservative throughout the twentieth century, and the attack on private property implicit in any increase in direct taxation drove most Liberal employers into the hands of the Conservatives.[19]

The 'New Liberalism' of the Liberal governments from 1905 to 1914 can thus be seen in terms of the elaboration of an inclusive social ideology, although it also served particular interests. The welfare benefits of the New Liberal State may well have represented an attempt by a political elite to preserve a national consensus around capitalism. However, they can also be seen as a means of creating social cohesion and national efficiency in a situation of international rivalry – a 'passive revolution' from above, as envisaged in the writings of the Italian communist leader, Antonio Gramsci.[20] The achievement of 'national efficiency' was seen as a means by which all classes of society could gain: the traditional landed classes and its military offshoot could allay their fear of how an urbanised industrial society could defend itself against the vast conscript armies of the Continental powers; capitalists could obtain a healthier and more educated workforce, and the hope of better industrial relations; the working classes were offered more rapid progress towards better standards of living and a more equitable society; and the professional classes gained greater power, prestige and wealth from manning this new state.[21] This was a further elaboration of that system of bounded pluralism that has sustained the British State in the modern period.

Moreover, at the same time as members of the working classes were being recognised as independent voters, the intellectual underpinnings of the belief in the moral autonomy of citizens was being assailed. A new set of paradigms of human activity was being elaborated that undermined the moral core of classical Liberalism. The early Victorian generation that had created the New Poor Law, civil registration and the census believed that the provision of information, and education in moral responsibility, would create a working population that could take advantage of the opportunities made available by the expansive forces of capitalism. The revelations regarding the poor physical condition of the population, and the surveys of Booth, Rowntree and their colleagues, had shown this optimism to have been ill-founded. The discovery that poverty was concentrated in old age, when people could not be economically active, and the demonstration by economists such as Alfred Marshall that unemployment might be involuntary, undermined the belief that want was caused solely by moral failings.[22] As Seebohm Rowntree put it:

> Nothing can be gained by closing our eyes to the fact that there is in this country a large section of the community whose income is insufficient for the purposes of physical efficiency, and whose lives are increasingly stunted. If the men and women … [of the working] class possessed, as a whole, extraordinary energy and perseverance, they might perhaps, notwithstanding physical feebleness and a depressing environment, raise themselves to a higher level: but it is idle to expect from them, as a class, virtues and powers far in excess of those characteristics than any other section of the community.[23]

The declining belief in the possibility of working-class salvation through personal moral exertion led to social theories that stressed the predominance of forces outside individual control. This can be seen in the debate in middle-class intellectual circles over the impact of 'nature' and 'nurture' on human behaviour. On one hand, eugenicists, following the ideas of Sir Francis Galton, believed that the poor were inherently unable to look after themselves because of their limited genetic endowment. The only answer to the problems of society lay, therefore, in selective breeding. As a committee of the Eugenics Society claimed, 'pauperism is due to inherent defects which are hereditarily transmitted. …'. These defects and inherited vices included:

> drunkenness, theft, persistent laziness, a tubercular diathesis, mental deficiency, deliberate moral obliquity or general weakness of character, manifested by want of initiative or energy or stamina and an inclination to attribute this misfortune to their own too great goodness and generally to bad luck.[24]

Other intellectuals, on the other hand, rejected such sweeping genetic determinism and argued that the poor were the victims of deficiencies in the workings of social and economic systems, and that reforms to these were required.[25] Many people, of course, believed in implementing both strategies in order to enhance national efficiency.[26] The ideal of the autonomous, moral individual, which classical liberalism had sought to create, was also undermined by the decline in religious belief, and the rise of a scientific view of the universe in which time, space and the processes of evolution dwarfed humanity.[27] Overall, theories that saw poverty in terms of moral irresponsibility were giving way to concepts of physical degeneration and environmental causation. As moralism declined, so did localism. This reflected, in part, the whole emphasis on *national* efficiency that could not be achieved via local action. Belief in the efficacy of the decentralised state was also undermined by the recognition of the limitations of local government. Although the late Victorian period was in some senses the golden age of municipal government, there were inherent weaknesses within the fabric of the local state that became increasingly apparent in the early decades of the twentieth century. Poor Law expenditure was growing throughout the 1890s, and increased greatly in the economic depression that followed the Boer War. Many local authorities in urban areas were faced during the Edwardian period with demands for public works from mass demonstrations of the unemployed.

As the widening franchise led to the election of working-class councillors, so there was an expansion of local interventionism in some areas. With charges on the rates continually expanding, the discrepancies between wealthy local authorities with few social problems and impoverished local authorities with many were increasingly highlighted. This led to legislation to equalise rates across London as a whole in 1894. Ratepayers, often themselves quite poor, were in open revolt against the cost of new social services. Local authorities were becoming progressively more dependent on central loans and subventions to carry out policies being elaborated nationally, or in response to economic downturns that reflected national trends, rather than local circumstances.[28] By 1890 the percentage of local-government expenditure in England and Wales met by central government was 25 per cent. This had risen to 31 per cent by 1910, and to 47 per cent in 1930.[29] Local government was losing its autonomy.

The period also saw the beginnings of a decline in the allegiances of elites to their localities. As José Harris has pointed out, during the late nineteenth century there appears to have been a shift in wealth and power from the industrial provinces and the countryside to finance capital and London. This process was facilitated by the emergence of a rentier class investing in the newly emerging joint-stock companies and limited liability companies legalised in the 1850s and 1860s, and also by the agricultural depression of the 1880s. The new fund holders looked to the London stock market, rather than to local trade, as the barometer of their fortunes. This increasingly cosmopolitan outlook was enhanced by cultural changes, such as the rise of mass communications and entertainment, and the absorption of the children of local elites, who once went to the old provincial grammar schools and dissenting academies, into the great, national public schools.[30]

Harold Perkin has also spoken of the 'nationalisation' of the middle classes as beginning in this period. As local industrialists sold out to, or merged their businesses with, the new giant, national corporations of the late Victorian period, so a middle class of cosmopolitan, and comparatively rootless, managers and administrators began to appear. These were very different from the local business and professional classes who had constituted the traditional middle classes. 'Spiralists' – career professionals and administrators who would move up by moving from local branch office to local branch office – began to replace the former 'burgesses', that is, the traditional local business and self-employed professional men whose whole careers would be spent in a particular locality. The professions also came to look increasingly to national associations, rather than to their local peers, for an orientation to professional and career development.[31] Thus, rather than the age of the classic Industrial Revolution, it was the period from about 1880 onwards that saw the true creation of a 'society of strangers'. This was the origin of that modern world of rootless men and women for whom the local community is merely where they sleep and park their cars, and whose interests and place of work lie elsewhere.

Such changes led to the erosion of local political elites, as large employers shifted their interests to the national and international stage. Joseph Chamberlain – often regarded as a shining example of the provincial industrial capitalist once dominant in local government – is a key example of a Midlands manufacturer who, in the words of Harris, 'moved his investments to London, his political concerns to the Empire, and his social circle to "Society" and the aristocratic county house'. This left local government in the hands of less wealthy men with a narrower outlook, and arguably less talent, who were unable to grapple successfully with the difficulties that faced England's traditional dispersed polity. At the same time, political leadership was increasingly passing from local political associations to mass parties organised at the level of Westminster and the nation state.[32]

The period saw the continued unravelling of that intertwining of sovereign, governing and disciplinary powers so typical of the early modern world. Sovereignty passed to national political parties organised in Parliament at Westminster. Government became the concern of professional administrators in Whitehall and local town halls. Disciplinary power became the province of professional groups such as the police and security services. There were, of course, close links between such groups but they took the form of formalised and bureaucratic flows of information. This was rather different from the understanding that had existed amongst the English county gentry of a former period, based as it was on shared values, interests and leisure pursuits. The state was becoming a set of components differentiated out of civil society, rather than the sum of dispersed interactions between elites. As this complex became 'nationalised', so it required more standardised information in order to make decisions, giving rise to the modern Information State. But although the period before the First World War saw the beginnings of this process, it was not until later that its full impact was felt.

The threat of organised violence to the integrity of the British state from both internal and external forces led to the creation, or revival, of centralised institutions for the collection of information. It is difficult, however, to see such forms of central information collection simply in terms of social control over the British working classes in the interests of capitalist elites.

Reactions to crisis: security and military preparedness

The British uniformed police of the mid-nineteenth century were poorly equipped and lacked the necessary skills to tackle the new forms of organised political violence. An example was the inability of the Metropolitan Police to locate a Fenian bomb that exploded against the walls of Clerkenwell prison in 1867, killing 12 people. This was despite the fact that a warning was received in good time from the British administration in Dublin. The débâcle appears to have been due to the fact that the warning had specified that the prison was to be blown *up*, and not *sideways*, thus leading to the police restricting their search to *underneath* the prison.[33] A force based on the principle of visible deterrence might be effective against rowdy drunks, petty thieves and even housebreakers but had little impact on committed terrorists. This was one of the reasons why the Home Office set up a 'Secret Service Department' in the 1860s to infiltrate Fenian organisations.[34] But mid-Victorian England was, on the whole, devoid of a well-developed 'secret state'.

The resurgence of Irish terrorism in the 1880s, which saw the bombing of town halls, army barracks, gasworks and Whitehall, led by 1883 to the establishment of a specialist 'Irish Bureau' within the Metropolitan Police Criminal Investigation Department (CID). The Special Branch proper, set up in 1887, was, however, a rather different sort of body. This was a national force rather than just Metropolitan, and reported to the Home Secretary as opposed to the Metropolitan Police Commissioner. It also had a wider remit, and was responsible for watching foreign anarchists resident in Britain as well as Irish republicans. The work of Special Branch involved screening suspects as they entered the country; creating dossiers on known anarchists; running agents and informers within Fenian and anarchist organisations; and harrying them via raids on their clubs. In the Edwardian period the Specials were also engaged in the surveillance of that other violent threat to the existing male constitution, the suffragettes.[35]

Special Branch was, in addition, to become the executive wing of the nascent security forces. A Cabinet Committee of Imperial Defence (CCID) had been set up in 1902 after the muddle of the Second Boer War to co-ordinate military planning. The War had revealed the poverty of British counter-espionage just as it began to be realised that a European power struggle was becoming inevitable.[36] In 1909 a sub-committee of the CCID suggested the establishment of a 'Secret Service Bureau'. According to their report its functions would be:

(a) To serve as a screen between the Admiralty and War Office and foreign spies who may have information they wish to sell to the Government.

(b) To keep in touch through the Home Office, who may nominate an officer for the purpose, with the county and borough police, and, if necessary, to send agents to various parts of Great Britain with a view to ascertaining the nature and scope of the espionage that is being carried out by foreign agents.

(c) To serve as an intermediary between the Admiralty and War Office on the one hand, and the agents that we employ in foreign countries on the other.[37]

If the Germans did invade, agents of the new security forces were to stay behind enemy lines as spies.[38] The military nature of the body explains why it was designated in its early days as 'Military Intelligence 5' (MI5).

By intercepting correspondence, Captain Vernon Kell, the head of the new bureau, was able to show the extent of German espionage networks. MI5 began keeping dossiers on spies from information supplied by the police, and on the outbreak of war the members of the German spy network were arrested.[39] This was the origin of MI5's famous, or infamous, Registry Section, an institution upon which Kell and his deputy, Eric Holt-Wilson, lavished much attention.[40] The centrality of the information-gathering function to the work of the security services was underlined in March 1914, when Kell made a presentation to the CCID, in the presence of the Prime Minister, Henry Asquith, on the work and records of the bureau.[41]

The entire German-born population, perhaps 80,000 in number, was seen as a potential fifth column for the invading armies of the Kaiser, and thus worthy of surveillance.[42] In order to do this MI5 compiled an unofficial register of Germans and Austro-Hungarians in the country, possibly drawing upon the manuscript records of the 1911 census. This would appear to be the implication of a statement in MI5's own official history of the period to the effect that

> the Registrar-General considered that the information in census returns had been obtained confidentially and that the police must not let it be known that they were being used for the purpose of [aliens] registration.[43]

In time the Central Registry was to contain a card index in which enemy aliens were helpfully classified, in order of support for the

British cause, as 'AA' (Absolutely Anglicized or Allied), 'A' (Anglicized/Allied), 'AB' (Anglo-Boche), 'BA' (Boche-Anglo), 'B' (Boche) or 'BB' (Bad Boche).[44]

The development and methods of Special Branch and MI5 were a fundamental departure in the history of central state surveillance, reflecting the enormity of the perceived threat to the nation. It also represented the importation of colonial forms of control into the imperial heartland, since many of the leading lights in the new 'vigilant' state were Irish, or had experience of administration in the Empire.[45] It should be noted, however, that in the years before the Great War the resources of Special Branch and MI5 were quite modest. At first Kell had to work by himself, and had difficulty getting any clerical assistance. In 1914 his department still had only four officers, a barrister, two investigators and seven clerks. Similarly, at the outbreak of war the Special Branch had only just over 100 officers. As will be shown shortly, however, the experience of war and its aftermath was to lead to a permanent expansion in the staffing and influence of both institutions.[46]

The threat of invasion also led to the creation of some less obvious forms of military surveillance, including the modern system of radio and television licences. Today such licences are, of course, used to raise revenue for public broadcasting but this was not the reason for their original introduction under the 1904 Wireless Telegraphy Act, which stipulated that wireless sets should be licensed with the General Post Office. What was really at stake here was the security of communications between naval vessels in the Channel, and of the fleet with Whitehall. The Admiralty had long realised the importance of imperial telecommunications networks in any future world conflict. Indeed, it has been argued that it was Britain's dominance of world communications networks that enabled it to survive in both world wars of the twentieth century. The Admiralty was the first and best customer for Guglielmo Marconi's new wireless transmitters. Marconi equipment had begun to be fitted to Royal Navy vessels as early as 1900, for both ship-to-ship and ship-to-shore communication. A year later the Admiralty ordered 50 wireless sets to equip all battleships and cruisers on the Home, Mediterranean and China stations, and in 1903 it made Marconi its sole supplier of wireless equipment for the next 11 years. Britain was not unusual in this emphasis on the strategic importance of wireless, and at this period the US Navy was trying to gain a complete monopoly of the US radio industry.[47] But what would happen if wireless transmissions could be intercepted or jammed by foreign agents on British soil? As the First Lord of the Admiralty stressed, when introducing the second reading of the 1904 Wireless Bill in the House of Lords,

> it was a standing danger to the defence of this country by land and by sea, that there was no method of controlling wireless telegraphy at all. It was perfectly possible for anybody who chose to do so to set up a wireless telegraph installation, and to communicate with anybody at sea or across the Channel ... If the coast were studded with wireless telegraph stations under no control and in competition with one another, the only possible result would be that they would be all quite useless, and ships, whether of His Majesty's Navy or of the mercantile marine, would be unable to communicate with the shore or with each other.[48]

The 1904 Act empowered JPs to issue warrants to agents acting on behalf of the GPO, Admiralty, Army Council or Board of Trade to seize unlicensed equipment. In the first days of the conflict of 1914 to 1918, police constables all over Britain, armed with information from the licensing authorities, went around confiscating or sealing up private wireless sets. By the end of August, 2,500 licensed sets, and 750 unlicensed sets, had been closed down.[49] It was only with the expansion of radio ownership in the 1920s, reaching over nine million by 1929, that the fiscal uses of licensing came to the fore.[50]

Military preparedness also lay behind attempts to revive the Registry of Seamen. In 1910, an Advisory Committee on Merchant Shipping proposed to the Board of Trade that a General Index Register of merchant seamen should again be created. Following legal advice that the Registrar-General of Shipping and Seamen was failing to live up to his statutory responsibility to maintain a register, the Central Index Register was established in October 1913 and maintained until 1941. Registration was made compulsory by the Registration of Merchant Seamen Order of September 1918 under the Defence of the Realm Act, and seamen were issued with numbered identity certificates, bearing a photograph. Although an improvement on previous attempts, the register became clogged with the names of about 1,250,000 men during the inter-war period, of whom over a million had ceased to be seamen but could not be cleared for lack of definite information as to their status.[51]

Reactions to crisis: the surveillance of crime

According to Martin Wiener, the late nineteenth-century decline in the belief in personal moral autonomy contributed to a shift in the treatment of the criminal. Rather than seeing criminal legislation as a means of enforcing personal moral responsibility, policy became increasingly restricted to the management and containment of the law-breaker.[52] This coincided with a shift towards the detection rather than the deterrence of crime. In the late 1860s the plain-clothes detective force of the Metropolitan Police comprised only 16 members, but the modern CID was set up in 1877 after four inspectors in the old detective branch were found guilty of corruption at the Old Bailey. The new CID had 250 officers but within six years had expanded to 800. Many, but not all, provincial forces had set up their own detective branches by the end of the century.[53]

The period also saw the adoption by the police of more 'scientific' methods for the centralised amassing of information about criminals. Following the publication in 1894 of the report of a Home Office committee of inquiry into the best means for identifying habitual criminals, the Habitual Criminals Registry was transferred from the Home Office to New Scotland Yard. It was expected that it would be amalgamated here with a new anthropometric registry also being set up as a result of the committee's enquiries. This was to supersede the rather hit-or-miss system of identification by tattoos or 'distinguishing marks'. These registries were to be kept separate from the existing Convict Supervision Office.[54]

The anthropometric registry was based on the system of identification elaborated by the chief of the police identification service in Paris, Alphonse Bertillon. Essentially, the Bertillon system entailed photographing a subject looking directly at a camera, and then in profile, with the camera centred upon the right ear. Besides the two photographs, the subject's height was recorded, together with the length of one foot, an arm and an index finger. This information was then archived as, or so it was believed, an infallible means of identification. In 1882, after some years of experimentation, Bertillon began using his system of criminal identification on offenders detained at the Palais de Justice in Paris, although it was not until 1893 that a Criminal Identification Department was established. The criminal was no longer a person to be reformed, helped and encouraged but a body to be identified.[55]

However, not all of Bertillon's contemporaries were convinced of the accuracy of his scheme of measurement. Francis Galton, the British father of eugenics and of modern statistics, was critical of Bertillon's system. In his work on human heredity, Galton had been concerned to establish the transmission of characteristics between generations through statistical correlations. This involved, in part, taking measurements of the bodies of differing generations of the same family. On the basis of his observations, Galton believed that Bertillon's system would result in an unacceptably high rate of false identification because no account was taken of relations between different bodily characteristics.[56] Instead, Galton was an enthusiast for fingerprinting. which he advocated in *Finger Prints*, published in 1892. Fingerprints had been scientifically described in seventeenth-century Europe, and first classified in 1823 by a Czech anatomist, Jan Evangelista Purkinje. However, the first extensive use of such prints for official identification was made by the British Raj in Victorian India. The British favoured such methods because they claimed that all 'natives' looked the same to the Western eye. Fingerprinting, eugenics and the belief in the inevitable inferiority of the 'lower' races and classes, were thus inextricably intertwined.[57] The new anthropometric registry at Scotland Yard also began to store such prints in conjunction with measurements taken on the Bertillon system by prison warders.[58] It was also found that in practice the anthropometric system was cumbersome to implement and required costly equipment and training.[59]

A further 'Committee to Inquire into the Method of Identification of Criminals' was established in 1900. This recommended that there should be one central office, called the Criminal Registry, in which the records of English, Scottish and Irish criminals could be collected, and in which all the work of identifying and registering criminals would be carried out. This led to the amalgamation of the Habitual Criminals Registry and the Convict Supervision Office. At the same time the Bertillon system was dropped, and superseded completely by the archiving of fingerprints. This represented the emergence of the modern system of centralised criminal identification.[60] However, in the period before the First World War the practical use made by the police of such information was patchy. Thus, in 1913 one finds Sir Leonard Dunning, HM Inspector of Constabulary, trying to set up a decentralised system of clearing houses for information relating to crimes and criminals. The clearing house in the north of England was set up in Wakefield in the North Riding of Yorkshire, whilst a less successful scheme was established for the south of England in Hatfield in Hertfordshire.[61] The Criminal Registry in London was plainly not always the first port of call for many provincial police forces.

Information on potential law-breakers was certainly collected for the purposes of social control, but was this always in the interests of social elites? The working classes may not have liked the police, especially during strikes, but were willing, on the whole, to call on their assistance when required. Grudging consent to policing was won through the provision of real public goods.[62] Similarly, the Information State might also be mobilised against others than the working classes. At the same time as the Criminal Registry was being consolidated, Parliament was also passing the 1903 Motor Car Act.[63] This laid down that all drivers of cars should have driving licences, which could be revoked or suspended for traffic offences; that cars and their owners should be registered with local authorities; and that motor vehicles had to carry number plates that would allow the police to trace their owners in such registries. Clive Emsley has seen this as an essentially localised system, since the registries and the enforcement of the law were locally based.[64] However, the system of identification used was elaborated centrally. The number plates issued were to carry a registration number made up of an alphabetical code, laid down in Whitehall, representing a local authority, and a number specific to the vehicle. 'WR', for example, meant the West Riding of Yorkshire.[65] The system was national in intent, if delivered locally. A central purpose of the registries was to allow the police in one county to collaborate with those in another to locate errant motorists who crossed such administrative boundaries.

The 1903 Motor Car Act needs to be seen in terms of the threat to the concept of community presented by the individualism and sheer anonymity of the motorist. Frequently the assumption was made that the motorist was an urban dweller on a spree, running down pedestrians, and invading the countryside in a cloud of dust. Members of Parliament were often moved to complain of the latter, alluding to the soiling of ladies' underwear on washing lines, and the virtual imprisonment of villagers by the noxious fumes and grit expelled from the cars of thoughtless motorists. Added to this individualism was the anonymity of drivers, who might speed through two or more counties in a day, evading the hapless police on foot or bicycle.[66] The anonymity of motorists was heightened by the protective garb that they wore. According to the Earl of Wemyss, speaking in the debates on the Motor Car Bill in the Lords, 'Men went about in goggles and in a ghastly sort of headgear too horrible to look at, and it is clear that when they put on that dress they meant to break the law.' In the committee stage of the Bill there was an unsuccessful attempt to get the wearing of such attire made a criminal offence.[67] These concerns might even be seen as a very faint echo of the eighteenth-century Black Acts, so ably described by E. P. Thompson, which made appearance on the highway whilst disguised for the purpose of hunting or poaching of game a capital offence.[68]

There was indeed a sense in which motorists were seen as people outside society, and thus a threat to law and order. They had certainly flouted the speed limit of 14 miles per hour that had been laid down for road vehicles by the 1896 Locomotives on Highways Act. In 1905, in the aftermath of the passing of the 1903 Motor Car Act, the Automobile Association was founded, and was soon at odds with the police. The latter were forced to prosecute AA patrols who warned motorists of speed-traps, and AA members knew that the failure by a patrolman to salute them was a sign that motorists would be well advised to slow down because of police activity in the area.[69] A certain sense of danger may have added to the thrill of motoring in its early days.

Non-motorists reacted to this novel menace by threatening to take the law into their own hands, with villagers proposing to lay boulders across the highway to keep cars out. At least one member of the hunting fraternity claimed that the best way to identify motorists was with a liberal sprinkling of swan shot.[70] The Earl of Camperdown recounted a story in the Lords that revealed the potential mayhem inherent in this emerging lawlessness:

A gentleman was cycling near Ealing, and he heard one of these motor-cars making a noise behind him. He thought that there was room for the motor to get by, but then saw another cyclist in front of him coming the other way, so he decided that there was no room and very wisely got down. He got into the hedge and the motor passed him, he says, at twenty to twenty-five miles per hour. When it reached the other cyclist who had brought up at a fence which he grasped, that cyclist whipped out a revolver from his hip pocket and fired two shots in rapid succession at the car. When the motor car had disappeared, cyclist No. 1 went up to cyclist No. 2 and pointed out to him that carrying revolvers was not permitted in this country, and that free firing was not allowed, and he replied – 'What can I do? I have hit one of his back wheels, I am quite certain, and I think that I have got them both.'[71]

Middlesex appeared to be descending into the dangerous condition of the American Wild West.

This seems a perfect example of the creation of a society of lawless individualists, a 'society of strangers', leading to the creation of an extensive system of state surveillance through information gathering for the purposes of social control. However, it would be difficult to see this as an example of the exercise of domination by social elites since it was just those elites who were being controlled by the new vehicle and driver registration systems. At a price of £130 or £140 for even the cheapest motor car, the Edwardian motorist was unlikely to be a member of the proletariat, or even of the lower middle classes. Part of the animosity towards motorists was derived from the perception that they were wealthy and feckless, and one left-wing MP even went so far as to describe motoring as a blood sport indulged in by the rich. Indeed, one of the few errant motorists mentioned by name in Parliament was none other than the Prime Minister, Arthur Balfour.[72]

The archetypal road-hog was not a member of the lower orders but that most famous 'furious' driver of the Edwardian period, Mr Toad, the anti-hero of Kenneth Grahame's *The Wind in the Willows*. The book was published in 1908 but was based on a series of bedtime stories told by Grahame to his son in about 1904, just after the passage of the 1903 Act.[73] Toad, the furious motorist and enemy of the police, was plainly not a lowly washerwoman, despite his disguise, but a member of the gentry, if not of the amphibious aristocracy. He had inherited a sizeable fortune from his father, which he was in the course of squandering on motor cars, and lived in a stately home – Toad Hall. The proletariat were plainly represented in Grahame's story by the weasels, stoats and ferrets of the Wild Wood, who invaded Toad's home when he was imprisoned for motoring offences and 'gross impertinence to the rural police'.

Rather than surveillance in the interests of an elite, the new system of information gathering was seen at the time in terms of the subordination of the few to the needs of the wider community. Lord Balfour of Burleigh, for example, believed that number plates were required 'so that those who misuse their privileges may be identified, and, if necessary, punished, and that the whole fraternity should not be prejudiced by the action of what I believe to be, comparatively speaking, a small minority'. He was seconded by the Earl of Rosslyn, who declared, 'It ought not to be permissible in a great democratic country like this, that there should be one law for the rich and another for the poor...'.[74] In this instance, elites were being incorporated into a pluralist democracy as much as the lower orders.

Reactions to crisis: information gathering and welfare

A key element in the means by which the working classes were incorporated into this pluralistic but bounded polity were the new welfare rights established in the Edwardian period. Old age pensions and national insurance were, however, fairly circumscribed benefits. The central state did not take over welfare provision, rather the 'mixed economy of welfare' was tipped in a statist direction. The national insurance system established by the 1911 National Insurance Act was at first only open to a small number of trades, such as shipbuilding, engineering and construction. These covered about 2.5 million workers, out of a total male labour force of slightly over 10 million. By design, such trades included almost no women; were skilled and well organised and provided stability of personnel; did not, by custom, see men being put on short time during a depression; and, it was hoped, were trades subject only to reasonable and predictable seasonal fluctuations. Nor was the scheme intended to deal with the long-term unemployment caused by structural problems, or an extended depression. National insurance also offered sickness benefits and basic medical care to those earning less than a specified annual income but not to their families and dependants. The system was administered by centrally registered approved societies – friendly societies, commercial insurance companies, and some trade unions.[75] From these modest beginnings the scheme was expanded in 1920 to apply to all persons of 16 years or over, who were employed under a contract of service, or apprenticeship. If they were non-manual workers, insured persons were not to have an income exceeding £250 a year. The scheme, however, still excluded those occupied in agriculture, forestry, horticulture, private domestic service, and many central and local government workers.[76]

The payment of old age pensions was also restricted by various eligibility clauses. The original Bill gave a 5s per week pension at the age of 70 to those with income less than £26 per annum. This was altered in Parliament during the committee stage to a sliding scale, giving pensions of 1s to 5s per week to those with incomes between £21 and £31 10s. But the elderly only received this provided that they did not receive poor relief after 1 January 1908; had not been imprisoned for any offence, including drunkenness, during the ten years preceding their claim; were not aliens or the wives of aliens; and could satisfy the pension authorities that they had not been guilty of 'habitual failure to work according to his ability, opportunity, or need, for his own maintenance or that of his legal relatives'.[77]

Such elements of overt social control were, however, soon abandoned. In the absence of detailed investigation the 'habitual failure to work' clause was never acted upon; the clause respecting the receipt of poor relief was dropped in 1910; and the disqualification of those who had been imprisoned without option of a fine proved unenforceable.[78] This left age as the main criterion for the receipt of the pension. Between 1910 and 1911 the number of men and women aged 70 or over who required outdoor poor relief fell from 132,235 to 8,420.[79] The original restrictions on payments reflected the continuation of assumptions implicit in welfare policy since the establishment of the old Poor Law. The real change was the transfer of responsibility for poverty amongst the elderly from local to central government.

But whereas pensions were directly funded from central taxation, national insurance was only so in part since the Treasury was opposed to further non-contributory social legislation in the wake of the Old Age Pensions Act.[80] Originally the worker's contribution to the insurance fund was 4d a week for men and 3d a week for women; the employer's contribution was 3d; and the state's 2d. Working-class leaders pointed out that employers could pass their contributions on to customers in the form of higher prices, whilst the state was avoiding taking full responsibility.[81] This system did not represent a transfer of incomes between classes but mainly within the lifetime of the worker.[82] Labour leaders could scarcely oppose the system, especially when they had nothing to put in its place, and according to Pat Thane:

> Many poorer people, throughout, were grateful for any amelioration of their hard lives. It is reasonable to conclude that very many people would have preferred, as an ideal, regular work, wages sufficient for a decent life, however defined, allowing them sufficient surplus to save for hard times and perhaps even to choose and pay for their children's education, their own house, or health care, leaving the state the minimal role of providing services which the individual could not, and for the minority who were unable for physical or other reasons to achieve this desirable independence.[83]

The working classes were gaining rights but they were circumscribed rights as citizens of a specific nation state. Nevertheless, and however limited such rights were, they were still an improvement on the New Poor Law, in which the receipt of welfare in the workhouse carried the threat of a loss of personal freedom and the right to a family life.

The partial centralisation of welfare in the Edwardian period led, over time, to an expansion in the use of central record keeping to prevent fraud, and to prove entitlement. If the Treasury was paying out funds centrally then it wanted them to be audited centrally as well. In part, this meant using existing records in new ways. The introduction of old age pensions in 1909, and the need to verify ages for pension officers, led to searches in census and civil registration data by the GRO.[84] By the end of 1910, the new Old Age Pensions Section of the Office comprised two second-division clerks, 19 assistant clerks, and six boy clerks, and was roughly comparable in size to the whole of its Statistical Department. Even then, the Registrar-General was asking the Treasury for permission to employ the Pension Section's entire staff on overtime because of the pressure of work.[85] In the inter-war period this organisation was to be supplemented by the establishment of a records branch of the Ministry of Pensions in Blackpool. By 1946 the latter employed approximately 4,000 staff and received nearly 40,000 claims each month.[86]

Over time the new national insurance legislation also spawned a comparable system of centralised surveillance. Records of payments into the new employment scheme were made by placing special stamps on books circulated for this purpose. Employers or employees kept these, and they were then lodged with an employment exchange when workers claimed unemployment benefit. The Ministry of Labour soon set up a Claims and Records Office at Kew, just outside London, where such claims were processed. By 1939 the Office was processing 5 million such transactions each year. Books were also collected from all insured persons annually, and new ones issued, leading by 1939 to nearly 15 million books arriving at Kew within a period of three weeks.[87] The whole process enabled the first comprehensive means of establishing the rate and distribution of unemployment via the 'claimant count'.[88] The Office also maintained a 'contribution and benefit account' for each insured person, to ensure that claimants had the necessary contributions to pay for the benefits claimed. The Kew Office undertook an audit of the weekly statements of benefit payments rendered by local offices to prevent clerical fraud.[89] By as early as 1921 the Claims and Records Office had 2,500 staff, and this rose to 3,600 in 1922. In the fiscal year 1924–25, the staff of this Office made up nearly a fifth of all the Ministry of Labour's employees, and outnumbered the Ministry's permanent headquarters staff two to one. Compared to the modest establishment of the Victorian GRO, this was centralised record keeping on an unprecedented scale.[90]

Such a shift in scale could be seen in terms of the creation of a new surveillance function of the state but it might more usefully be conceived as a change in the way in which the state carried out its existing tasks. As already noted, welfare benefits had been delivered under the Poor Law system for centuries, and had involved detailed scrutiny of individual circumstances. Such benefits also carried with them implicit, and often explicit, conditions informed by a distinction between the deserving and the undeserving poor. But this surveillance was dispersed throughout parishes, and undertaken by oral interviews that generated local record keeping, or none at all. A centralised system of surveillance could not function in this manner, and had to elaborate impersonal means of information gathering that did not necessitate what Anthony Giddens has termed the 'co-presence' of the parties involved.[91] It would hardly have been possible for all claimants of unemployment benefits to have presented themselves at the Claims and Records Office at Kew for interview. The vastly increased scale of the information flows involved led inexorably to the creation of bureaucratic systems of data gathering based on paper forms, in which the information regarded as relevant to a claim could be narrowly defined and processed centrally. Such means of reducing complexity had, of course, already been pioneered by bodies such as the GRO in the Victorian census. Census schedules and bureaucratic forms are as much about excluding communications considered irrelevant as about collecting data. Such forms of control over information flows were essential if government information systems were not to be overwhelmed with extraneous material.

The creation of such systems as a consequence of the increasing scale of information flows was not confined to the state. In the period 1850 to 1920, with the increasing size of capitalist enterprises,[92] a new philosophy of management based on system and efficiency had arisen, in which the amassing, analysis and dissemination of corporate data along systematically structured lines of internal communications came to serve as a mechanism for managerial co-ordination and control. JoAnne Yates has summed up this revolution as follows:

> Procedures, rules, and financial and operational information were documented at all levels, making organisational rather than individual memory the repository of knowledge. Impersonal management systems – embodied in forms, circular letters, and manuals – replaced the idiosyncratic, word-of-mouth management of the foremen and owners of earlier periods. Information and analysis, increasingly in statistical form, were drawn up the lengthening hierarchies to enable upper management to monitor and evaluate processes and individuals at lower levels.[93]

This movement of 'systematic management' was the informational equivalent of the contemporary movement for 'scientific management' on the workfloor, associated with Frederick W. Taylor and his followers.[94] It was also associated with changing technologies within the office – the development of the file, the typewriter, carbon paper, early duplicators, and mechanical calculators for accounting purposes.[95]

Such centralised means of bureaucratic control are certainly oppressive but the physical and temporal distance created between the organs of control and those controlled enables the latter at least some room to 'work the system'.[96] 'Paper-mongering' often has a point and the relative anonymity of interaction via forms might be preferable to the minute personal interrogation of the overseers of the poor, and the local justice of the peace. This form of impersonal information gathering was also preferable to some of the other forms of surveillance being advocated in the late nineteenth century. Charles Booth, for example, suggested that the solution to poverty was to remove the lowest, supposedly unproductive, strata of the working classes to labour colonies. Here they could be watched by the state and forced to work. They or their children would only be allowed back into society when they had learnt work discipline. Booth argued that such a policy of 'limited socialism' would relieve the 'respectable' workers from unnecessary competition and so raise wages.[97] However, a general 'Arbeit macht frei'[98] model of social welfare was never seriously implemented in Britain. Rather than being supervised as deviants, the recipients of the New Liberal largesse were monitored to ensure that they had the entry qualifications for a comparatively privileged club.

Reactions to crisis: information gathering and statistical production

The creation of a more centralised and pluralist state, the need to increase national efficiency, and the relative eclipse of moralism, can be seen as leading gradually to the increased generation of data to inform central intervention in local government and society. This period saw the further expansion within government of the cadre of experts that supported this function, although their impact was still, as yet, modest. Such a strategy served the ends of this administrative elite but also paralleled the need of existing political elites to respond to electoral, social and imperial pressures. Such factors led to the creation of new institutions such as the Labour Department of the Board of Trade, that in various guises from 1886 onwards collected and analysed data on strikes, trade union membership, and wage rates and conditions of work. This was in addition to its use of the new employment exchanges to gauge unemployment levels already mentioned. The extent and importance of such new departures should not be exaggerated, however, since bodies such as the Labour Department were hamstrung by lack of funds. Powerful groups within government, especially the officials of the Treasury, were opposed to the extension of state intervention on ideological, professional and financial grounds.[99]

There was, moreover, a gradual reorientation of the work of existing information-gathering organs of the state, to take account of this shift of emphasis, although this was not always welcomed by statisticians steeped in older traditions of data collection. This can be seen in the activities of the GRO. The census, for example, began to be less a means for pushing forward a narrow medically based project for encouraging local, personal and scientific activity, and more a general tool for research and centrally sponsored initiatives. This can be seen in the deliberations of the 1890 Treasury Committee on the Census, which arose out of the deputation of social scientists, led by Charles Booth and the economist Alfred Marshall, to the Chancellor of the Exchequer and the President of the Local Government Board (LGB). The formal demands of the deputation included:

- a quinquennial census;
- that the census should be the 'care of a special department' which should be in continuous existence;
- that a question on employment status should be added to the census schedule; and
- that there should be revisions to the occupational classification.[100]

Simon Szreter has seen this deputation, and the resulting Committee, as an attempt by social scientists and economists to wrest control of the occupational census from the GRO. Hence the appeal to the GRO's paymaster and then parent department, the Treasury and LGB respectively. Booth and Marshall were trying to shift the underlying organisational principles of the occupational census away from Farr's medical model of the effects of working with materials on health, to those more suitable for economic and social analysis.[101] The GRO managed to fight off some of these demands, which threatened its own autonomy, but the question on employment status was introduced in the 1891 census at the insistence of the LGB, and despite the GRO's continuing opposition. The Office tried to claim that the Census Act did not give the GRO authority to collect the data – an interpretation which was resisted by the LGB.[102] The staff of the GRO plainly resented being diverted from their epidemiological and public health role.[103] Although the GRO declined to analyse the data on employment status collected in 1891, since it claimed that the returns were unreliable, the question reappeared, in a modified form, in 1901.[104] As Szreter notes, the GRO henceforth included representatives from other government departments in internal committees planning the decennial census.[105] A question on home working was introduced into the 1901 enumeration to help the Home Office deal with the control of 'sweated' trades. This was at a time when attempts were being made in Parliament to extend the Factory Acts to home workshops via a system of licensing.[106] Similarly, it was the Board of Trade that suggested the splitting of the occupation column in two – one for occupations, and the other for the trades or industries in which the occupations were performed – which was a feature of the 1911 census. This was to allow the Labour Department to obtain some idea of the overall impact of downturns in trade on particular industries.[107]

Similar concerns underlay changes in the GRO's treatment of mortality data. Whilst the registered birth rate had fallen from 35.3 per thousand in the decade 1871–80 to 26.6 per thousand in the period 1901–11,[108] the infant mortality rate had failed to improve in the late Victorian period in line with the experience of other age cohorts.[109] Edwin Cannan had argued in the *Economic Journal* in 1895 that the declining replacement rate would lead to a stationary population, whilst the manpower of Germany and the USA was expanding rapidly.[110] As already noted, such an eventuality would have dire consequences for British society, the economy and the Empire. It was at this point in Britain that population became a political issue requiring urgent attention, rather than in the eighteenth or early nineteenth centuries.

As Jane Lewis, Deborah Dwork and others have argued, predictions with respect to the declining size of the population engendered a public debate over infant and maternal welfare, especially after the shock of the Second Boer War.[111] The President of the LGB, John Burns, held a series of national conferences on infant mortality in 1906 and 1908, which were attended by large contingents of local medical officers of health.[112] The latter were the officers in local authorities responsible for public health measures. These meetings led to the development of a general child-welfare movement that sought to prevent the loss of infant life through the delivery of local authority welfare and health services. In order to allow local medical officers of health and the LGB to gauge the efficacy of such measures, the GRO began to publish tables in 1907 showing mortality from the principal causes of death in each of the first four weeks after birth, and in each month in the first year of infant life.[113] As well as the new tables already noted, a distinct section on mortality amongst infants and young children was introduced as a standard component of both the GRO's *Annual Reports* and its *Decennial Supplements*.[114] Central state information gathering was beginning to address the population issue, although in a very tardy manner compared to the Continent, because military manpower was now becoming an issue for the British State and Empire.

But the GRO was not only concerned with issues of *quantity*, it also became embroiled in a debate over the best way to improve the *quality* of the population. Responding to pressure from the eugenicists, the GRO introduced a question on marital fertility into the 1911 census, and elaborated a classification of socio-economic groupings, to see what social-class differentials existed. This classification was based on placing households into certain groupings based on the occupation of the male head of household. These groupings were supposed to be made up of occupations requiring similar levels of skill.[115] The results appeared to show that the lower orders were indeed out-breeding their 'betters', although the relevant analysis was not published until the First World War and its aftermath.[116] By this date, of course, any argument for the reduction of the reproduction of any social group was likely to fall on deaf official ears if it meant slowing the replacement of men lost during the War.

The 1911 fertility survey was an important development in its own right but what was just as important for the future was the consequences this had for the data-processing capabilities of the GRO. In order to analyse the fertility data, and that gathered by the other new census enquiries, the Office introduced the use of Hollerith machine tabulators. These had been developed in 1890 for the US census of that year, and were being introduced into state statistical offices across Europe. The take-up of such technology was a consequence of the increasing size and complexity of national census enumerations across the Western world as a whole, in a period of increasing state engagement with social issues. Existing manual methods of data processing simply could not cope with the demands now being placed upon them.[117]

Machine tabulation broke data analysis down into two stages. First, information on individuals was punched on a card as a series of holes, and secondly, the information on the cards was read electronically. In essence, pads with spring-loaded pins were brought down on individual cards, and if the pins passed through a hole they completed a circuit through which electricity passed to move the hands of a dial on a counter on one position. The dials could be wired up via relay keys to undertake complex calculations.[118] Punched cards remained one of the principal methods of automated data input until the 1970s. What this two-part process did was to separate data capture from data analysis, since the cards could be analysed in differing ways, and as many times as necessary. At a stroke the bottlenecks in the GRO's manual system of data processing were removed, opening up whole new possibilities for statistical manipulation, and the new technology was soon used to create new and more complex forms of epidemiological and public health data.[119] As the then Registrar-General put it:

> Once the labour of preparing the cards required for the routine tabulation as previously carried out has been accomplished, it becomes a very simple matter to obtain records of additional combinations of the facts recorded, whereas under the system previously employed each additional tabulation had to be undertaken independently, the record of one combination of facts not contributing in any way to the preparation of that of another.[120]

This was the invention of the modern, machine-readable database, predating the electronic computer by over half a century.

However, if this innovation allowed the GRO to aggregate the characteristics of whole populations, it also had the potential to identify individuals with particular characteristics within that population. By November 1914 MI5 was reporting at a CCID sub-committee that the GRO had already compiled an unofficial register of about 70,000 Belgian refugees, and had 'carded certain facts about them'. This may have referred to Hollerith cards, although the evidence is inconclusive.[121] Whatever the technology used, this was surveillance for the purposes of centralised action, rather than local debate, representing another reorientation of the role of the GRO. As will be discussed in a subsequent chapter, the new potential for information retrieval and combination inherent in the database would eventually lead to public disquiet about the powers of the state.

The withering of local taxation systems

The relative decline in decentralised forms of administration can also be seen in the gradual withering away of the local state's control over the taxation. This is especially evident in the chequered history of the income tax, which became the principal form of assessed tax in the course of the Victorian period. Income tax was first introduced by William Pitt in 1799 to finance the war with France, but the tax was repealed in 1802, and then reimposed in 1803 for the duration of the conflict with Napoleon. So unpopular was the tax that on its second abolition in 1816, those documents relating to it, including assessments, that were held centrally by the Commission for the Affairs of the Taxes were ordered to be cut into small pieces and conveyed to a paper mill. Here they were pulped before the eyes of one of the commissioners. However, the effectiveness of this rather grandiloquent gesture was somewhat undermined by the retention of duplicate assessments in the records of the King's Remembrancer of the Exchequer.[122]

Sir Robert Peel reintroduced the tax in 1842, as a means of balancing the budget, for an 'experimental' period of three years. The experiment became, of course, the cornerstone of modern state finances. Peel's tax, at a rate of 7d in the pound on incomes over £150, was a tax on the middle and upper classes. One of the ways in which he sweetened the pill was to include in the Income Tax Act an arrangement by which taxpayers could elect to be assessed by special officers employed centrally, rather than by the usual, locally appointed, commissioners. Appeals against assessments could also be made to special, as opposed to the local general, commissioners. According to Peel, the appointment of special commissioners was an attempt to reconcile 'the impartial and just imposition of the tax and the prevention of evasion and fraud'. But he was also concerned lest,

any one objected to go before the local authority, and this might happen where the commissioner was a competitor in trade or a rival in manufactures, or where the disclosure of a person's income before a particular commissioner might be prejudicial or vexatious.[123]

As the profits of trade came to replace land as the principal source of wealth, so privacy and secrecy became a political issue. A landed gentleman could not hide the source of his wealth from view, indeed he tended to flaunt it as the visible symbol of his status – hence, perhaps, the vogue for aristocratic representations of land in seventeenth- and eighteenth-century British art.[124] This was not the case, however, with the new mercantile and capitalist classes, for whom commercial confidentiality was of paramount importance in their business dealings. For them the 'paraphernalia of gentility' lay in their private homes, carriages and retinues of servants.[125]

Various attempts were made by Victorian governments to bring the collection and administration of income tax under full central control. This culminated in a proposal in 1883 that all collections under schedules D and E should be transferred to the officers of the Inland Revenue. The Chancellor, Hugh Childers, suggested that this would complete the transfer of collection of the tax 'from the irresponsible collector on poundage to the responsible collector on salary – that is, a public officer'. He also claimed that the proposal had been pressed on him by the Association of Chambers of Commerce on the grounds that the collector might be a 'neighbour who may possibly be a rival in trade'.[126] However, the change was opposed by many members of parliament as 'compulsory centralisation'. W. H. Smith, the retailer and future Conservative leader in the Commons, claimed that:

> The principle upon which the income tax was originally established was this – that there should be Commissioners representing the people who should appoint their own clerks, their own assessors and their own collectors and that, on the other hand, the Crown, the Chancellor of the Exchequer and the Commissioners of the Inland Revenue should have their Surveyor and their Inspector to see that the Crown received no damage and that the duties, as charged, were realised.[127]

This assertion of the traditional division of responsibility between the central and local state, which could have come from a seventeenth-century Whig, carried the day, and the Government was defeated by 167 to 161 votes.[128]

This was, however, merely a victory of form over content. The increase in the proportion of GNP (gross national product) passing through central government, itself a function of rising central expenditure on welfare and defence, undermined the decentralised forms of revenue collection. By 1920, the Royal Commission on Income Tax found that local general commissioners were indeed still responsible, in theory, for appointing clerks to the commissioners, local assessors and, frequently, the collectors. They could also receive assessments, hear and determine appeals, and could imprison defaulting collectors and taxpayers. In practice, however, the sheer complexity and scale of the process of making income tax assessments meant that much of the work had to be done by full-time inspectors of taxes responsible to the Board of Inland Revenue. The general commissioners, often distracted by numerous other private and public duties, merely gave 'some kind of formal covering authority' to the work of the civil servants. The Royal Commission believed that if the local process of taxation was undertaken solely by the general commissioners this 'literally would result in a breakdown of the machinery ... [of taxation]'.[129] Leisured country gentlemen could afford to spend time organising the minutiae of local revenue collection amongst their tenants, but company directors and the managers of local branches of national banks had neither the time, the inclination nor the authority to do so.

The Royal Commission recommended that the post of local assessor of taxes should be abolished and that the work such officials performed should be taken over by the central inspectors of taxes. They further argued that henceforth the duties of the general commissioners should be confined to hearing appeals since the taxpayer often 'looks upon the general commissioner as a natural safeguard interposed between himself and the Revenue authorities'. The returns, assessments and other documents relating to the tax, which were formerly the property of the general commissioners, would in future be the property of the Board of Inland Revenue.[130] However, these sweeping proposals for centralisation were not acted upon immediately, and it was not until the 1931 Finance Act that the appointment of all collectors of taxes in England and Wales fell to the Board of Inland Revenue. Even then, the process of collecting taxes in the City of London was not assimilated into the central state until 1945. In theory assessments could still be made locally by general commissioners until the passage of the Income Tax Management Act of 1964. Even in this most critical government function, the decentralised state of early modern England lingered on, if in a degenerate form, into the modern world.

The gradual centralisation of overall control of taxation in Whitehall during the late Victorian and Edwardian periods may help, in part, to explain the revolution in national fiscal statistics in these years. Revenue statistics had been placed before Parliament since the English Civil War, and the Board of Inland Revenue began issuing reports from 1857 onwards. But these mostly contained measurements of receipts, rather than of the size and composition of the tax base. It was only in 1893 that the Board of Inland Revenue appointed its first official statistician, J. E. Chapman. Chapman set to work to analyse the returns relating to estate duty, another centralised tax, which had been introduced in 1894. The returns provided the Board, for the first time, with comprehensive information about the ownership and composition of the wealth of the country. The estate duty tables devised by Chapman, showing the distribution of capital in ranges, and its composition by reference to types of property, were still in use in the Inland Revenue in the 1940s.[131]

Further estate duty statistics, showing the distribution of capital by age and sex of the deceased, were prepared to facilitate the computation of national capital, based on a method suggested in 1908 by Sir Bernard Mallet, a commissioner of Inland Revenue. Mallet became Registrar-General in 1909 but still found time to examine the impact of British budgets on the wealth of various sections of the population in his *British Budgets, 1887–1913*, published in 1913.[132] Josiah Stamp, later Baron Stamp and assistant secretary at the Inland Revenue in the years 1916 to 1919, followed this up with his own *British Incomes and Property* in 1916.[133] A Statistics and Intelligence Division was set up by the Board in 1919, and was responsible for the preparation of budget estimates, for estimating the cost and yield of changes in taxation, and for general statistical work.[134] As the central state came to monopolise the power of national wealth extraction, so the calculation by Whitehall of what that wealth amounted to became both desirable and practical.

Conclusion

The period from about 1880 to the beginning of the Great War emerges, therefore, as the crucible of the formation of the modern

Information State. British economic and imperial decline, and the decline of moralism and localism, forced the beginnings of a radical reappraisal of the balance between centre and locality, and between personal or communal autonomy and the needs of Empire. At the same time, the working classes were being incorporated into the political nation, and their interests catered for, or perhaps reformulated, within the parliamentary process. These factors all helped to create new forms of central and local data collection and analysis, and new methods of mechanical information processing. In some ways Britain was being forced to conform to a more general European pattern of state formation.

But only in some ways. Britain did not become a new Prussia overnight, and there were still limits to which centralisation could be pushed. As already noted, many of the innovations of the late Victorian and Edwardian periods were initially small in scale, or took decades to work through the administrative and legislative systems. However, the increasing demands made by the population on the Welfare State, and for the purposes of crime and terrorist prevention, helped to increase the scope of central surveillance. Nor did external threats to Britain decline, and in an age of fascism and world communism such threats became intertwined with internal dissent. These general themes will be the subjects of the next chapter.

6

The Information State in total war and total welfare

The generalisation of the New Liberal State

Although the decades either side of 1900 may have laid the groundwork for the modern Information State, its development prior to 1914 was strictly limited. It was the intensification of military threats to Britain and its empire in the twentieth century, and the deepening and widening of the Welfare State, that pushed forward state expansion. Thus, the number of civil servants increased from 107,782 (excluding industrial grades) in 1902 to 547,000 by 1980, plus some 157,600 industrial grades. Altogether the state came to employ no less than 17 per cent of the occupied population, 25 per cent if the nationalised industries are included. There was also a thirty-fold increase in government expenditure in real terms, or nearly tenfold as a proportion of national income, from £77.9 million in 1897–98 (£105.3 million at 1913 prices), to £66,800 million in 1978–79 (£3,389 million at 1913 prices). This represented a rise from about five per cent of the net National Income to about 47 per cent.[1]

This expansion almost inevitably brought the population into ever-closer contact with the central state, and the increasing scale of information exchange between the two drove the state collection and analysis of personal data to new heights. Yet for much of the century there were certain limits to these processes, reflecting both the older liberal traditions of the polity, the relatively modest aims of the regime of personal benefits and taxes, and the limitations of the data-handling technologies available to the state. Although it is usual to see the pre- and post-Second World War periods as being very different in British history, they form a unity when discussing the development of the Information State.

However, the years from the 1960s onwards, which saw the rise of computerised data processing, represent a rather different set of issues in the field of information, and will be the subject of the next chapter.

Citizenship and the World Wars

Although in 1805 Horatio Nelson had signalled to his fleet at Trafalgar that, 'England expects every man to do his duty', this was to be understood in a strictly local sense. If a nineteenth-century Englishman did not want to do his military duty by the nation, he was under relatively little compulsion to do so. The exceptions were if he was unlucky enough in the early decades of the century to be in or near a port, and come to the attentions of the press-gang, or was chosen locally by lot to be drafted into the militia and was unable to pay for a replacement. But after the Napoleonic Wars the Royal Navy had less need of men, and the Victorian army was an even lower priority. Indeed, Britain hardly had a regular army at all in the nineteenth century. In 1844 the British Army numbered a mere 138,000 men, of whom only 30,000 were at home, the rest being dispersed across the expanding Empire. This was a volunteer force, and one that preserved many features of the military life of the eighteenth century – the purchase of commissions did not end until 1871; officers' pay remained constant from 1806 to 1914 despite inflation; and although only eight per cent of the British labour force were employed in agriculture in 1912, 65 per cent of senior officers in 1914 came from a rural background. The British Army was hardly the modern, industrial 'nation in arms'.[2]

As already noted, this lack of obligation on the British citizenry to perform military service was unusual in the European context. The concept of the conscript army based on the *levy en masse* had come out of the French Revolution, when the new Republic was threatened by foreign invasion. Responding to the cry of 'Le patrie en danger', France had over a million men in arms by August 1794. The Revolution thus helped to link citizenship with conscription. As Hew Strachan has put it:

> The Revolution had transformed the ethos and size of the French army, and had based it spiritually and physically in the heart of the nation (or at least the revolutionaries' view of the nation). The outbreak of war meant that the

army assumed simultaneously the defence both of France and of the new order, and in consequence all three – army, nation and Revolution – were identified together.[3]

The French Republic fell, as did the subsequent Empire, but the association between citizenship and military service continued, and became generalised in a situation of almost constant European confrontations. In the course of the mid- to late nineteenth century most European states introduced some form of military conscription, which implied the national registration of citizens. Only Britain and the USA did not maintain conscript armies, since the British placed their reliance on the Navy, and the USA was remote from European warfare.[4] Nor, as has already been noted, did Britain have the population registers, or the internal passports, that were found in many Continental states.

But this lack of systematic national registration could not survive the total warfare of the years 1914 to 1918. By 1915 it was plain, at least to Lord Kitchener as secretary of state for war, that the conflict with Germany could only be won if the entire human resources of the nation could be mobilised.[5] Given the rate of attrition at the front in battles such as the Somme, the old British Army would have been wiped out in a matter of days. A series of reports produced by the Jackson and Landsdowne Committees on National Registration called for the establishment of a system that would facilitate military conscription but also enable the claims of industry and agriculture to be taken into account.[6] There was no point in raising a vast conscript army if it could not be armed and fed because of labour shortages on the Home Front.

Under the resulting 1915 National Registration Act, the GRO became the central military registration authority for the country, with the metropolitan and municipal boroughs, and urban and rural district councils, acting as its local agents. The Act also authorised the creation of a register of all men and women aged 15 to 65 years who were not members of the armed forces, or resident in certain institutions – prisons, lunatic asylums, Poor Law hospitals and so on. Registration forms, asking for the required data[7] on each relevant member of the public, were sent to the local registration authorities by the GRO. When these had been completed and returned, registered citizens were issued with a certificate that they had to sign and keep in their possession. Individuals were required to notify the local authorities of changes of address, and were then issued with new, corrected certificates.[8]

Each local registration authority was to keep its forms arranged alphabetically within occupations, and another set was kept for all males of military age. The GRO acted as a clearing-house in the inevitable doubtful cases, and received returns of the numbers in particular occupations from the local bodies. Duplicates of the registration forms were also held by the military authorities, and when it was decided to recruit a particular group of men, their forms were sent to the GRO for distribution to the localities. The registration system was also used by the Ministry of Munitions and Board of Agriculture to gather information on potential munitions workers and agricultural labourers. The chief inspector of mines and the Railways Executive Committee also used the register in a similar manner. The organisation of the nation for total war was thus facilitated.

The GRO also tabulated the occupations affected by military conscription to provide information to central government on the impact of such recruitment on the industrial workforce. By January 1917 the GRO was employing 59 members of its staff on national registration work alone.[9] In the later stages of the War, the GRO was also responsible for issuing ration books and sugar tickets to the public via the local registrars of births, marriages and deaths.[10] The Office also maintained a Central Register of War Refugees to guard, in part, against the creation of a fifth column ready to fight for the enemy if the German Army should invade.[11] The GRO continued to supply information on enemy aliens to MI5, and co-operated in the calculation in 1915 of the proportion of them that would be of military age, and the totals interned and at large.[12] Unfortunately it is difficult to tell if this was based on a reworking of the original census totals, or the tables in the published *Census Reports*, since the MI5 file dealing with the setting up of systems for the control of enemy aliens is unfortunately said to be 'Wanting' in the PRO lists.

Thus, in the crisis of the nation state, the underlying function of the registration system as a means of enforcing obligations and maintaining the very integrity of the nation state, was brought sharply into focus.[13] Whether such obligations were 'just' depends, of course, on how one evaluates war in general, and the First World

War in particular. Nor should this be taken to imply that citizens' rights and obligation, in T. H. Marshall's sense, were simply the reward granted by the state to citizens in return for fighting for the nation, since many such rights had already been established prior to 1916.[14] But the war certainly underlined the link between citizenship and fighting for the nation/state. The state even promised to reciprocate with a 'Land fit for heroes', although the reality fell somewhat short of the rhetoric.

The overall success of these administrative arrangements encouraged T. H. C. Stevenson, the GRO's then superintendent of statistics, to suggest in 1916 that the national registration system should be continued after the War.[15] He envisaged this leading to the issuing of a single document that would be a general means of identification to replace all the official documents issued by various government departments – an identity card in all but name. As a result of Stevenson's musings, and with the active support of the Registrar-General, Sir Bernard Mallet, a Committee on National Registration was set up in May 1917 by the President of the LGB. The original members of the committee included Hayes Fisher, parliamentary secretary to the President of the LGB; Mallet; Horace Monro, permanent secretary at the LGB; Seebohm Rowntree, the Liberal social reformer; Stevenson; Sylvanus Vivian from the National Insurance Commission; and Beatrice Webb, the Fabian socialist activist. The War Office was supportive, since a national register would provide the means of furnishing its Recruiting Department with the information it required concerning youths of military age.[16] The Committee was thus an amalgam of senior civil servants and left-leaning social scientists.

Webb, in typical Fabian fashion, saw the proposed national register in terms of both citizenship and administrative convenience. As she argued in a letter to Vivian:

> The identification of every individual within a community is necessary in order (a) that each shall be made responsible for the fulfilment of his legal obligations; (b) that he shall be ensured his rights as a citizen; and (c) that he shall receive all that is due to him, not merely in respect of protection of life and property, but also with regard to any collective services to which he is entitled ... The second purpose of a National Register is to discover statistical facts about the population or any particular section of the population, partly for the purpose of record, but also to permit administrative action to be taken to remedy overt dangers or redress grievances.[17]

The National Registration Committee reported in July 1918, and advocated the continuation of the national register for the reasons outlined by Webb. The list of administrative uses of the proposed system given in the report included:

- the improved registration of births, marriages and deaths;
- increased accuracy of the census;
- better administration of Poor Law chargeability;
- allowing the estimation of the population of districts for medical purposes;
- tracing those with communicable diseases;
- providing against 'overlap, neglect or fraud' with respect to all the differing bodies responsible for public assistance and war pensions – boards of guardians, local health authorities, National Insurance Committee, local education authorities, local war pensions committees, employment exchanges, etc.;
- enforcing school attendance;
- and facilitating registration for military service.[18]

The Committee envisaged that local authorities would employ canvassers to create local registers, which would in turn be the basis of a central register.[19] Ominously, they were vague as to the cost of the project, mentioning figures of £100,000, £150,000, and even £500,000, per annum, depending on the assumptions made with respect to the scope of the register and the adminis-trative structure employed.[20]

These recommendations reveal the potential intertwining of positive rights, obligations and state surveillance of the individ-ual, but in practice there appears to have been little chance of their leading to any political or administrative action. This was partly due to the cost to local authorities[21] but the main stum-bling block was the perceived limits to the extent to which the central state should monitor citizens. In September 1916, even before the National Registration Committee had been set up, Monro was writing to Fisher, noting that,

It is no doubt worth considering whether after the war public opinion will tolerate a system of universal registration, which involves the continual reporting of removals &c. and a considerable amount of interference with individuals. Two years ago this would certainly have been regarded as a 'Prussianizing' institution, but we have got used to various things since then and it is quite possible that it would not be viewed with so much hostility now. At the same time it has the great defect that it must inevitably put a duty on millions of individuals, failure to perform which must render them liable to penalties. There will thus be an enormously enlarged field of 'crime' opened and a corresponding necessity for official surveillance. The former result would be unfortunate, the latter both irritating and expensive.[22]

Significantly, neither Fisher nor Monro appears to have signed the Registration Committee's report.[23] An internal GRO memorandum, from the period after the report was issued, also advocated the postponement of the introduction of the scheme because of public hostility to 'Prussianism'.[24] By February 1919 Webb was writing to Mallet and commiserating with him that the scheme had been, 'held up without being considered'. Five months later, in July 1919, a senior civil servant was apologising to Mallet with respect to the 'discontinuance of the National Register'.[25] During the financial stringencies of the 1920s, the subject of national registration simply vanished from view, as with most of the state controls of the war period.[26]

This approach to information gathering, or rather non-gathering, was evident in other parts of the state. In 1918, for example, the short-lived Ministry of National Service suggested that all servicemen should be fingerprinted to prevent fraud in the payment of war pensions. The Ministry of Pensions, on the other hand, believed that this 'would be unpopular and would tend to produce hostility to the department initiating the practice', whilst the War Office turned the proposal down flat.[27] As the Ministry of National Service ruefully admitted,

the British public is so accustomed to associate it [fingerprinting] with the identification of members of the criminal classes that public opinion would be offended and scandalised by its application to the discharged soldier and sailor.[28]

Such modern technologies of identification were not to be generalised to create a universal system of identification, rather they were a mark of infamy that placed certain groups, such as criminals, beyond the pale of citizenship. Some other countries, such as the USA, were, however, less circumspect in their use of fingerprinting.[29] In South America, fingerprinting had been associated with a system of identity cards proposed by Juan Vucetich in 1905, and became a feature of the majority of countries in the region by the 1930s.[30]

However, although the system of internal registration was dropped in Britain, control of movement to and from other states was intensified. During the nineteenth century people had moved into and out of Britain quite freely. Indeed, most of the people who migrated to the USA from Europe passed through British ports such as Liverpool. But this system of *laissez-faire* was another victim of the First World War. The 1914 Aliens Restriction Act, passed in August of that year, gave the government greater powers to restrict such movement. This increasing sensitivity to perceived threats from abroad was shared by states across the developed world, and led to the creation of the contemporary system of international passports. The first modern United Kingdom passport was issued in 1915, when the 1914 Status of Aliens Act came into force. This contained the personal description of the holder, giving the shape of the person's face, their features (nose: large; forehead: broad; eyes: small) as well as their complexion, a photograph and their signature. The passport was valid for two years and could be renewed for a further four two-year periods.[31] The wartime restrictions were extended after the period of conflict by the Aliens Order of 1920, which laid down that anyone wanting to enter or leave the country had to carry a passport indicating his or her nationality and identity. In a world in which citizens were being mobilised for total warfare, all foreign nationals became a potential threat.[32]

The events leading up to the Second World War, and the threat of another European conflict, reactivated interest in the subject of internal passports. As early as 1922 a sub-committee of the Committee of Imperial Defence was insisting that any decent system of national service would require a good system of national registration.[33] However, the preparations for a new registration system appear not to have begun in earnest until 1935, due, in the words of Sylvanus Vivian, the Registrar-General from 1921 to 1945, to 'the recent international disturbances'.[34] In that year Vivian was chairing a sub-committee of the Cabinet's Committee on Imperial Defence on the subject, and a draft National Service Bill had been drawn up.[35] A plan for the enumeration that was to be the basis of the register was drafted in 1936, and an experiment in one county was proposed to find out how much work would be involved. It was also noted by Vivian that, 'as the operation will be useful in the preparation for the 1941 census plans it cannot be considered as lost labour'.[36] Subsequently, the preparations for the national register and the census ran in tandem.

The National Service (Armed Forces) Act was passed on the same day that war was declared on Germany in September 1939, which gave authority to issue royal proclamations imposing a liability for service with the Armed Forces on men between the ages of 18 and 41. The enumeration machinery was activated for the compilation of a national register by the end of that month, and in 1941 a little over 7 million men had been registered. As in the First World War, the register was used to issue identity cards; for rationing purposes; and for the deployment of labour in the military and other essential services. The population figures produced by the enumeration of 1939 were seen by the GRO as the nearest thing to a census likely to be taken in war conditions, and as such they were first circulated for official use and then published in 1944.[37] In the run up to the Great War, the census apparatus had been adapted to the needs of military preparation but in the Second World War the national register provided a substitute for the decennial enumeration.

At the same time, a Registration for Employment Order allowed the Ministry of Labour to order men and women to register at local labour exchanges, and to give details of their present employment. Women were also to give information on their marital status, household responsibilities and whether they had children under the age of 14. Those people whom local officials felt could be transferred to essential work would be interviewed and 'advised' of jobs they could take to aid the war effort. If they declined to participate in war work they could be legally compelled to do so. This led to mass mobilisation of the civilian population. In 1939, for example, about 5 million women were employed in the forces, industry or commerce, out of a total of about 16 million women of working age. By 1943 a further 2.25 million women had been drawn into employment. In all, 90 per cent of single women aged 18 to 40 years were so engaged, as were 80 per cent of married or widowed women who had no children.[38]

The mobilisation of the entire population for warfare made other forms of registration possible. The Second World War allowed the failings of the inter-war Register of Merchant Seamen to be rectified. During the first 18 months of war, those responsible for manning ships were often at their wits' end to find crews.

Many of those who had left the sea, however willing they were to return, could not leave their shore jobs, many of which had become vital to the war effort. It was essential that sailors should be directed to ships, and a substantial reserve built up, so as to avoid delaying vital convoys.[39] The Essential Work (Merchant Navy) Order of 1941 created a Merchant Navy Reserve Pool. To ensure that seamen would always be available to crew vessels, the government paid them to remain in the Reserve Pool when they were ashore. Now that continuous paid employment, instead of casual work, was available to all seamen, and the state controlled exits from, and entrance to, the mercantile marine, comprehensive and effective registration became possible. All those who had served at sea during the previous five years were required to register with the Registrar-General of Shipping and Seamen, and a new Central Register of Seamen was established. This Central Register was maintained until 1972.[40]

The onset of the Cold War, and the continuation of the state direction of the economy, meant that national registration was not abolished after the defeat of Germany in 1945. According to a Cabinet memorandum drawn up in 1951, national registration was being used at that date for organising National Service in the forces, NHS registration, food rationing and the investigation of crime.[41] The security services were also said to,

> rely on the National Register to obtain evidence as to the identity of people who are the subject of investigations. The number of those people is large and growing, and the method used helps to ensure that news of the enquiry does not reach the individuals concerned.[42]

The maintenance of such a system for the enforcement of national obligations upon vast numbers of citizens during 'peacetime' was, and is, unique in British history. However, despite its usefulness, and against the wishes of the security services and police, national registration, and the issuing of identity cards, was wound up in 1952.[43] This was partly on the grounds of expense, since the system cost £500,000 per annum and required 1,500 civil servants to run it. But the carrying of identity cards, and the need to register changes of address, were also associated with the administrative controls of the austerity programme of postwar Labour governments, which came to be widely regarded as unnecessary and oppressive.[44] Conservative and Liberal peers objected strenuously in Parliament to what they saw as 'Socialist card-indexing'.[45] Even the Bench was turning against the need for citizens to produce identity cards for the police in petty disputes, a practice Lord Goddard described as 'wholly unreasonable' in a legal judgment in 1951. He felt that this undermined law and order since 'such action tends to make the people resentful of the acts of the police and induces them to obstruct the police instead of to assist them'.[46] The abandonment of identity cards was in stark contrast to other European states, such as France, which had introduced them after the Second World War.[47]

Such sentiments could be found in numerous cultural forms, from Orwell's *Nineteen Eighty-Four* of 1949 to the Ealing comedy *Passport to Pimlico* of the same year. In the latter film the population of a small London borough discover that they are ancient Burgundians rather than British, and use this as an excuse to lift all the rationing and bureaucratic restrictions associated with 'Austerity Britain'. The neighbourhood becomes an oasis for black-market transactions, and of drinking into the early hours of the morning. The British government responds by creating a frontier around the mini-state, controlled by officials scrutinising identity papers – hence the 'passport' of the title. But the plucky Burgundians are saved by Londoners, who throw food packages across the barbed-wire barriers, and by milk and live pigs delivered by helicopter and parachute. This can be seen as a reference to the Berlin airlift of the previous year, in which the beleagured citizens of West Berlin had been supplied by the West in order to enable them to hold out against a communist blockade. National registration had thus become associated, if facetiously, with the totalitarianism of the Left, which was perhaps understandable given the use of internal passports to control the population of the Soviet Union.[48] The identity card system was a casualty of the election of a new Conservative government late in 1951, although National Service was not abolished until 1960.

The national register did not fade away entirely, however, since it was used to prepare the NHS Central Register (NHSCR), which was subsequently kept up to date by the local registrars of births, marriages and deaths, and by family practitioner committees. For those people who held national identity cards in 1952, their identity number became, and still remains, their NHS number. The NHSCR was later used to monitor the transfer of patients between general practitioners; for the issue of NHS numbers; and in order to notify family practitioner committees when people died, went abroad, or for any other reason no longer needed health care.[49] By 1951 the GRO was employing no fewer than 870 staff, out of a total of 1,486 in sections dealing with various aspects of registration and the provision of direct services to the public.[50]

The history of national registration reveals, therefore, both the potential of the Information State in Britain but also the limits to how far general state surveillance could be justified in times of peace. Extremely effective systems of information gathering could be elaborated when they were required in emergencies but were dismantled when those emergencies passed. How far this reflected an in-built virtue in the British system, or the relative lack of immediate threats, is difficult to determine. However, the concept of privacy certainly did not apply to communities within the UK that posed a threat to the state, as in the case of Northern Ireland. In the 1950s there were also various other sources of information on individuals upon which the state could now draw for security purposes, such as national insurance records.[51] In addition, in the subsequent 50 years, efficient means of combining such sources to create profiles of individuals were to be developed that perhaps made national registration unnecessary. Both these issues will be discussed in more detail in the next chapter.

The expansion of the Secret State

The almost constant warfare, or preparation for war, of the twentieth century facilitated the expansion of the security services and the deepening of their penetration into British society. During the First World War the size of the counter-subversion forces increased markedly. MI5 grew from 14 officers and staff in July 1914 to 844 by the end of the war, whilst Special Branch expanded from 114 in November 1914 to 700 officers. The combined budgets of the two organisations rose from £25,000 to more than £200,000, and their remit expanded to cover all those whose activities might possibly be seen as hindering the war effort – pacifist organisations, socialist societies, trade unions, strikers, and potential fifth columnists.[52] In all, 32,000 male enemy aliens were interned as a result of the lists created by MI5, and up to 20,000 men, women and children were repatriated out of a total of 75,000.[53] After the Russian Revolution of 1917, MI5 immediately began making enquiries regarding Russian, Finnish, Polish and Czech officers, and investigated 'activities in connection with Bolshevism, strikes and Pacifism in the U.K.'.[54] Section H.2 of MI5, the Registry, expanded into a complex information processing system. By 1917 its work involved receiving information on suspects from government departments, chief constables and private individuals, from which it created registered files. These were subsequently printed for ease of use. The Registry distributed files to other divisions of MI5, and kept track of their movements. H.2 also produced various name, ship, subject and place indexes to the information in its records, the geographical indexes being organised down to the level of streets in London and large towns.[55]

To a certain extent, the ordinary police were drawn into this system through their work in arresting enemy aliens. The First World War brought other new responsibilities for the traditional 'bobby', such as guarding vulnerable points, enforcing lighting restrictions, and dealing with the consequences of air raids. Similarly, chief constables sent information to Special Branch on strikers, and police even visited the homes of munitions workers when they were absent from work. The Chief Constable of Hull had plain-clothes police occasionally riding trams to identify those spreading rumours that could undermine morale. A new degree of centralisation in policing was also introduced by the establishment of district conferences of chief constables, and a central conference of delegates from the districts that met for the first time at the Home Office in 1918. The Home Office thus began to supply a degree of leadership, and acted as a point of contact with the security forces.[56]

However, the immediate post-war period saw the marked contraction of this Secret State. MI5 shrank after 1918 under the impact of financial stringency, and by 1925 its staffing had fallen to a mere 30 officers. Indeed, in that year the organisation was nearly absorbed into MI6, the security service active overseas, and its role was reduced to one of counter-intelligence in the armed services, with a brief to prevent communist infiltration. Special Branch now dealt with civilians, undertaking extensive surveillance of communists in the inter-war period. MI5's fortunes began to recover in 1931 when it was given the brief of civilian security as a whole, and at this point it ceased to be a section of the War Office and was officially renamed as the Security Service. In 1933, when Hitler came to power in Germany, MI5 began to collect information about Nazi sympathisers in Britain. After the Munich Crisis in 1938, telegrams ordering the police to arrest British fascists, as well as those suspected of German espionage, were kept at readiness by MI5 for dispatch at a moment's notice. These were indeed sent out in September 1939.[57]

But on the eve of war in 1938 MI5 was still a comparatively small organisation, with 30 officers, and 130 secretaries and registry staff. The onset of hostilities led once more to the expansion of the Secret State, MI5 having 234 officers and 634 support staff by January 1941. During the first few days of the war, 415 enemy aliens were arrested on the basis of lists prepared by MI5. Internment was subsequently the fate of many Germans in Britain, including some who were refugees from the Nazis. Following Italy's entry into the war in June 1940, all male Italians aged between 16 and 70 with less than 20 years' residence in Britain were interned, as well as those Italians, male or female, on MI5's suspect list. It appears that MI5 also exercised a veto over individual releases of enemy aliens from internment and took a narrow security view of such matters. Lord Lytton, the chairman of the body that advised the Home Office on the release of enemy aliens, had twice offered his resignation prior to January 1941 because his council's recommendations had been overridden by the security services. Trade unionists had to obtain permits to visit protected places such as factories engaged in war work, and no permits were issued until MI5 had checked on the applicant. MI5 was also involved in keeping a watch on the activities of communists and Trotskyists in factories.[58]

This intensification of its activities swamped MI5's old paper-based Registry, which had all but broken down by June 1940. Large numbers of 'omnibus' files, covering vague subject headings such as 'Communists in Northumberland', were created in preference to individual personal files, making information retrieval extremely difficult. The resulting breakdown in efficiency led to the introduction of a business efficiency expert recruited from Roneo, Reginald Horrocks, as deputy director. Horrocks modernised MI5's antiquated filing system, breaking up subject files into individual personal files, and adopting a numbering series for personal records. By March 1944 the Registry possessed an index to its records containing one and a quarter million cards. Horrocks also introduced Hollerith punch-card machines to speed up information retrieval.[59] As in the case of the original introduction of such technologies into census work, it was the increased scale and complexity of information handling that necessitated automation. This was also the beginning of that mechanisation of the work of the security forces that has driven a great deal of the subsequent reorganisation of the British security apparatus.

During the Second World War MI5 still relied on the police for much of their information and for the making of arrests, and the constabulary's surveillance role became more intrusive. It has been claimed that MI5 virtually took over the Metropolitan Police Special Branch in the 1930s,[60] and this relationship with the police was strengthened after 1939. The Aliens Order gave the police power to detain, or impose restrictions on, any person in order to safeguard public safety and defend the realm. Acting under it, the police took into custody enemy aliens and others marked out for detention by the security forces. They also enforced restrictions on certain proscribed individuals with respect to their places of residence, movements, and their possession of prohibited articles, such as cameras, cars, binoculars, maps and radios. The police also reported to regional headquarters on any cases of improper disclosure of secret information, and acted throughout the war as an intelligence service, reporting on the state of public order and morale; the conduct of the public during air raids; the effect of enemy propaganda; and signs of industrial unrest.[61]

The Second World War also saw further moves towards police centralisation. By Defence Regulation 39, the Home Secretary was empowered to give to any police authority or chief constable,

> such general or special instructions as appear to him necessary or expedient in the interests of the public safety, the defence of the Realm, the maintenance of public order, or the efficient prosecution of the war.[62]

These statutory powers were revoked in 1945 but the 1964 Police Act gave the Home Secretary a duty to take initiatives 'to promote the efficiency of the police' by developing co-operation between forces; provide common services; and amalgamate police areas. He could also call for reports from chief constables, approve the appointment of senior officers, and compel the retirement of inefficient chief constables.[63]

As with national registration, the onset of the Cold War meant that the cessation of open hostilities with Germany in 1945 did not lead to a contraction in MI5's staffing or influence, as had been the case in 1918. The need to maintain surveillance on British communists, and to introduce the vetting of civil servants to prevent the infiltration of the state by Soviet agents, resulted in the expansion of the Secret State.[64] Shortly after the Second World War, MI5's expenditure was running at about £3 million per annum, but had risen to £40 million by 1979, and to £140 million by 1999. Some, but not all, of this increase was caused by inflation but a similar expansion can be seen in terms of employees. In 1999, MI5 disclosed that it had 1,900 staff, and 20,000 active files on individuals, although far higher figures have been claimed.[65] Duncan Campbell, for example, has asserted the figure to be as high as 500,000, although this may reflect a misunderstanding as to what a computer 'file' signifies.[66] Similarly, in the financial year 1998/99, the Metropolitan Police Specialist Operations (which include Special Branch, the Anti-terrorist Branch, the Directorate of Intelligence, and the National Identification Service, as well as the Fraud Squad) took up 13.2 per cent of the £2.33 billion budget of the Metropolitan Police, or in excess of £300 million.[67] Local forces have, of course, their own, much smaller, Special Branch forces.

This continued expansion of the Secret State can be seen in terms of the protection of existing economic elites. With the consolidation of foreign powers, especially the USSR and China, on the basis of communism, many of the international threats to the British state could be seen as meshing with internal opposition to capitalism. In the depths of the Cold War, fringe political parties, 'fellow travellers', trade unionists, peace activists, and numerous other groups became targets for surveillance. The distinction between geopolitics and internal class politics had been blurred. The security forces have also been closely linked with employers' organisations, as in the case of the Economic League. The League was founded in 1919 by Admiral Sir Reginald 'Blinker' Hall, who had just retired as Director of Naval Intelligence. He was co-operating at this date with Basil Thompson, head of Special Branch, to establish a new co-ordinated domestic security intelligence agency for the UK, which was intended to supersede MI5. From 1925 onwards the League built up its information dossiers on socialists and 'subversive' organisations. By the mid-1930s card indexes of individuals were being compiled and the information passed on to companies. A formal vetting system was established in the context of the Cold War, when requests for information about individuals increased rapidly. The service was started in the London region and was based on records supplied by a senior Special Branch officer. By the mid-1980s the League had over 2,000 subscribing companies, and files containing the names of 30,000 people. In 1986, it carried out 200,000 name checks on behalf of companies. The League supplied information to Special Branch, an exchange facilitated by the fact that both made use of national insurance numbers as identifiers.[68]

However, it would be misleading to see the activities of the security forces simply in terms of a defence of capitalism, which in the context of the Cold War was not an unpopular activity in itself. The other main focus of increased surveillance by the Secret State in the post-war period, Northern Ireland, involved a threat to the integrity of the United Kingdom, rather than to the existing economic system. By 1999, international terrorism and that related to Northern Ireland accounted for over half of MI5's budget.[69] The latest official definition of terrorism in the 2000 Prevention of Terrorism Act,

> The use of serious violence against persons or property, or the threat to use such violence, to intimidate or coerce a government, the public, or any section of the public for political, religious or ideological ends

has given MI5 a potentially wide remit. In recent years the security forces have also become involved in the prevention of serious crime, and in the monitoring of such groups as animal liberation movements.[70] The extent to which the surveillance activities of the Secret State protect the state itself and the general population, rather than any particular elite within it, is a moot point. It can, and does, but is that its only activity?

The expansion of the Welfare and Taxation State

Just as the twentieth century saw the continued expansion of the Secret State, so it saw the rise of an all-encompassing Welfare State.

Whilst the nineteenth-century Poor Law had been a deterrent, and the Edwardian National Insurance system a privilege, the arrangements that grew out of William Beveridge's famous *Report on Social Insurance* of 1942 were intended to cover the entire population from cradle to grave. Only by making welfare rights part of the general content of citizenship would it be possible, it was argued, to eliminate the stigma from receiving benefits, and remove them from party-political conflict. Also, whilst earlier welfare systems had been organised locally, or via independent 'approved societies', the payment of benefits in the twentieth century was to come increasingly from the central state. Despite Beveridge's own intentions,[71] flows of incomes were no longer within local communities, or across an individual's own life cycle, but increasingly across the nation, and from generation to generation. This led, in turn, to a vast expansion in the contacts citizens had with the central state, either as the recipients of welfare, or as the payers of taxes. These created huge flows of information and the elaboration of ever more sophisticated and anonymous systems for their storage and manipulation.

The creation of this new Welfare State could be seen in terms of a deeply premeditated attempt to control the actions of the masses, and it certainly helped to maintain the system of bounded pluralism elaborated in the period before 1914. Payments under the new welfare arrangements certainly assumed an engagement with the capitalist system and certain forms of behaviour. However, many of the new social rights gained were popular, especially on the left of the political spectrum, whilst increasing centralisation was hardly a conscious process. As José Harris has put it,

> Throughout the period [1870 to 1940] the increasing scale of economic organisation, the inadequate tax-base of local government, the erosion of paternalist community structures, the impact of demographic change and the inescapably 'national' character of certain key social problems (especially unemployment) all combined to shift the British welfare system in the direction of centralised financing and control, without anyone specifically willing that this should come about. To a certain extent the free market itself facilitated and even compelled state intervention by subverting many of the traditional local and voluntary relationships on which the so-called 'minimal state' relied.[72]

As already noted, the expansion of the Welfare State could also be seen in terms of forwarding the interests of the civil servants and policy experts that found employment within it.[73] However, in the period after 1914, as before it, many state bureaucrats appeared unwilling to expand their remit, lest this undermined the private sector. The greatest obstacle to state expansion was perhaps not capitalism but the civil servants of the Treasury.[74]

Some of the first examples of the new citizenship of welfare were not, in fact, a result of popular agitation, or bureaucratic ambition, but arose out of the exigencies of war. The mass mobilisation of Britain during the years 1914 to 1918 saw the creation of new, centrally funded, rights to transfer payments from the taxpayer to special categories of citizens. The war years, for example, saw a flood of searches in the GRO to assist dependants of men serving at the Front to obtain evidence of marriage and of the birth of children under 16 years of age. This was in connection with claims for army and naval separation allowances.[75] Many of these allowances had, of course, to be converted to war widows' pensions by 1918. During 1914 the GRO made nearly 30,000 searches on behalf of the wives and dependants of servicemen. In the immediate aftermath of the Great War, the GRO's 'War Section' was completing between 2,000 and 3,000 searches per week, 'in connection with liability for service in the Army under the Military Services Acts, claims for separation allowances, pensions, special allowances, service in the State Munitions Establishments, liability of young soldiers for service abroad, etc.'.[76] Rights to central funds flowed from obligations under a national citizenship. This was, of course, a particularly gendered concept of citizenship because such payments as widows' pensions and separation allowances went to women not in their own right but in recognition of the status, or actions, of their husbands.[77]

Despite the criticisms that have been made of welfare provision during the inter-war period,[78] the amount spent on welfare increased markedly. Whilst £2.40 was spent per head of population on welfare payments at the beginning of the period, this figure had risen to £12.50 by 1939. In 1918 2.4 per cent of the Gross National Product was devoted to the social services, compared with 11.3 per cent in 1938.[79] Access to pensions, for example, was gradually extended by political parties of all hues. In 1929 the Labour Government added potentially 500,000 people to the existing pensioned population, by giving pensions at age 55 to the widows of insurable men who had died before 4 January 1926, the date at which widows' pensions became payable. Similarly, by the Widows', Orphans' and Old Age Contributory Pension (Voluntary Contributors) Act of 1937 the Conservative government extended pension rights to many independent workers.[80] The expansion of welfare provision and party-political advantage were still linked in the period, and centralised welfare provision increased as a result.

At the same time, the voluntary and localised basis of the National Insurance system was called into question. The actuarial basis of the unemployment fund established by the 1911 National Insurance Act was gradually undermined in the inter-war period in order to meet the problems of long-term unemployment. Increasingly unemployment benefits came to be paid from centrally raised taxation, rather than from savings. The local provision of benefits was undermined by the sheer scale of the problems in some localities that demanded solutions at the national level. Unemployment reached 2,888,000 in 1931 but was most heavily concentrated in areas, especially in the north and west of Britain, dominated by the old Victorian staple industries – iron and steel, textiles, mining and shipbuilding. In 1934 the Unemployment Act created a new three-tier system of relief controlled by two 'independent' bodies, the UISC (Unemployment Insurance Statutory Committee) and UAB (Unemployment Assistance Board), and the local authorities.

The responsibility of the UISC was to ensure the solvency of the reformed unemployment insurance scheme, by which the majority of the unemployed were to be helped. The responsibility of the UAB was to devise and implement a national system of standardised means-tested benefits for approximately 500,000 to 700,000 uninsured claimants. This left the local Poor Law to cater for approximately 30,000 unemployed persons who – like vagrants – were able-bodied but enjoyed only a tenuous connection with the labour market.[81] This complex system led to the vast expansion of intrusive local information gathering via the institution of the hated means test to determine eligibility.[82] Although local authorities still handled the majority of social service spending, central civil servants were also being drawn into new areas of policy, and a new relationship with the public, paying out annually £115 million in over 200 million separate weekly transactions.[83]

The central state also gradually turned against the medical arm of the National Insurance system because of what were seen as its inefficiencies. Transactions between members and societies, as well as between societies and central authorities, between doctor and patient, between doctor and local insurance committee, all translated into administrative expense and higher costs. Friendly societies that policed their members to prevent unnecessary claims lost members to more lax commercial companies. Doctors tended to sign sickness certificates on demand to keep registered patients, and also the per capita fee that went with them. Nor did the approved societies give equitable treatment – as actuarially based commercial organisations they preferred the young, healthy and regularly employed. Older entrants had to pay higher premiums, and women were accommodated in separate branches of friendly societies, where their lower wages and worse sickness record would not affect the rest of the membership.[84] Thus, Beveridge's plans for the post-war Welfare State can be seen in terms of economies of scale, and lowering costs, as well as of fairness and equity. The expansion of central welfare provision also reflected the experience of the central planning of health services, labour and social benefits during the Second World War. The sheer scale of the problems involved in mobilising the population for war defeated local government, and established the central departments as the main focus of interactions between the citizen and the state.[85]

However, the Beveridge welfare system was based on certain assumptions that proved unsustainable in the long run – full employment, stable demographic structures, improving health, and a continued political consensus. Beveridge had assumed that Keynesian demand management would maintain high levels of employment. But during the Oil Crisis of the mid-1970s, Keynesianism was abandoned across the Western world and unemployment levels soared. They have subsequently come down in Britain but have never returned to previous levels. The Beveridge model assumed the maintenance of conjugal households, and a stable working population to support the young and the old. But the increase in the levels of divorce created large numbers of one-parent families that came to depend on the welfare system. At the same time, an aging population meant that a smaller portion of the population was at work and so able to support the elderly on old age pensions. Beveridge had assumed that the new health services would make people healthier, and so lead to a decline in demand for health care. But as science extended the possibilities of health care, and as the population grew older and frailer, so the National Health Service demanded more and more resources. Lastly, under Margaret Thatcher in the 1980s the political consensus around the Welfare State was undermined, and increasing attempts were made to 'roll back' the public sector. Taxpayers in the West, including Britain, were unwilling to pay the taxes required to maintain Beveridge's ediface.[86]

The new national Welfare State came in time, therefore, to institutionalise the concept of the means test associated with local relief for the unemployed. In 1900 only about two per cent of the population received poor relief, and were assessed by relieving officers. By 1970 almost eight per cent of the population were supported by a means-tested income supplement. By 1982, taking into account income-related assistance such as housing benefit, the figure had risen to 12 per cent.[87] The Welfare State was becoming less a general system of rights, and more a safety net for the poorer members of society. With the 'targetting' of benefits came an increasing emphasis on proving eligibility.

The development of a welfare system based on universal eligibility for benefits and means testing created ever larger and more bureaucratic forms of information gathering. A vast new Central Office was established at Newcastle upon Tyne in the late 1940s to handle claims and contributions within the welfare system, superseding or supplementing the previous record offices of the Ministry of Labour and Ministry of Pensions. By the end of the 1950s the Newcastle Central Office held 100,000 ledgers, each containing 300 sheets, relating to claims for benefits. In order to collect the necessary claimant details the Central Office received punched cards prepared in the local benefit offices. It also had a batch of teleprinters linked with the regional offices in case of emergencies. The flow of cards varied from 150,000 a week in the summer to something approaching 400,000 to 500,000 a week during a winter epidemic. In all, some 10 million cards were handled each year. By the early 1970s the Central Office employed 10,500 staff, of which 4,000 worked within its Record Branch, and the facility was believed to be one of the largest clerical installations in Europe.[88] As one can see from Table 6.1,

Table 6.1 Number of new claims processed by the Central Office, Newcastle, 1970

Benefit	Claims
Sickness benefit	10,632,000
Unemployment benefit	3,159,000
Maternity allowance	901,000
Maternity grant	901,000
Retirement pension	780,000
Widow's benefit	70,000
Death grant	537,000

Source: James B. Rule, *Private Lives and Public Surveillance* (London: Allen Lane, 1973), p. 148.

the information flows passing through the Central Office by this date were enormous.

Even when Conservative governments attempted to curb welfare payments in the 1980s and 1990s, this only created another point of contact between the state and its citizens. By 1999, the Child Support Agency, set up in 1993 to enforce the obligations of estranged parents to support their children, had a caseload of 'live' and assessed cases of nearly one million (998,500).[89]

In addition, the benefits that citizens could draw from the central state were balanced by an increasing obligation to pay taxes to support that state. This can be seen perhaps most clearly in the case of income tax. In 1901 J. E. Chapman at the Board of Inland Revenue's Statistical Department estimated that there were 5,000,000 persons in the 'income tax paying classes' in the UK, i.e. living in families with incomes over £160. But this implied only 1,000,000 active payers of income tax since the figure of 5,000,000 was obtained by multiplying the payers by a notional five persons to a family. This was out of a total population of 41 million.[90] The First World War saw the reduction of the exemption limit from £160 to £130, and an inflation that raised nominal wages, so that by 1918–19 the number of taxpayers stood at nearly 3.55 million. The numbers declined in the interwar period but never fell below 2.2 million.[91] The wage inflation of the Second World War and its aftermath led to a similar expansion, and by 1949–50 some 20,750,000 individuals had incomes above the effective exception limit of £135. Of these, 15 million paid tax after allowances were taken into account. By the fiscal year 1989/90 there were 21,900,000 income taxpayers.[92]

In order to establish the tax codes, and assessments, of taxpayers, the Board of Inland Revenue needed to amass vast amounts of information on the incomes and financial responsibilities of individual citizens. This it did via individual tax returns, or by requiring private companies to act as its local agents via the Pay As You Earn (PAYE) system, which was established in 1944. At the height of 'War Socialism' private enterprises were being used to ensure flows of incomes and information to the state. The involvement of employers in the management of state-mandated income flows had, of course, begun with the handling of contribution cards and stamps under the 1911 National Insurance Act. In the course of the twentieth century, however, both in wartime and without, such statutory involvement expanded endlessly, or at least so it seemed to employers. By the beginning of the twenty-first century even small firms were expected to provide the state with information on employees, or maintain information for inspection, relating to income tax, national insurance contributions, tax credits, statutory maternity pay, statutory sick pay, student loan deductions, cars provided for private use, and so on.[93]

Superficially such a use of local agents was similar to the long-standing decentralised system of information gathering found in the British polity of the early modern period. But this was actually a very different form of decentralisation – compulsory rather than voluntary, and feeding into central systems rather than reflecting local activity. Employers have been forced against their will to become the 'front end' of the central state, rather than willing and responsible partners providing local goods and services in the name of the monarch. This reveals the manner in which the modern state has come to be differentiated out of 'civil society', in a way that would have been inconceivable in the earlier period. Today one's position in society is not marked by state office holding but to a considerable extent by one's purchasing power. This, in turn, is linked to one's position in capitalist organisations, and to the profitability of the latter. Whilst local elites in the early modern period regarded performing such activities for the state as a mark of their status, or as a constitutional right, the modern Confederation of British Industry (CBI) sees them as 'red tape' and a burden on business.[94]

The creation of this vast system of surveillance brought huge numbers of people into contact with the central state officials responsible for taxation for the first time in British history. Thus, in the fiscal year 1999/2000, the Board of Inland Revenue dealt with 74 million items of post, and 38 million telephone calls. Its 300 Enquiry Centres dealt with 4.4 million enquiries face-to-face, whilst mobile advice centres visited 545 venues and were visited by 87,000 people for help and information.[95] Such a level of interaction with the general public would have been inconceivable, and indeed alarming, to Victorian civil servants. In 1895, for example, the GRO, one of the most public of government departments, saw a mere 53,289 individual searches in its registers of births, marriages and deaths, and its entire surviving correspondence for the period 1836 to 1912 is contained in 16 letter books.[96] Dealing with officers of the central state, and supplying them with information, is now one of the common vexations of life for all social classes.

The rise of the government social survey

The requirements of military preparedness, and of the Welfare State, also led to the expansion and strengthening of the statistical apparatus of the central state. As already noted, the use of population statistics for military purposes probably goes back to the origins of the first census in 1801, and the Victorian GRO had shown some interest in the subject. But such exercises in military statistics became less hypothetical, and more urgent, in the century of total warfare. In 1920, for example, Parliament passed the first permanent Census Act, which facilitated the establishment of a permanent Census Branch within the GRO. This was predicated on the assumption that a quinquennial census could be taken every five years if authorised by an order in council, always providing that the Treasury was willing to pay for it. This was partly to improve the calculation of intercensal mortality rates but the expanded statistical apparatus of the GRO also had a military purpose. Winston Churchill wrote a Cabinet Memorandum from the War Office supporting the taking of more frequent censuses, in which he maintained that a quinquennial enumeration was 'essential to the proper solution of recruiting and man-power problems'.

He also believed that if a new military service system was to be established, 'in a future emergency, it will be impossible to administer it until reasonably accurate vital statistics are available'.[97] The resulting 1920 Census Act provided for the taking of all future censuses, whether decennial or quinquennial, although the subsequent reassertion of Treasury control in the inter-war period prevented a true quinquennial census ever being taken.

The continued belief that the British population was in decline in a period of renewed international tension also led to the passing of the 1938 Population (Statistics) Act.[98] This authorised the introduction on 1 July 1938 of additional questions to be asked at the time of birth registration, including: the age of the mother; and, for legitimate births, the parents' date of marriage, and the number of live and still births to the mother within the marriage. The GRO subsequently used this extra data in its published discussions of marital fertility. The civil tables in the Office's *Statistical Review for 1938*, for example, covered numerous facets of the subject, including: the ages of mothers; legitimate and illegitimate fertility; sex ratios and regional distributions of births; multiple births; an analysis of previous children of all marriages; the duration of marriages; first maternities; family size according to marriage duration; infertility; and so on.[99] Public concern over the 'population question' led to the appointment of a Royal Commission on Population in 1943, with the remit 'to examine the facts relating to the present population trends in Great Britain; to investigate the causes of these trends and to consider their probable consequences; to consider what measures, if any, should be taken in the national interest to influence the future trend of population; and to make recommendations'.[100] The Commission, which reported in 1949, drew upon the assistance of the GRO for a number of special enquiries.[101] But in the post-war period the relationship between population and military preparedness became more tenuous, as the Empire was dissolved, as Britain was absorbed into NATO, and as warfare became a contest of hardware and skilled professionals rather than crude manpower.

It was also during and after the Second World War that the government social survey gained a new role in central planning. If the population was to be mobilised for war, economic survival, and also as voters, users of the Welfare State and taxpayers, then the central state needed to know how government policies would affect their morale, their well-being and their pockets. In April 1940 a Wartime Social Survey was established by the Ministry of Information, which undertook wartime investigations into a myriad of subjects, including: civilian morale; the supply of consumer goods during wartime; the diets of workers; the objections of women to joining the services; the difficulties of parents getting their children immunised; heating and lighting in domestic buildings; and a multitude of other pressing matters. Such investigations, including one into ladies' foundation garments, based in part on asking women leaving munitions factories what they were wearing,[102] led to the officers of the Wartime Social Survey being known as 'Cooper's Snoopers' after Duff Cooper, the Minister of Information.[103]

At the same time, the fear of massive civilian casualties from aerial bombardment, and the need to relocate large numbers of citizens, led to the establishment of a national Emergency Hospital Service (EHS).[104] Percy Stocks, the GRO's chief medical statistician from 1933 onwards, rapidly appreciated that the new centrally planned arrangements required data on morbidity to function efficiently. He tackled the issue from two angles. First, he organised a one-in-five survey of civilians being admitted to the EHS to discover their ailments and patient histories.[105] In addition, in 1943 he negotiated with the Wartime Social Survey to undertake a 'Sample Survey of Sickness' amongst the population to discover the nature and severity of their illnesses.[106] Significantly, the latter was measured according to the amount of time someone was incapacitated for work, perhaps indicating Stocks's priorities.[107] As Stocks explained to the Survey's admirably named Miss Pixie Wilson in 1944, the purpose of the survey was to 'give the Ministry [of Health] a guide to what is happening to the health of the population as a whole, which may help them to take necessary action'.[108] By July of that year, Stocks was advising the Ministry's chief medical officer that the survey would enable it to measure the 'total loss of working time and total service by doctors', and help in 'guiding policy in the building up of health services'.[109] This new form of data collection was shown to be superior to the existing system for notifying the Ministry of Health of notifiable diseases, which it subsequently superseded for statistical purposes.[110] The survey continued to be taken until 1952, and its findings were published regularly in the GRO's *Quarterly*

Returns.[111] The Survey of Sickness also provided information for the Ministry of National Insurance on the likely fluctuations in the take-up of sickness benefits, as in the case of the flu epidemic of 1951.[112]

It is difficult, of course, to estimate directly the effect that the scientific knowledge of the impact of diseases had on the health of the population in Britain. However, it is known from modern studies that the effect can be striking. In certain districts of modern Tanzania, for example, when surveys were undertaken to determine the burden of particular diseases on the population and spending on medical care adjusted accordingly, infant mortality rates fell by 28 per cent. In turned out that malaria was the most deadly disease but it had not been the first priority in health-care expenditure. Fewer sick children subsequently allowed parents to work more hours in the fields, and so increased general prosperity. Statistical information allows limited health-care resources to be used to the greatest effect.[113]

As the Second World War drew to a close, Stocks and the GRO moved to consolidate their new field of responsibility. A Working Party on Hospital Records was set up in 1945 to consider whether the experiment of collecting statistics by sampling the records of patients admitted to beds in the EHS hospitals could be extended more generally.[114] Stocks drafted a summary form for use in collecting statistics of hospital in-patients, which included questions on the reasons for a patient's admission; their length of stay in hospital; the length of time they had to wait for admission; and the patient's age, sex, occupation, social class and civil status. Stocks saw such information as 'essential for the purposes of efficient direction of a national hospital scheme, answering parliamentary questions and guidance in the matter of reducing waiting lists and provision of new hospitals'.[115] At the end of 1947, the Working Party on Hospital Records recommended to the chief medical officer of the Ministry of Health that a pilot survey should be started in selected hospitals as soon as possible.[116] This proved a success and since 1949 the GRO, and its successors, have continued to run a Hospital In-Patient Enquiry (HIPE) along the lines originally suggested by Stocks for the purpose of allocating resources within the NHS.[117]

The Government Social Survey Department also expanded its remit in the post-war period. A National Food Survey had been set up in 1940 to survey the food and drink consumption and expenditure of households, which was superseded, in part, by the Family Expenditure Survey in 1957. This collects data from a sample of households on the expenditure and incomes of each member of the household aged 16 years and over on a regular basis. The General Household Survey was introduced in 1971 to collect information systematically from about 15,000 households a year on fertility, housing, health, car ownership, employment, education, and a range of other matters of interest to state departments. From 1973 a Labour Force Survey supplemented the activities of the employment exchanges in measuring employment and unemployment. Yet another general, ongoing, longitudinal programme, the Family Resources Survey, was instituted in 1992 to monitor of the effects and cost of changing the social security system.[118] This was in addition to numerous other one-off investigations required by government departments.

The increasing overlap between the medical and census work of the GRO, and the work of the Social Survey Department, led to the amalgamation of the two bodies in 1970 to form the Office of Population Censuses and Surveys (OPCS). This was subsequently integrated with the Central Statistical Office in the 1990s to create the Office for National Statistics (ONS). The latter body employed over 3,000 staff (2,453 in its statistical sections and 654 in its central registration services) at the beginning of the twenty-first century, at a total cost of over £100 million per annum.[119] This could be compared to the mere 48 staff in the GRO's Statistical Department in 1921, or the 200 officers of the Government Statistical Service as late as 1966.[120] Similarly, whilst the great social surveys of the late Victorian period were undertaken by private individuals such as Charles Booth and Seebohm Rowntree, all social scientists, whether civil servants or university academics, now look predominantly to official statistics for their raw data. The statistical apparatus of the British State has expanded in a manner that would have overjoyed a man like William Farr, although it would have horrified his colleagues in the Victorian Treasury.

This is plainly a vast and impressive project of state data collection on a regular, ongoing basis. But what is its historical significance? For some social scientists such statistical production represents nothing less than the democratisation of the

British State. Catherine Marsh, for example, sees the relationship between the social scientist and the public going through a threefold development over the last 200 years. In the first stage, predominantly in the nineteenth century, the social researchers would only interview other professionals, acting as *informants*, giving proxy information to the researcher on a somewhat suspect populace. John Rickman's early censuses and the parliamentary reports produced by Edwin Chadwick might be seen in this light. This gave way in the later nineteenth century to a second relationship, in which researchers such as Seebohm Rowntree surveyed directly those about whom they wanted to make generalisable statements. They treated people as *respondents*, providers of data who were, nonetheless, still 'subjects'. The censuses from 1841 can be understood in these terms. The growth of egalitarianism since the Second World War has, Marsh argues, encouraged a third view of the subjects of study, namely as *citizens*, of a status equal to that of the researcher. She links this, in turn, to the development of citizenship in the terms put forward by T. H. Marshall. Statistics are part of the process of public consultation in a modern democratic society.[121] For Sir Claus Moser social indicators could be developed to the point at which they were 'coterminous with all that relates to the quality of life', and citizens could become the 'consumers' of such statistics.[122]

Other social scientists take a rather more jaundiced view of state statistical production. Miles and Irvine, for example, see this official activity in terms of facilitating the administration of the populace, and argue that the bulk of social and labour statistics relates to the productive efficiency of the workforce and the economy.[123] The data collected reflect the needs of the administrative system, rather than of advocacy on the part of the disadvantaged, or of general education.[124] Thus, they claim,

> there is a plethora of information on fire-damage to properties, but little on industrially-related diseases; the number of house-starts is well documented, but figures on homelessness are miniscule; and the measurements of social-security scrounging is clearly given priority over tax evasion, the consumption of consumer durables over poverty, and so on.[125]

Again, there are rather poor statistics on the health of the people but an awful lot on mortality, the use of health facilities and statistics on absences from work.[126]

The British State has also been comparatively uninterested in its citizens in statistical terms. Thus, between 1931 and 1971, the number of questions in the British census increased from 12 to 30, but was then reduced to only 21 in the 1981 census. By way of contrast, the 1980/81 censuses of Australia, Canada and the United States contained far more questions – 35, 42 and 60 respectively.[127] In Britain, government ministers depend for advice and guidance in general on the administrative Civil Service rather than upon social scientists.[128] Official statistics thus give a misleading view of society, although Miles and Irvine argue that this bias is created by the relatively narrow interests of the state, rather than by a definite attempt to mislead or mystify the public.[129]

The truth may well lie somewhere in between these optimistic and pessimistic extremes. Government departments may have very narrow, instrumental reasons for creating statistical series but these may in turn reflect broader political considerations. The collection of data to facilitate the workings of the NHS, or of the social security system, is not a bad thing in itself, although it may reflect a somewhat restricted vision of what the 'Good Life' means. The state, it could be argued, applies first aid to the problems of health or social exclusion, rather than considering a root-and-branch approach that might call into question the economic and political structures that lay outside the boundaries of public debate in the system of 'bounded pluralism'. Similarly, this does not mean that individual state statisticians are not committed to the welfare of citizens, or that independent researchers cannot use official statistics to shift accepted views of society.[130]

However, there are plainly limits to the impact that statistics can have upon government policy, as shown by the fate of the Black Report. This was the product of a Committee under the chairmanship of Sir Douglas Black, set up in 1978 to examine health inequalities by social class in Britain. It concluded that, 'Social and economic factors like income, work (or lack of it), environment, education, housing, transport and what are today called "lifestyles" all affect health and all favour the better-off.' On average the poor die earlier, in some cases much earlier, than the rich. The Committee's recommendations included improvements in information, research and organisation; redressing the balance of the health care system to place more emphasis on prevention, primary care and community health; and radically improving the material conditions of the poor, especially children and people with disabilities, by increasing or introducing cash benefits, and developing new schemes for day nurseries, antenatal clinics, sheltered housing, home improvements, and so on. The report was submitted to the new Conservative government of Margaret Thatcher in April 1980 and summarily dismissed by the new Secretary of State for Health and Social Security on the grounds of cost – £2 billion per annum.[131] Despite growing evidence of the gap between the life expectancy of the rich and poor in Britain, the recommendations of the Black Report have never been seriously acted upon by any subsequent administration because of the political implications of their price tag.

Indeed, the Thatcher government of the early 1980s was not keen on state statistical production outside that required for administrative purposes narrowly defined. The Government Statistical Service (GSS) was one of the first targets of Sir Derek Rayner's efficiency scrutinies, introduced by the Conservatives to 'tackle waste and ineffectiveness in government'. This led to a 20 per cent cut in the budget of the GSS, and a greater concentration on servicing the government of the day.[132] As with identity cards, this aspect of state information collecting has tended to be a project of the political Left, rather than of the Right.

However, although the direct political effects of statistics might be circumscribed, the process of statistical information gathering has had more subtle, but far-reaching, effects. This is because of the manner in which the collection of information via forms of one sort or another influences how the state sees society. Form filling is ubiquitous in modern society but it is only in the last two centuries that the *pro forma* has changed from being the form in which texts were written by state officials, to a means of acquiring information from the public. Historians have examined individual forms in detail but there has been little attempt to understand how and why this generic bureaucratic device was developed. Nor have historians thought how forms affect the state that uses them, and the society with which it interacts.

One of the few sets of forms studied in depth have been the nineteenth-century census forms for England and Wales development by the GRO.[133] What emerges from this analysis is that forms and their associated instructions enabled the GRO to control its interactions with the public. Census forms:

- reduced communication with citizens to the exchange of information – the GRO permitted only certain information to be considered 'relevant', and defined its meaning;
- standardised exchanges so that information flows became predictable and, therefore, more easy to handle;
- reduced the amount of information entering the GRO, so matching it to the internal resources available for its processing – vital when the increasing volume of information gathering threatened to overwhelm its analysis techniques.

This truncation of communication allowed the GRO to establish working hypotheses as to the nature of its external social environment, and so underpinned purposeful state intervention in society. But because this hypothetical reality was based on truncated information flows, it was partial, if not skewed. Interventions in society based on such data gathering were likely to have unforeseen results.

In the late nineteenth century, for example, male householders were no longer asked to indicate if their female relatives were actively employed in businesses based in the home. This, and changes to the way in which women were presented in the published census tables, helped to give an impression of women as non-economically active, and as dependants. This may have been fed back into society via the *Census Reports*, thus helping to strengthen the belief in the 'separate spheres' of men and women in society, with the former in the public sphere and women in the home.[134] The manner in which the results of state information collection have been fed back into society, so influencing its conception of itself, has been explored in general terms by Ian Hacking and Anthony Giddens. Neither, however, has looked closely at the role of information-gathering technologies such as forms.

A number of the other bureaucratic means of information gathering pioneered by the British state may have had similar effects. One might include here the introduction of death certificates into civil registration in 1836, and how this encouraged the understanding of mortality in terms of specific pathogens rather than the general unbalancing of the body in humoural medicine.[135] Diseases were understood in terms of germs, rather than the impact of diet, stress or working conditions. Similarly, the routine, central collection of income tax and estate duty via forms in the late nineteenth century led to the development of a particular concept of wealth in the Board of Inland Revenue's Statistical Department, and in the national wealth accounting of the likes of Bernard Mallet, Josiah Stamp and Arthur Bowley in the early twentieth century.[136] Wealth was what could be taxed, rather the intangibles of skill and enterprise.[137] Yet again, the systematic collection of information on employment and unemployment via the stamped books introduced under the 1911 National Insurance Act, constrained much of the subsequent understanding of unemployment.[138] It has only been in the last few decades that the number of people 'signing on' has ceased to be the sole economic indicator relating to the labour market, although the movement of the measure is still fraught with political meaning. The issue of unemployment, or underemployment, amongst women and the young, has been obscured. How state and society have conceived of health care, and incentives for wealth creation and economic growth, have all been affected by such processes of information collection, or non-collection.

This is not to say that germs are not involved in ill health, that monetary incomes are not wealth, or that people seeking unemployment benefits are not unemployed. The flu virus, pay packets and the 'sack' are not 'discursive formations' formulated by experts, as some post-modernists might believe. They exist in the real world and have effects upon us but they are not the whole story. State information gathering and statistical production is not a process of 'making up the world' from nothing but of chopping it up into bits, and presenting those partial views as the whole. In the world of the blind the one-eyed man is king but he still only knows half the truth.[139]

Conclusion

Much of the history of the Information State in the twentieth century can thus be seen in terms of elaborating the structures and state strategies of the late Victorian and Edwardian crisis of British imperialism. War, and the threat of war, required information and surveillance, as did the creation of a planned Welfare

State. It is difficult to see these processes solely in terms of a simple model of social control in the interests of economic elites. Often it was the state itself that was threatened, rather than capitalism. On the whole, non-elites saw the defence of the nation and the extension of social rights in a positive sense, although the information collection this entailed was viewed as irksome, or even alarming. Also, information collection was often to support state activities advocated by the Left, such as the Welfare State. If one wanted a planned society, then the collection of information was, and is, essential. This might explain why the continuation of national registration and the issuing of identity cards in peacetime, at least until the 1950s, was advocated by those who regarded themselves as socialists rather than by those on the Right. The belief that liberty from state interference is an exclusively left-wing concern is historically inaccurate.[140]

7
The Information State in the age of information technology

Information technology and surveillance

By the 1950s the British State had built up a vast apparatus for the ongoing and systematic collection and analysis of data about its citizens, although this fell short of some of the thorough-going systems of population registration found in continental Europe. On the whole, this apparatus had been created without much popular dissent, despite opposition to some specific elements, such as the means test, form filling, and the need to carry an identification card. General questions about why the state should collect and hold information, and whether it needed as much information as it possessed, were seldom raised in any systematic manner. But from the 1960s onwards, information became a live political issue, although not one that could be said to have been at the forefront of public debate. In 1971, for example, the Liberal Party launched a national campaign to persuade people to refuse to fill out their census schedules, and groups such Charter 88 and the Freedom of Information Campaign began to press for safeguards over the use of information by the state. In 1984 Britain passed its first data protection legislation, and this was followed in 2000 by a Freedom of Information Act.

This increasing concern over the extent of the Information State can be put down, in part, to the sheer proliferation of contacts between citizens and civil servants that took place in the twentieth century. Given the amount of form filling that now became a part of everyday life, it was impossible for citizens to be unaware of the amount of material held by government officials. In a society in which liberty was generally seen in terms of freedom from the state, rather than freedom though the state, as in the continental European tradition,[1] increased contact with state officials was likely to increase concern. But this was also a state to which people were far less deferent than in former generations, partly because participation in the political process, however tangential, had undermined something of the mystique of public authority. In addition, respect for civil servants and politicians has been eroded by imperial and national decline,[2] and by the propagation of the right-wing belief that the state had to be 'rolled back', although not, it should be noted, where this related to policing functions. Even the modern political Left was less sanguine than the likes of Beatrice Webb about the use of the state to change society for the better. As José Harris has put it:

> Englishmen in the 1900s greatly admired their country's system of government, but on the whole expected it to do very little. By the 1960s they were much more critical of the whole range of government institutions; but their expectations of and demands upon government were incomparably more ambitious than they had been a half century before.[3]

But an additional reason for the growing concern over the power of the Information State was the increasing data-handling capacities of government due to the advent of the modern information technology. The 1960s saw the beginnings of the replacement of punched-card technology with electronic computers such as the IBM 1401 series.[4] Electronic computers speeded up the processes involved in manipulating information by reducing mechanical operations, thus making the regular identification of data relating to particular individuals a practical possibility. In addition, the world dominance of US computer companies such as IBM and Microsoft meant that the file structures and software applications in which differing datasets were stored were similar across computer systems. Information collected on individuals by differing bodies for differing purposes could be swapped between machines and merged, as long as those individuals could be identified consistently.

This compatibility between data storage structures was an international phenomenon. When, for example, the GDR (East Germany) collapsed in 1989/90, archivists from the West German Federal Archives discovered that they could reconstitute the computer records kept by the ex-communist state on its citizens and Communist Party members because they were in IBM formats, or in Russian formats based upon them.[5] In the 1990s, the development of means of exchanging data between computer systems via the Internet at ever greater speeds further dissolved the boundaries between datasets. Personal information in the state and elsewhere became, in theory at least, a single, seamless resource. These technological developments were not necessarily driven by the needs of the Information State but they greatly enhanced its capabilities.

The potential power conferred upon the state caused increasing unease. As the Younger Committee on Privacy, an official body of inquiry, put it in 1972,

> We found that the computer's facility to store, link, manipulate and provide access to information gave rise to suspicions that complete personal files on a great number of people could be compiled; that information could be used for a purpose for which it was not initially collected; that some information could be inaccurate; that it facilitated access to confidential information by many people scattered over a wide area; that its powers of correlation were so superior to traditional methods that it made practicable what had hitherto been impracticable; and that it encouraged on an entirely new scale of information-gathering and of organisations to do it.[6]

This apprehension was especially strong because the potential of the new technology caught the imagination of the public. It is unlikely, for example, that HAL, the rogue computer in Stanley Kubrick's *2001: A Space Odyssey*, would have seemed so sinister if it had been a punched-card tabulator. The British State undoubtedly took advantage of this technology to integrate data to achieve many of the objectives it had traditionally pursued. However, it would be over-simplistic to assume that this was done without some hesitation, or at least without divided counsels.

The manner in which personal datasets can be integrated makes any attempt to compartmentalise the history of the relationship between information technology and the Information State a difficult, and perhaps misguided, task. In what follows, however, an attempt will be made to look at the use of information technology in the Welfare/Taxation State, and then, separately, in policing and counter-terrorism. In practice, computer systems in both spheres have been increasingly integrated. In addition, the '30 year rule' that prevents government files from reaching the public archives until three decades after the date of the last dated paper they contain, also prevents an exhaustive analysis of the subject. However, enough material is in the public domain to allow at least some initial generalisation to be made about the processes involved, and to link them to the previous history of state information gathering.

Information technology and the Welfare/Taxation State

The amount of state expenditure in Britain on information technology has been phenomenal in recent years. The 1970s saw an enormous initial expansion of computing in government in terms of bulk data processing to reap economies of scale. Large computer installations were established at the Department of Health and Social Security (DHSS) central offices at Newcastle; at the DVLA in Swansea; at the central Passport Office in Peterborough; and at the Inland Revenue's PAYE processing installation in Reading. This investment has continued down to the present day. In the financial year 1995–96, central UK government spent £2,311 million on information technology, and local government spent £1,040 million. The largest purchasers of IT were still the large-scale processors of personal data, such as the Inland Revenue, Customs and Excise, the Ministry of Agriculture, the Department of Social Security (DSS), as well as the Ministry of Defence.[7] By 1985, according to Duncan Campbell and Steve Connor, there were over 450 central government computer installations in use, or on order, for general and administrative purposes.[8] Such a calculation would be almost meaningless in the networked computer environment of the early twenty-first century. As already revealed in Table 1.1, by the late 1970s the information systems in government departments already held files on millions of individuals, and such datasets have been growing apace ever since. In 1978, for example, the Lindop Committee found that the DHSS had 45 million computer records relating to national insurance contributions, whilst seven years later Campbell and Connor claimed that it held 54 million such records.[9]

Most informed commentators concur in believing that the expansion of information technology in this field has not been driven by any sinister desire to create a police state but by considerations of efficiency and economy.[10] As the government claimed in 1975, in *Computers and Privacy*, its response to the

Younger Report on privacy, although the use of computers has implications for civil liberties,

> Their actual and potential benefits are great: in the saving of routine clerical work; in the economy, accuracy and speed with which information can be processed; in forecasting, planning or matching supply to demand; and, in the service of central and local government, in making public administration more responsive to the needs of the individual citizen and his family.[11]

In an age of tight financial controls over government expenditure, political pressures to reduce taxes, and constant Treasury 'efficiency scrutinies' of government departments, the expansion of the use of electronic means of data processing was perhaps inevitable. Such technologies enabled government departments to undertake their traditional functions – paying benefits, preventing fraud, creating statistics – at lower costs, through removing clerical error and by reducing staff. The whole apparatus of the Welfare State might, of course, be seen in turn as a means of creating a docile and pliable society – but this is not the same as the creation of a police state.

With the elaboration of information networks across government, data sharing and data profiling became easier, and much more common. Data sharing can be seen as the swapping of information between government organisations, whilst data profiling involves the pooling of information on particular individuals. Much information sharing in the recent past reflected perfectly sensible administrative arrangements. The DHSS and the Inland Revenue, for example, shared information in the 1970s and 1980s because the Inland Revenue collected national insurance contributions from employers on behalf of the DHSS, whilst the DHSS notified the Inland Revenue of any taxable benefits it paid.[12] Data sharing also means that the state eliminates the cost of collecting the same, or similar, information more than once.[13]

By the end of the 1980s, the technical means of such sharing had become institutionalised through the creation of a Government Data Network connecting the DHSS, Customs and Excise, the Inland Revenue, the Home Office, and the police.[14] This new information network helped carry forward the continuing integration of taxation and state welfare systems. In 1999, the government announced that the Child Support Agency would also be given authority to contact the Board of Inland Revenue in order to deduct outstanding maintenance payments from absent parents' incomes.[15] By the end of the twentieth century a government department such as the DSS supplied personal information to, amongst others, the Inland Revenue, Customs and Excise, the Home Office, the Department of Health, the Department of Employment, the National Audit Office, the Legal Aid Board, the Post Office, police forces, local authorities, banks, building societies, grant-maintained schools, and so on. It was also involved in the trading of personal data.[16]

In April 2002, the Cabinet Office's Performance and Innovation Unit published a report entitled *Privacy and Data-sharing: The Way Forward for Public Services*, which advocated more data sharing within government. This was seen a way of providing 'joined-up and personalised public service delivery', or at least services that were cheaper to deliver. But enhancing the state's ability to deal with crime and fraud was also an important incentive. The report also recognised public disquiet about the way in which government used personal data and underlined the need for greater data 'privacy' and accuracy. However, by 'privacy' the report seems to have meant ensuring the confidentiality of information once it had been collected by the state, not the right to refuse to provide information. As the Prime Minister, Tony Blair, put it in his introduction to the report, the aim was to provide 'better, more personalised, more efficient public services which handle personal information in a way that commands public trust'.[17]

The dangers potentially inherent in the practice of data sharing can be seen in the case of the 1997 Social Security Administration (Fraud) Act, that placed the exchange of personal data for the purpose of detecting fraud by the DSS, taxation departments and local authorities, on a legal basis.[18] Some local authorities, however, interpreted this legislation as giving them vast intrusive powers, for, as the Data Protection Registrar, the official data watchdog, noted:

A number appear to believe that the Act gives them the power to demand the wholesale disclosure of pay roll information from employers, such as supermarkets, the Post Office, and, in one case, a Formula 1 racing team, whereas the Fraud Act gives them no such powers. Others have assumed that they have the power to use data held for other local authority purposes such as pay roll and personnel in data matching exercises, whereas the Act is concerned only with data held for benefits purposes. Yet others have sought to extend the purpose of their data matching exercises from the detection of benefit fraud to more general income maximisation and debt recovery.[19]

The sharing of information on this scale allows data profiling, or matching, to become possible, and then widely practised.[20] A composite dataset created on an individual could be used for numerous purposes – to see, for example, if they were eligible for the benefits they claimed given their employment status and income. This might involve the pooling of information held in taxation and social security databases. But, as the Data Protection Registrar noted in 1989, such developments

offer possibilities: for the wide use and disclosure of information without an individual's knowledge or consent; for the use of information out of context to the detriment of individuals; for the wider replication of errors; for unjust decisions about individuals simply on the basis of a 'profile' which causes them to fall into a group with certain selected characteristics; for automatic decision making on facts of doubtful completeness, accuracy or relevance; for the surveillance of individuals; and for influencing peoples' lives.[21]

This was merely echoing the views of the Lindop Committee a decade earlier.[22] In North America concerns over the potential abuses associated with data profiling led to the official limitation of these practices. Since 1988 the USA has regulated profiling by a Computer Matching and Privacy Protection Act, whilst Canada has an official policy on 'Data Matching and Control of the Social Insurance Number'.[23]

The linking of data matching and social insurance numbers in this manner in North America reflects the requirement for unique personal identifiers in order to allow data to be integrated. This is because relational database systems require there to be at least one unique variable that is common to each of the component databases to be merged. Names cannot be used for this purpose, since there will be bound to be more than one 'John Smith' in any large data file.[24] Although British citizens do not have an official number, a few obvious candidates for the function of providing a unique form of identification have been emerging in recent decades. The use of national insurance numbers (NINOs) has spread across government, and they are now the primary income tax reference, besides being used for Personal

Equity Plans (PEPs) and Tax Exempt Special Savings Accounts (TESSAs). At one point it was suggested that the NINO should be used for processing student loans, although this proposal was subsequently dropped.[25] Similarly, the new driver's licence number introduced in the 1990s was but a thinly disguised amalgam of the driver's name and date of birth.[26] Other proposed personal identifiers have included a pupil identification number to aid the production of data in connection with assessing the performance of schools, and the use of NHS numbers to underpin a national medical records network.[27]

Such willingness on the part of the modern Welfare State to circulate and pool information on individuals is in striking contrast to official policy at the inception of the modern system of state benefits. Almost as soon as the national insurance system had been set up in 1911, the police attempted to gain access to the personal information it contained. In 1913 the matter was discussed at the highest possible level, and, according to an internal Insurance Commission memorandum,

> The Cabinet have decided that the rule that the addresses of insured persons should not be disclosed to the police by insurance officials, is to remain in force. If, however, the special circumstances of a particular case seem to warrant a departure from this principle, the Insurance Commissioners, with the consent of the responsible minister, may authorise such disclosure.
>
> Acting on this decision, the Home Office instructed police authorities not to apply to members of the outdoor staff of the Commission, nor to approach societies and insurance committees for information regarding particular insured persons, but, if the circumstances appeared to be exceptional, application should be made by the police authority concerned direct to the Commission.

Subsequent official records in the years before the First World War reveal cases where the police, county courts, county medical officers of health, the wives of absconded husbands, and creditors, had requests for information turned down by the Commission.[28] Such a contrast with the situation in the early twenty-first century reveals the manner in which the British State's concern for personal privacy has been eroded in the twentieth century, although in pursuit of a widely held definition of the public good.

However, it would be misleading to assume that this has been a process without certain boundaries. As yet British citizens are not allocated a single official identifier, as people are elsewhere. In the old GDR, for example, each person was given a *Personenkennziffer* (*PKZ*), made up of numerical codes for their data of birth, sex, century and location of birth, and a control digit. This identified them throughout their lives in their dealings with an all-encompassing state.[29] Such practices were not, however, confined to communist countries. By the 1970s, for example, as impeccable a democracy as Norway held vast amounts of information on individuals in its official National Central Register (see Table 7.1).

It could be argued, therefore, that Britain has merely been 'catching up' with practices widely accepted by citizens in other European states.

Table 7.1 The basic categories of data held in the Norwegian Central Register of Individuals in the early 1970s, and their frequency of updating

Attribute	Frequency of registration		
	Continuous	*Annual*	*Every nth year*
Birth date, place	X		
Commune of residence	X		
Name	X		
Address	X		
Marital status	X		
Date/place of death	X		
In/out migration	X		
Birth no. of mother	X		
Birth no. of father	X		
Birth no. of spouse	X		
Income data		X (from 1967)	
Property data		X (from 1967)	
Tax data		X (from 1967)	
Baccalaureat		X (from 1968)	
Family data			X (dec. census)
Education			X (dec. census)
Occupation			X (dec. census)
Branch of economy			X (dec. census)
Housing data			X (dec. census)
Electoral participation			X (election)
Social support		X (from 1966)	
Criminal action		X (from 1966)	

Source: Martin Bulmer, 'Maintaining public confidence in quantitative social research in Britain', in Martin Bulmer (ed.), *Censuses, Surveys and Privacy* (London: Macmillan, 1979), p. 204.

Information technology, policing and counter-terrorism

Whereas information and communication technology can be seen as building upon traditional working methods in the Welfare/Taxation State, it has transformed the very nature of policing. Welfare and taxation systems in the twentieth century had always been about handling data via large bureaucratic systems, but traditional policing, as already noted, was mainly about physical surveillance. Since the 1960s, however, policing has increasingly been subordinated to the collection and central processing of information. This has changed the way in which the police operate, and lies, in part, behind contemporary concerns over the absence of a police presence on the streets.

Pressures on resources and new communication technologies began to change the traditional pattern of police work from the 1950s onwards. The more effective and efficient use of telephone and radio communications allowed the Metropolitan Police in 1957 to open a new 'information room' to receive incoming 999 emergency calls, and to mobilise men and police cars to deal with incidents more quickly. Other provincial police forces subsequently set up information rooms along these lines. In the 1960s such methods were extended into the 'unit beat' system. Here a team of constables, a police car and driver, a detective, and a sergeant 'collator', were responsible for an allocated area. The constables acted as the local eyes and ears of the team, and maintained radio contact with the sergeant at the police station. The sergeant collator co-ordinated the team by radio, and recorded all the information sent in. This helped to create a daily record of all information relating to crime, and an index of criminals or suspects working in the area, their habits, cars and associates. Additional information on people with driving disqualifications or drug offence convictions was also collated. From such data a monthly survey and analysis of the patterns of crime in the area could then be produced to direct local policing operations.[30]

In time the boundaries between these new police beats broke down. For officers in police cars, distinctions between areas became meaningless as the pressure of work rose, and such officers came to be a resource to be directed anywhere within the police district. At the same time, the sergeant collator transmuted into the 'divisional intelligence officer', supplying information to local officers across the whole division but increasingly to CID. In place of information designed to act as a back-up and supplementary resource to a small group of officers working an 'area', divisional intelligence was now intended as a policing tool in relation to populations often in excess of 200,000 persons.[31] The police in Birmingham initiated research into the use of such 'command and control' policing, and introduced an information system linking the city's 12 sub-stations in 1972 – the first in the UK and Europe.[32] Information systems were now used to direct a highly mobile police force to 'incidents' at specific points within a police district, and the patrolling of space became a secondary activity. In essence, policing became predominantly responsive, rather than preventative.

As a result, 'thief-taking' became more and more the prerogative of the CID, whilst the work of the uniform branch was directed increasingly to the rather loosely defined 'provision of ground cover', the prevention of crime, and the collection of information.[33] As the emphasis of policing shifted to the 'rapid response' of 'tinned police' in patrol cars and the central processing of information, so the traditional 'bobby' on the beat tended to be less in evidence. As the centres of modern cities were hollowed out to become retailing and entertainment zones, especially for the young, there was increasing anxiety over the relative lack of physical police surveillance in public spaces. However, this concern did not result in a wholesale return to traditional policing. Instead, 'law and order' was increasingly provided by the proliferation of private security guards, the ubiquitous 'bouncers', and CCTV systems, which in themselves became grounds for further public concern.[34]

The large-scale information systems elaborated by the police inevitably leant themselves to the use of computer technology. In 1964, five years after an initial Home Office unit had been set up to explore the use of computers in various government departments, including the Metropolitan Police, a study was initiated to examine the possibility of creating a Police National Computer (PNC). In 1969 the then Labour government decided to establish this in a building near the Metropolitan Police training centre at Hendon. The two Burroughs B6700 computers used initially had the capacity to hold 40 million records, and these were soon upgraded. By 1973 each of the 47 police forces in England and

Wales had at least one terminal accessing the central database.[35] According to the Lindop Committee, in the late 1970s the PNC was connected by a network of private lines provided by the Post Office to some 300 wholly dedicated terminals situated in police stations across the country.[36] Divisional intelligence officers were thus given access to a national dataset that could be interrogated at speed.

One of the first sets of information to be put on the new PNC were the lists of cars and their owners held on computer at the Driver and Vehicle Licensing Authority (DVLA) at Swansea. An important reason for the creation of this central installation in the late 1960s had been the Labour government's desire to provide the police with a national information service to give quick and accurate data on vehicle ownership.[37] By the early 1980s over 19 million vehicle registrations had been downloaded onto the PNC. Other files on the new system included an index to all the 3,250,000 fingerprints kept by the National Fingerprint Unit, and an index to all the criminal records held at the Central Criminal Records Office. The latter was said to contain the names of at least 3.8 million convicted criminals, and to have the capacity for 5.7 million records.[38] The PNC also held a file of all those under suspended sentences, a list of disqualified drivers, a list of wanted and missing persons, and a stolen vehicle register. The system rapidly became central to day-to-day policing operations. According to the Lindop Committee on data protection, by the late 1970s the PNC's index of vehicle owners was interrogated about 9,000 times a day, whilst there were 20,000 transactions (enquiries and updates) per day relating to the computer files on stolen and suspect vehicles.[39] Campbell and Connor were claiming by the mid-1980s that 11 million checks were made on people via the PNC every year, mostly in the street, and that 19 million interrogations were made with respect to vehicles.[40]

Local police forces were also developing their own IT systems. The Metropolitan Police at the same date had its own Criminal Intelligence Computer, holding files of the Fraud, Serious Crimes and Drugs Squads, and of the Illegal Immigrants Unit. This was installed in 1977 with the initial purpose of computerising Special Branch files. New databases were created by the Metropolitan Police as its policing priorities changed. Thus, in 2000 it was announced that the names and details of more than 13,000 known or suspected racists were being gathered onto a single database in an attempt to link racially motivated incidents, and to target serial offenders.[41] In a similar manner, the Thames Valley Police established an intelligence system in 1974 to collate information on those living in Berkshire, Buckinghamshire and Oxfordshire who might be of interest to the police. By 1981 the number of persons on the system was 142,000, of whom 120,000 had criminal records. In 1979 there were said to be 77,834 addresses on the computer, and records of 66,998 occurrences and 5,943 crimes.[42] Police constables on duty could consult the VDU operators at the local station via radio, and immediately be given what information was held on any of the persons whose names appear on the index. The holdings of this computer system were claimed to be equal to about 10 per cent of the population of the police authority's district,[43] although the coverage of certain groups – young males, or particular ethnic minorities – would, of course, have been much higher. By the mid-1980s it was claimed that between a quarter and one-third of all adult males in the Thames Valley area could expect to have records on the local police computer.[44]

Much of the routine work of the police is now subordinated to collecting information for such systems. According to the Merseyside Police standing orders, for example, in the mid-1990s the resident beat constable was advised that:

> To obtain information, it is useful for the area constable to make himself known to local officials, shopkeepers, tradesmen, garage proprietors, and other reliable persons who regularly visit or reside in each road or street in the area. He should aim at having a contact who is confident in him in every road and street.

The constable was also told that, 'The amount of information passed to the collator by the area constable will indicate his effectiveness.'[45] Regarding the duties of the collator, the standing orders noted that:

> All items, however insignificant, will be recorded and indexed and will be available to all persons at all times. ... It should be borne in mind that the Collator's Office should be an Information Bureaux [sic] in addition to a Criminal Intelligence Office and information of all kinds should be encouraged on the premises [sic] that we do not know today what we will need tomorrow.[46]

Similarly, in the mid-1980s, a collator in the Merseyside Police was required to set up and maintain six indexes:

1 a daily record sheet (an event/date index of all information coming in);
2 an intelligence index on people;
3 a vehicle index;
4 a local modus operandi index (notable criminal methods);
5 a street index;
6 a miscellaneous index.

Similar 'section intelligence – subject index' cards used by the Metropolitan Police provided space to record racial 'identity codes', descriptions and 'associates'. A 'beat–sheet index' was used to identify houses and premises that beat officers should keep under surveillance.[47]

The whole process of 'stop and search' in the streets became a means of collecting information, via the identification of people who associate with known criminals. The automatic collation of stop-check records provided an historical record of where people had been. Suffolk Constabulary standing orders in the mid-1980s regarded three successive stop-checks at night in a four-week period as *prima facie* evidence of suspicious behaviour on the part of those stopped. Each of these people would then be permanently entered on the computer as a 'suspect'. Similarly, the City of London Police issued standard 'random vehicle check' forms to police officers, on which they were to enter details of the vehicle checked, the driver, all passengers, including their names and addresses, and where they were seated. An officer who did not report the results of a sufficient numbers of checks was regarded once more as underperforming.[48]

As already noted, records on criminal convictions held in the Central Criminal Record Office were used by the police themselves for the purposes of preventing and detecting crime. In addition, magistrates, justices of the peace, barristers, solicitors, and solicitors' managing clerks, of course, had access to the information in order to administer justice. Courts, for example, needed evidence on previous convictions for the purposes of sentencing. Moreover, the police also made this information available to a number of public and professional bodies with regard to

> doctors, dentists, nurses, persons employed in the care of children, and youth leaders, 'because they stand in a position of trust to vulnerable members of society'; civil servants, atomic energy and Post Office temporary and permanent staff, 'in the interests of national security'.[49]

In the early 1990s an internal 'Efficiency Scrutiny of the National Collection of Criminal Records' was undertaken by the Home Office; it recommended putting all criminal records, both national and local, onto an integrated national computer system. This was to allow wider use of criminal records for vetting individuals in order to protect children and other groups at risk.[50] By 1994 a comprehensive national criminal records system, PHOENIX, had been installed on the second version of the PNC.[51] In 1998 the then Home Secretary, Jack Straw, announced that employers and voluntary organisations would have the right to insist that job applicants and volunteers should produce a certificate detailing their criminal convictions from a new Criminal Records Bureau.[52] But the introduction of the system was delayed because of complaints from the official Information Commissioner about the high number of inaccuracies in the information held by the police.[53]

Claims were also made in the 1980s that the NHS Central Register in Southport and Edinburgh, and the DHSS National Insurance General Index in Newcastle upon Tyne were used by MI5 and the police as central population registers through which individuals could be traced. Wholesale trawls, for example, were made through the Newcastle national insurance contribution files during the hunt for the Yorkshire Ripper in the 1970s. Some 17,000 men and their DHSS records were investigated in the search for a Sunderland man who had later moved to West Yorkshire. This was because a Sunderland accent had been detected on tapes that the police believed, erroneously, they were receiving from the Ripper.[54] Police access to such material was, of course, facilitated by the development of the Government Data Network in the 1990s.

Similarly, under the provisions of the 1994 Criminal Justice and Public Order Act, the police also began to build up computer databases of DNA profiles of material taken from individuals either convicted or charged with recordable offences. This technology was developed in Britain in the 1980s as a by-product of research into the genetics of blood anomalies, and uses a chemical process to force the DNA strands to separate into shorter elements that can be arranged to create a set of horizontal bars resembling a bar code. The system has been used in high-profile cases to identify several perpetrators of rapes and murders in Britain, and is being used extensively in the USA. The state of South Dakota, for example, collects DNA samples from all those who are merely arrested for particular crimes.[55] In Britain there have even been suggestions by the Home Affairs Committee of the House of Commons and the Metropolitan Police Commissioner that a DNA database of the whole population would be of considerable use to the police.[56] This is an extension of the general trend in the recent past for information gathering to shift from surveillance of what individuals claim about themselves to surveillance of their bodies, and from surface features to the very make-up of the human cell.[57]

In addition, non-state bodies in the UK are being integrated into digital systems of information storage and surveillance. Under the 2000 Regulation of Investigatory Powers Act, all commercial providers of telecommunications and Internet services are obliged to keep records of mobile phone calls and Internet connections made by citizens. These can then be accessed by the police and security forces fighting terrorism and organised crime. These arrangements have subsequently been extended via Europol, the European-wide system for sharing criminal intelligence.[58] The latter gathers and exchanges hard information on criminal suspects across Europe, and analyses a much broader range of information to indicate trends/patterns in crime. As with commercial firms handling taxation and welfare schemes, the state is again decentralising itself but via extremely unwilling agents in civil society. As the spread of the Internet allows ever easier interchange of information, these forms of information collection are likely to expand.

However, some of the more extreme forms of mass surveillance have not, as yet, been put in place in mainland Britain,[59] and this probably reflects a reluctance to apply forms of surveillance associated with criminals to the population as a whole. Rather than providing a means of social control of the entire population, scientific means of identification such as DNA have become a badge setting the criminal apart. However, when the British State was attacked directly, as in Northern Ireland, it was quite capable of elaborating thoroughgoing information systems covering entire communities. The British Army, for example, was intimately involved in the surveillance of the population of Ulster during the 'Troubles' of the late twentieth century. It has been claimed that as many as one-fifth of the members of each army battalion were at one point engaged in full-time plain-clothed intelligence, or covert surveillance operations.[60]

Aided by Special Branch, the Army organised local censuses on a street-by-street basis to build up a register of the population, houses and businesses. An index of 'P cards' was established in the early 1970s of known or suspected terrorists, and of their families and friends. This contained extensive personal information – descriptions of houses, telephone numbers, cars owned, lists of all occupants of houses, their dates of birth, schools attended by children, and so on. This index, later computerised, was cross-referenced to intelligence summaries, so that a complete dossier, including photographs, could be compiled for any particular individual. Information was fed into this system from reports supplied by soldiers on mobile and foot patrols, or undertaking snap searches at vehicle checkpoints, as well as from covert operations involving infiltration, captured documents, informers and defectors.[61] In 1974 it was estimated that the British Army had information on computer relating to 40 per cent of the Northern Ireland population.[62] In recent years one of the features of the situation in Ulster has been the plethora of – sometimes conflicting – surveillance bodies in action, including MI5, MI6, Special Branch and the Royal Ulster Constabulary, as well as Military Intelligence.[63]

It was perhaps inevitable, moreover, that in a period of heightened concern over crime, asylum seekers and terrorism, especially in Northern Ireland, that the whole issue of identity cards should be resurrected. In a reversal of earlier patterns, calls for the introduction of such cards tended to emanate from the Right of the political spectrum, and to be concerned predominantly with policing issues. In 1989 two private member's bills were introduced into Parliament for the setting up of a national identification system. Although the then Home Secretary made it clear that the government did not favour a compulsory national registration system, he also stated that he would examine the feasibility of a voluntary system.[64] In the early 1990s concerns were expressed that the introduction of photographs and personal identity numbers on driving licences might turn the latter into a de facto identity card. The government again made it clear that although it planned to make all driver details available to the police in 1992, drivers would not have to carry their licences at all times.[65] Similarly, the DSS was looking at the possibility of replacing benefit books with a social security payment card, although this proposal was subsequently abandoned as too costly.[66] Demands for the introduction of identification cards surfaced in Parliament once more in 1994, and the then Prime Minister, John Major, stated that he believed that there was a strong case for such means of checking identity. At the same date, the Association of Chief Police Officers (ACPO) dropped its opposition to the issue of a voluntary machine-readable card.[67]

A subsequent government green paper, and comments by the Home Secretary at that time, implied that the government favoured a combined driving licence and identity card.[68] The Prime Minister argued, however, that there were 'practical difficulties' in introducing such a card, reflecting the fact, no doubt, that the driving licence database is probably the least accurate of the existing information systems covering a large part of the population. The British driver licensing procedures were not designed for identification purposes, since there are no checks on the identity of the applicant; no existing set of photographs of drivers prior to the mid-1990s; and it is known that multiple licences are held.[69] In other countries some licensing systems require the production of a birth certificate and fingerprinting, as a well as a photograph, before a driving licence can be issued.[70]

A change of government in 1997 did not lessen the pressure for identification cards to prevent 'bogus' asylum seekers entering the country, or to combat international terrorism in the wake of the bombing of New York and Washington DC in 2001.[71] The new Labour administration was certainly willing to introduce cards for specific target groups. For example, in reaction to the case of Harold Shipman, an NHS general practitioner who may have murdered hundreds of his patients, the government announced that doctors were to be issued with a 'smart card'. This would hold a record of pre-employment checks and of the doctors' suitability for work with children; their police records; and any disciplinary proceeding against them by the General Medical Council.[72] In July 2002, the Home Secretary, David Blunkett, issued a consultation paper on 'Entitlement cards and identity fraud', suggesting the establishment of a national register, and the issuing of an identity card that would not need to be carried at all times. This would do away with the need for multiple databases in government, help people gain entitlements, and guard against illegal immigrants gaining welfare benefits and employment. Similar arguments lay behind the decision to introduce national ID numbers for all citizens in Japan in August 2002.[73] The issuing of identity cards was not necessarily a cause of disagreement between the front benches of the major political parties.

This did not lessen public disquiet, however, and many objections to entitlement cards were summarised by the Information Commissioner at the beginning of 2003. He was concerned over:

- the need to guard against 'function creep' – especially the risk that greater state monitoring of individuals' activities will be helped by recording these in a central register;
- the problems of relying on existing databases of questionable quality;
- keeping personal details accurate and up to date;
- stopping the card itself becoming the target for identity fraudsters;
- the difficulties in restricting the wider use of the card and the unique personal ID number in situations where these are not really needed;
- the excessive amounts of information displayed on the card and the dangers of misuse by others who see this.[74]

At the beginning of the twenty-first century, therefore, the government appears to be caught in a cleft stick. On the one hand, it sees the advantages of identity cards in terms of policing, and of cost-effectiveness – a 'swipe card' with a photograph and signature would speed up so many state transactions with the public. The carrying of an identity card with a unique personal identifier would, for example, help in creating a unified, and automated, medical records system in the NHS. It is, in part, the inability of the public to remember their NHS numbers that has led to the endless duplication of records across hospitals, GP practices and health centres. On the other hand, the government is concerned at the political costs of appearing to treat the citizen body in the same manner as it has traditionally administered criminals. To do so could be seen in the British context as treating the public as under general suspicion, undermining the line drawn between the 'respectable' working classes, and the 'dangerous classes' in the course of the nineteenth and early twentieth centuries.

This may explain why the issue of identity cards is being pursued so cautiously, and why such a system may be created in the end via a gradual build-up of the new driving licence database, despite all its faults. Plainly, the creation of a consistent national register in one go may only be possible, in political terms, during such national emergencies as 1916 and 1939. Whether the events in the USA in September 2001 constitute such a national emergency in Britain waits to be seen. Certainly, if identity cards are to be used to prevent terrorists hijacking jets in Dublin or Paris to attack London, this points towards the need for an EU-wide identification system, which might not be acceptable to the political Right. One need not necessarily follow Michel Foucault in seeing the emphasis on threats to 'law and order' as being merely a means of justifying such technologies of surveillance and social control.[75] Preventing crime and acts of terrorism can plainly be seen in terms of the state providing social benefits to its citizens, and a political party that was not seen as providing such goods would soon find itself in trouble. However, one might query whether the creation of vast information systems to meet what seems to be almost every threat faced by the polity is not just a quick technological fix that leaves underlying social and geopolitical problems unsolved. Indeed, the elaboration of such databases in an ad hoc and inconsistent manner may create new problems by alienating specific communities singled out for such surveillance,[76] or by creating databases so filled with inaccuracies that they loose credibility.[77] Of course, this may be an argument for a single identity system based on reliable and verifiable information, rather than for the suppression of the Information State itself.[78]

The politics of data protection and freedom of information

It should also be noted that the vast expansion of the Information State in the late twentieth century has not been achieved without the provision of some checks and balances, although one may have legitimate doubts about their effectiveness. As already noted, the period saw the passing of some significant pieces of legislation to help regulate information gathering and use within both the British State and civil society.

Whilst it is probably true to say that the British State has collected comparatively modest amounts of information on its citizens compared to other European countries, what information it has held has been guarded jealously. Whereas a country such as Sweden passed its first freedom of information legislation in 1766,[79] the UK did not achieve this until 2000. In the late nineteenth and twentieth centuries, British civil servants were bound by draconian legislation, starting with the 1889 Official Secrets Act, by which they were exposed to prosecution if they transmitted any document to any person who 'ought not' to receive it. The bounds of impermissible communication were defined in terms of that which was not in 'the interest of the State or otherwise in the public interest'.[80] Official records were normally only opened to the public when they had been selected for permanent preservation at the national archives, the Public Record Office. Even then, under the terms of the 1958 Public Records Act, government departments only had to do this when records were 50 years old. Under the 1967 Public Records Act, this period was later reduced to 30 years but government departments could still obtain a Lord Chancellor's instrument to close records for longer periods of time on the grounds of personal and commercial confidentiality, and of national security. Records could also be held back for 'continued administrative use'. The actual records selected for public preservation in this way were only a tiny fraction of those ever created.[81] Indeed, the whole public records system was not designed to allow access to current state records but to create an historical archive – a distinction lost on many journalists.

The ability of the British State to collect what information it wanted, and to prevent members of the public looking at it, began to be questioned in the late 1960s. In 1967 the MP Alex Lyon introduced a Right of Privacy Bill into Parliament. Although this failed to get a second reading, the National Council for Civil Liberties (NCCL) launched a privacy campaign at the same time. Justice, the British section of the International Commission of Jurists, also started to draft potential legislation in this field. This was followed in 1970 by another Right to Privacy Bill introduced by Brian Walden, then a Labour MP. Walden's Bill was adapted from the draft by Justice, which had just published a report on privacy and the law.[82] In time-hallowed fashion, the response of governments in the 1970s was to set up a series of committees, especially the Younger Committee on Privacy and the Lindop Committee on Data Protection already mentioned, to consider the issues involved. The latter collected information from most government departments, and suggested important principles upon which data protection legislation might be based, although it could obtain little co-operation from either the Metropolitan Police or the security services.[83]

A cynic might see such developments as a mere holding operation but in the 1980s it became ever more difficult for the British State to drag its feet. In 1981 the Council of Europe's Committee of Ministers approved the *Convention for the Protection of Individuals with Regard to Automatic Processing of Data*, which set out basic citizens' rights with respect to the personal data held by commercial and public bodies on computer.[84] The provisions of the convention were due to come into force in 1985, and British firms feared that they would be debarred from international data processing business if Britain did not have a data protection system.[85] The British State was also bound by European treaties to introduce such legislation. This led in 1984 to the passing of the Data Protection Act, which laid down certain principles for regulating the computer storage and manipulation of personal data. A Data Protection Registrar was appointed in 1985 in order to administer the Act, and to organise the registration of computer systems the legislation required. In broad terms, the new data protection principles were similar to those proposed by the Lindop Committee, these being that:

1 data subjects should know what personal data relating to them are handled, why those data are needed, how they will be used, who will use them, for what purposes, and for how long;

2 personal data should be handled only to the extent and for the purposes made known when they are obtained, or subsequently authorised;

3 personal data handled should be accurate and complete, and relevant and timely for the purposes for which they are used;

4 no more personal data should be handled than are necessary for the purposes made known or authorised;

5 data subjects should be able to verify compliance with these principles.[86]

In addition, personal data was not to be transferred to a country or territory outside the European Union, unless that country or territory ensured an 'adequate' level of protection for the rights and freedoms of 'data subjects' in relation to the processing of personal data.

However, Schedule 2 of the 1984 Act gave sanction for data processing in those cases where it was required:

1 for the administration of justice;

2 for the exercise of any functions conferred by or under any enactment;

3 for the exercise of any functions of the Crown, a Minister of the Crown or a government department; or

4 for the exercise of any other functions of a public nature exercised in the public interest.

An exemption from the Act was also given in those cases where giving individuals access to information relating to them was likely to prejudice 'the prevention or detection of crime', or 'the apprehension or prosecution of offenders'.[87]

This plainly gave the state considerable room for the use of information untrammelled by restrictions, as in the case of the information on the PNC. A new EU Data Protection Directive was issued in 1995 to take effect across Europe from 1998,[88] which was implemented in the UK in the form of a new Data Protection Act in 1998. Amongst other things, this Act will extend data protection principles to personal records held in non-electronic form by 2007. However, the Act still provides exemption in cases where data is processed in order to safeguard national security, prevent crime, or facilitate the collection of a tax or duty. Data protection legislation thus provides some limitations on the official use of information but it can also be seen as a means of heading off more fundamental demands for a total right of privacy. It is perhaps inevitably a compromise between the requirements of state and the protection of individual rights.[89] The British citizen cannot be said to have had a right of privacy, rather he or she has had a right to confidentiality,[90] although this may be challenged after the incorporation of a Bill of Rights into UK law.

Similar limitations apply to the 2000 Freedom of Information Act, which will give citizens a legal right to see information held by national, regional and local government, and also by some other organisations working on behalf of the state. However, of the Act's 88 sections, a quarter relate to documents that are exempt from its major provisions. These exemptions include, amongst other forms of information: that relating to security matters, defence, international relations, law enforcement and the courts; the formulation of government policy; or material the publication of which would prejudice 'effective conduct of public affairs'. This appears somewhat restrictive compared, for example, to the provisions of the 1996 US Freedom of Information Act.[91] Certain aspects of existing data protection legislation overlap with the new Freedom of Information Act, not least the provision for the disclosure of information. It seems appropriate, therefore, that the Data Protection Registrar should also have been given the responsibility of implementing the Act, and renamed the Information Commissioner.[92]

At the heart of this reluctance to let go of control over information appears to lie a fundamental constitutional principle – in Britain, until quite recently, liberty resides in a sovereign, representative Parliament untrammelled by outside power, rather than in the fundamental rights of citizens. England's political revolution of the seventeenth century led to the removal of external impediments to the power of Parliament, in the form of the royal prerogative, rather than to the idealisation of individual rights, as in the American and French Revolutions a century and more later.[93] As Margaret Thatcher put it, in reply to freedom of information campaigners when prime minister:

> Under our constitution, ministers are accountable to parliament for...the provision of information. A statutory right of access would...transfer ultimate decisions to the courts....Ministers' accountability to parliament would (therefore) be reduced, and parliament itself diminished...I firmly believe that major constitutional changes such as your campaign is proposing are inappropriate and unnecessary.[94]

The sovereignty of the British Parliament is, however, being undermined by the increasing influence of the EU in its affairs.

It can been argued, for example, that Britain would not have its current data protection legislation without the issuing of European directives.[95] Moreover, as crime and terrorism have become international, so has the information compiled to combat it. By the early 1990s the Data Protection Registrar was expressing concern about the development of common police information systems across Europe.[96] In response to these developments EU Data Protection Commissioners met in Lisbon in 1995 to discuss the implications of the establishment of the Europol system of criminal intelligence.[97] A European Joint Supervisory Board was subsequently established to audit the processing of data by Europol, with national data protection authorities auditing the relevant national units.[98] The process of European integration was further facilitated by the appointment of an EU Data Protection Commissioner.[99] This decline in British informational autonomy was strikingly revealed in the chapter of the Data Protection Registrar's *Report* for 1993 relating to the EU Draft Directive on Data Protection, which was simply entitled, 'The United Kingdom – a part of the European Community'.[100]

Conclusion

Information technology can thus be seen as resulting in a radical change in the capabilities, but not the aims, of the Information State. It could not be argued that the state is doing anything new in the late twentieth and early twenty-first century, although it is certainly working in new ways. Elites still maintain their authority and power in ways that would have been understandable to politicians such as David Lloyd-George in the 1920s, or to social reformers such as Beatrice Webb. Information technology has not changed the basic nature of the system of bounded pluralism within which citizens live. Indeed, the computer has enabled that system to deliver rights, liberties and social goods with greater efficiency. State information systems may undermine the right to privacy but they help underpin other forms of rights to welfare and freedom from crime. Changes in the nature of social and political systems at this level cannot be explained in terms of technological determinism. However, if the basis of the British polity were to change, and elites sought to maintain their authority through undemocratic means, they would have at their disposal instruments of almost limitless capacity.

The advent of the computer has, however, seen a change in the attitude of citizens towards the Information State, and the first attempts to regulate its activities. A means of surveillance such as the SPECs system described in the Introduction would have been inconceivable to the likes of William the Conqueror, but so would a Freedom of Information Act. Norman barons and even commoners might appeal to Domesday Book in adjudicating disputes with the monarchy,[101] but when in the thirteenth century landowners were being asked by what right ('quo warranto') they held their land, one is reputed to have appealed not to official records but to an old rusted sword used by his ancestor at the Battle of Hastings.[102] The implication of this, perhaps apocryphal, story is that brute force rather than legal documents, and thus the law, lay at the root of political relationships. That modern citizens have a right of access to information via freedom of information and data protection legislation, however imperfect, thus reflects the existence of a rather different polity.

Also, much of this book has been concerned with delineating a national polity that was self-contained, and somewhat different from its neighbours. This exceptionalism now appears to be greatly reduced, although not extinguished. In part this reflects the decline in the importance of the physical and institutional barriers that allowed the British State in earlier periods to maintain its authority and cohesion without many of the administrative means used by Continental states. However, the English Channel is no longer a barrier to external threats. The gradual integration of the British state into a broader European polity has also led to the adoption of more 'normal' state systems of information gathering, and safeguards against their abuse. The national Information State is giving way to new, more global, forms of surveillance.

8

Towards a conclusion: social control or a hegemony of citizenship?

After this, admittedly brief, survey of state information gathering over the past 500 years, it is possible to return to an evaluation of some of the ideas discussed in Chapter 2. It is to be hoped that enough evidence has been provided here to show that many of the key arguments respecting the Information State found in the existing literature require considerable qualification, and in some cases wholesale rejection. However, the present work has been concerned only with the development of the Information State in England and the UK, and any conclusions reached must, therefore, be provisional.

Official information gathering, or at least information gathering by officials, of English men and women was, arguably, not something that had its genesis in the Enlightenment of the eighteenth century, or in the Industrial Revolution of the nineteenth. Indeed, these periods saw a relaxation of certain forms of information gathering for the purposes of surveillance, especially in the religious and moral spheres. Office-holders under the Crown had been imposing discipline at every level of society in Tudor and Stuart England down to that of the parish, in order to meet perceived threats to 'good order'. Some of the forms of information gathering and punishment used in this earlier period would indeed appear outrageous to modern eyes. Such information gathering was undertaken via the co-operation, or symbiosis, of the elites of local communities and the central state, although neither of these can be understood in terms familiar to modern sociology.

Local communities in the early modern period were not homogenous *gemeinschaft* in which control was exercised solely via the institutions of family, service and neighbourliness. Such communities were often riven by internal dissentions, and prey to

194

troublesome interlopers. Nor were they necessarily stable, 'timeless' entities, since many localities were undergoing comparatively rapid economic and social change. Local elites, the gentry and the 'middling sort' drew upon the authority of the state to patrol local society to protect property, life and patriachal structures. Rather than simply imposing itself on the localities, the monarchy won their consent to rule by providing various public goods. This can be seen especially in the case of legal services, and the provision of the force and prestige necessary to back up the law. In turn, the monarchy expected counties and parishes to appoint local officers to implement official policy and raise taxes. To a certain extent, what we think of as local communities in the early modern period were actually creations of this relationship – the civil, as opposed to the ecclesiastical, parish was the area over which certain local officers such as the constable, the overseers of the poor and of the highways, had jurisdiction. These were all office-holders undertaking duties laid down centrally, and answerable to other officers, especially the JPs, who could be removed by the Crown.

At the same time, the state itself was not simply a set of central institutions – Westminster and Whitehall – that had extended their control over the rest of English society. Rather, the state was a series of interlocking and ongoing processes to which a large number of individuals contributed, both centrally and locally, to preserve 'good governance'. The state emerged rather than was imposed. What 'good governance' meant varied from place to place, and from level to level, within this constellation of forces, and much of the history of the period can be understood in terms of the playing out of these differing interpretations. However, if the centre appeared to become too powerful, as during the reigns of Charles I and James II, or during the Protectorate of Oliver Cromwell, the localities were quick to reassert themselves. This decentralised polity was not, however, a weak state – for much of the early modern period it maintained internal peace and order in an exemplary manner, whilst defeating, or at least successfully countering, the Papacy, Phillip II of Spain, Louis XIV of France, the Mogul Empire, Napoleon Bonaparte and Manchu China. This was a state on its way to becoming the first world hegemony.

These activities have left few central records because in a decentralised polity their locus was local. In addition, because they were small scale, such forms of information gathering and surveillance were often oral in form. However, evidence of the activities of parish officers, JPs, ecclesiastical courts and the like, can be found spread across the country in local and dioscesan record offices. As the records of Earls Colne show, such evidence can provide a fine-grained understanding of the life of past communities, but only when it is combined with modern information technology. The central state of the early modern period created comparatively few of the comprehensive record series on its subjects that are associated today with the modern central state because most government took place in the local state. However, where the creation of such records facilitated its most pressing concerns, such as preserving its position within the decentralised polity and fighting wars, the monarchy could create surprisingly comprehensive information systems. This can be seen in the case of oaths of allegiance and the pay records of its fighting personnel.

The subsequent history of the English State can be seen not in terms of the expansion of power and authority from a central point outwards but as a contraction inwards. The state ceased to be a set of processes involving elites across the whole society undertaking tasks on an unpaid, amateur basis. Instead it became the preserve of a centralised, salaried core of civil servants and party politicians. The industrialisation of the late eighteenth and early nineteenth centuries certainly played a part in this, through making governance at the parish level increasingly unworkable. The period also saw the rise of a cadre of middle-class, professional experts, exemplified by the likes of Edwin Chadwick, for whom the central state was both a source of employment and a means of social reform. However, the initial strategy of this modified English State was not to centralise surveillance via information gathering but to introduce the physical surveillance of the police, prison and lunatic asylum, and to re-establish local government on a new basis. Physical surveillance was an alternative rather than an adjunct to social control via the collection of information. Central information gathering in the early to mid-Victorian period, in the form of the census and civil registration, was also more about encouraging personal and local activity than central planning. This was not surveillance in the narrow sense but the creation of more stable personal rights to property, rights to environmental health, and ultimately political rights within a party political system.

It was the late nineteenth and early twentieth centuries that really saw the genesis of the centralised Information State. It was then that the central collection of information for the purposes of central activity came to the fore. This reflected, in part, the need for political elites to incorporate the working classes into the existing polity via welfare and electoral reforms, and the need to counteract Irish nationalism. But there were also external threats to British world hegemony – in the form of industrial rivals such as Germany and the USA – that required the elaboration of systems for secret surveillance and military mobilisation. The traditional, decentralised polity was seen as unable to cope with the threats facing it. Centralised welfare and warfare in an age of rival mass democracies and totalitarian states led to centralised record keeping. The organisation of vast information flows through central nodes of communication could not be undertaken orally, and required the development of vast paper-tracking systems. In the case of Britain, therefore, the rise of the modern Information State can be seen as reflecting the relative decline of the power of the ruling elites rather than its expansion. An accommodation had to be made with the masses, whilst internationally the power of Britain was diminished.

Moreover, the rise of the central state, with the concomitant rise of a specialised political and administrative class, can also be seen in terms of the decline of the local political elites of the former period. In an earlier society, status was concomitant with state office holding, and local standing was dependent on the ownership of property rooted in the community, such as land. In the twentieth century, status accrued more to position within a capitalist firm, and the ownership of highly visible, and essentially mobile property, such as a particular type of motor car. The rich came to see themselves as being *in* a locality rather than being *of* a locality. Local elites, in some senses, simply ceased to exist, whilst the remorseless globalisation of economic, professional and intellectual life undermined the belief that local problems could be solved by local action. The central state increasingly had to step in to fill the gap left by the relative decline of local governance. Anyone involved in local community activity in Britain over the past 20 years will bewail the narrowing of the scope and ambitions of local authorities, and the manner in which local politicians see their activities as merely a stepping-stone to national party politics.

This analysis of the British Information State raises issues about the reasons for information gathering, in addition to the timing of its inception and its role in local–central relations. Debates regarding the function information plays in the state tend to revolve around the issue of social control. However, the latter is such a flexible term, with so many contested meanings, that it is difficult to use the concept with any degree of precision. At times it is simply used to designate what elites do to reproduce themselves as elites, which is almost a tautology. Social control has been taken to refer, amongst other things, to the following social processes:

- the identification of those who deviate from the norms of a society, so that the members of that society can protect themselves against those deviants, and thus maintain society's cohesion and the good things that spring from social life – this was inherent in the original insights of, for example, G. H. Mead and E. A. Ross;
- the identification of those who deviate from the norms of a social system, so that system as a system can protect itself against those deviants, and thus maintain its cohesion and identity – the position of Talcott Parsons and other systems theorists;
- the identification of those who deviate from the norms of a society, so that dominant elites within that society can protect themselves against dissent, and thus maintain the good things that accrue to them from their dominance of society – some Marxist theorists and Anthony Giddens (in at least some of his writings);
- the socialisation of members of society into the norms of a society that supports inequality, especially via education, so that dominant elites within that society can protect themselves against dissent, and thus maintain the good things that spring from their dominance of society – some Marxist theorists;
- the provision of generalised civil, political and social rights by social elites, which creates a 'life world' in which alternative conceptions of what might be possible become impossible to conceptualise, and which thus safeguard the position of social elites based on the status quo – Corrigan and Saoyer.

Elements of all these models can be found in the story told in the present work. The case for state information gathering, allowing the identification of potential deviants from the norms of an elitist society, can be made. Much of the information gathering in early modern England was to enable surveillance in order to protect the authority, property and safety of the monarch and the landed classes, and the patriarchal rule of the 'middling sort'. One can conceptualise the early development of the uniformed police in terms of the creation of a specialised force by political and economic elites to combat Chartism and trade union activity. Modern police computing, the data analysis powers of the security services, and the spread of CCTV, can all be seen in terms of the creation of a 'Big Brother State'. Information gathering in modern welfare systems can also be understood in terms of enforcing work discipline on a reluctant workforce through the 'availability for work' test. The collection of 'data' by the state, and its use in the production of statistics, can be seen as an attempt to educate the working classes in the virtues of a capitalist society, or to facilitate their administration.

However, the use of personal information as a means of identifying deviants for the purpose of maintaining the positions of elites should not be overdrawn, and there are other ways of conceptualising these activities. It is also very difficult to see many modern forms of central data gathering, such as censuses and civil registration, in terms of the identification of deviants much before the twentieth century, if then. Victorian data-processing technologies simply did not lend themselves to such purposes. In the twentieth century, however, especially since the advent of the modern computer, the Information State has had the ability to use records in this manner. Yet in many ways the British State has been reluctant to use its potential power to the full, as can be seen from its unwillingness to sustain a system of national identity cards. However, the case of Northern Ireland might indicate that this was only because the structures of British society have not been called into question by a revolutionary, or insurrectionist, working class. But equally important has been the unwillingness of politicians and civil servants to pursue policies that appeared to efface the line drawn in the Victorian period between the respectable working classes and the criminal 'mob'.

This points to a more fundamental interpretation of the Information State in Britain, as the underpinnings of a whole raft of rights and benefits that has helped to incorporate the masses into the structures of the modern nation state. Political elites cannot sustain themselves simply by the repression of deviants, or through overt brainwashing, since their power has never been sufficient enough, nor the populace gullible enough, to allow this. Such was the lesson taught by the collapse of communism in Eastern Europe in the late twentieth century. Elites need to gain consent to their rule, and this has usually involved the provision of services and public goods. One might argue, for example, that *in the final analysis* the uniformed police are there to protect the existing political and economic status quo. However, if they did not also help to protect the person and meagre property of the poorest members of society, their position as defenders of the law would soon become untenable. State information gathering has helped to underpin the property rights of all social classes, maintained equitable voting rights, and helped to plan the supply of health services and welfare benefits, and ensured the taxes necessary to fund them. State information gathering is not simply something against which civil, political and social rights have been erected as a defence, as Anthony Giddens has argued on occasion. Instead it underpins many of those rights, as Giddens has argued on other occasions.

However, as Corrigan and Sayer have pointed out, the provision of such rights and benefits can lead to a restriction of what entitlement can mean in a society. Chadwick and Farr's model of medical rights in terms of sanitary reform in the early nineteenth century restricted what a right to a healthy life might imply. It certainly did not imply the redistribution of wealth envisaged by the Black Committee in the late twentieth century. The property rights maintained by civil registration, and the host of places of record established in Legal London in the nineteenth century, related to individual private property, rather than to a generalised right of access to the wealth created by society. The use of birth certificates to regulate the life course of children as an adjunct to the Factory Acts, and other legislation, may have increased the incomes and authority of male household heads through the removal of their competition. This was not, however, a means of ensuring a more equitable distribution of national wealth *between* families. The provision of welfare rights has been the cornerstone of the modern social compromise but came to be dependent upon proving certain forms of behaviour that might be seen as conducive to the reproduction of the existing economic and social system.

But this should not be seen solely in terms of the propagation of a 'false consciousness' amongst the masses, or a simple sleight of hand to gain consent to the hegemony of the ruling classes. Many of the civil, political and social rights gained in the process of modern state formation fulfilled, if only in part, the aspirations of non-elites. These aspirations can be seen in the early nineteenth century in the Chartist demands for the reform of the franchise; in the opposition to the restriction of access to welfare under the New Poor Law; in the alacrity with which members of the working classes appear to have registered the births, marriages and deaths of their kin via the new civil registration; in the creation of working-class friendly societies to facilitate saving; and their recourse, if reluctantly, to the police in time of need. Organised labour wanted the vote; the protection of property and person; financial independence; and some security against the vagaries of economic cycles and old age. The genius of the established political classes in modern Britain was to provide these rights on their own terms, in exchange for acquiescence in the capitalist and party political systems. Within these bounds there was room for a pluralistic accommodation of most social groups, which necessitated, in turn, the collection and analysis of information to facilitate government intervention. The rise of the Information State in England and the UK was thus a creative process, rather than just a defensive reaction. The extent to which the modern state meets the aspirations of the population, if in a particular form, explains its stability and relative orderliness. Identification means recognition as well as control.

Such rights and liberties were, of course, won within the context of a particular nation state, and helped to ally the working classes with political elites in the protection of the autonomy of that polity. Much state information gathering can be seen not in terms of internal domination by elites but as an aspect of the defence of the country from external enemies. Hence the genesis of the modern Information State in the crisis of imperialism at the end of the nineteenth century, and the expansion of its powers during the two world wars. The nineteenth century had been a period of unparalleled peace for Britain, and it resulted in the absence of many of the information-gathering structures found in Continental European states. The twentieth century was a period of almost incessant hot and cold wars, and saw the vast expansion of information gathering by the state. But for most of the population the defence of the realm was a popular cause. British citizens may not have liked the idea of a Secret State collecting information on them, and found the restrictions on their customary liberties imposed by war and national registration irksome. However, most were, and are, prepared to put up with such forms of information gathering to protect the nation state to which they belong (and from which they derive benefits) from real, or imagined, enemies.

Here perhaps lies the paradox of the modern Information State – as something that everyone fears but no one can live without. The vast and intrusive powers of information gathering of modern government could be turned to oppressive purposes, as they have been in other countries, and on occasion within the UK itself. Once social or political movements threaten the boundaries of the pluralist compromise, the State can deploy its powers with great dispatch. However, these same powers maintain society's cohesion and the good things that spring from social life. Welfare may involve the rationing of entitlements but this is perhaps inevitable in any situation of scarcity. As long as the Information State helps to provide the benefits of the existing bounded pluralism, and there is no viable alternative on offer, it is difficult to see how or why it would be dismantled. As a totality its scope and power may be unsettling but its individual manifestations often appear benign and welcome.

This takes one back to the plot of Charlie Chaplin's *Modern Times*, with which this book began. What is striking about the factory in which the film opens is that it creates nothing of any obvious value – its output is a flat plate with two nuts that Chaplin's character and his co-workers have to tighten endlessly. The entire process of production is presented as pointless from the start. But what if the factory was producing consumer goods for the sort of ideal home that the little tramp later dreams about, or if the film portrayed Chaplin enjoying the fruits of his labour? One might argue that the provision of such goods could be provided by other forms of production, and do not justify the curtailment of civil liberties portrayed. In practice, however, and in the absence of working alternatives, citizens have tended to accept the

restrictions and disciplines of modern, industrial society in order
to obtain the benefits it can produce. It was not surveillance that
kept the masses in the factories of the 1930s but the fear of unemployment and the dream of a better life, if one envisaged and
propagated by large corporations.

In conclusion, it is probably true to say that as long as there is
a modern state, it will be an Information State. That is, one that
has to collect information in order to fulfil its functions. One may
cavil at the amount of information held by government but there
will always appear perfectly valid reasons why data collection
should be increased. Immediate benefits often obscure concerns
about the possible adverse effects on civil liberties of the collection
of information that might be put to dangerous uses by a regime
at some future date. Despite the arguments of political theorists,[1]
modern states tend to work in terms of maximising short-run
utility rather than in protecting the social contract between government and citizens. The alternative to the Information State
may be the creation of private organisations, which are both collectors and users of personal data, to undertake state functions but
without some of the public controls over official information handling. One might call for the strengthening of such controls but
in the end these can be overcome when the state declares that
'national security' is threatened. This is exactly what has happened
in the USA after the terrorist attacks of September 2001. What is
important, therefore, is not the nature of information collection
but the nature of the state, and the degree to which it is willing,
or constrained, to work within due process of law, and for the benefit of all social groups. How these are defined, and the extent to
which they can be achieved, within the present system of bounded
pluralism, are issues that carry one beyond the narrow confines of
the present work.

In these circumstances, those who oppose the expansion of the
Information State are, perhaps, in denial. It is difficult to see how
it will be 'rolled back', as one noted advocate of state surveillance
put it. A more fruitful strategy for those concerned about the misuse of personal information by the state might be to ensure that the
flows of information in state information systems can be properly
monitored. If, for example, personal information was held on one
central database, and citizens had the right, and ability, to access it
and a log of its use by government organisations via a swipe card,

this would help to expand civil liberties. Citizens could ensure that the information held on them was accurate, and that its use by the state was appropriate. If the Information State became a two-way process, and there appears to be nothing in the technology that prevents this, it would become a means of expanding the control of citizens over the state. This would still enable the state to save money, and prevent it having to rely on the pooling of suspect information from across numerous and separate databases, the results of which can do unnecessary harm to the rights and well-being of citizens. Given the history of the Freedom of Information Act, such a suggestion might appear somewhat utopian but it would go with the grain of technological and state development, and would also put the onus on the state to justify its secrecy. Perhaps the circle can be squared by greater transparency rather than by an attempt to prevent interaction with the state and commerce. But this raises the whole issue of the right to privacy, and is the subject of another book.

This exercise in historical reconstruction also raises issues about the relationship between theoretical models and the 'patterned mess' that can be seen in the past. Human beings cannot get away from models and theories, and those who claim to be thoroughgoing empiricists often turn out to be making the most fundamental assumptions when they approach the archives. But the application of theory to historical events has to be an iterative process that engages with documentary evidence. History may be storytelling but it cannot be done in a vacuum – there are 'things' out there with which the story needs to be consistent. When discussing state information gathering some authors have made sweeping generalisations based on theoretical models, without much knowledge of actual historical structures and processes as revealed by the archival sources. They have factored a temporal dimension into their work, without really taking on board the content of the past. Rather than proceeding in this manner, scholars should be attempting to build theory on historical case studies. This is not to denigrate theoretical work, merely to call for the construction of a more robust theory that will not be undermined by its first brush with historical artefacts. Attempting to integrate theory and empiricism may create poor history and worse sociology but it should at least be attempted. Inevitably this means working on comparatively small subjects, although some will doubt that examining England over half a millennium counts as such. The role of information gathering in state formations requires in-depth research into differing states, and only then can a comparative typology emerge. To do otherwise is to place the theoretical carriage before the empirical horse.

Notes

1 Introduction

1 H. C. Darby, *Domesday England* (Cambridge: Cambridge University Press, 1977), pp. 4–5.

2 Elizabeth M. Hallam, *Domesday Book though Nine Centuries* (London: Thames & Hudson, 1986).

3 Darby, *Domesday England*, pp. 9–11; John McDonald and G. D. Snooks, *Domesday Economy: A New Approach to Anglo-Norman History* (Oxford: Oxford University Press, 1986), pp. 53–8; W. L. Warren, *The Governance of Norman and Angevin England* (London: Edward Arnold, 1987), p. 36.

4 M. T. Clanchy, *From Memory to Written Record: England, 1066–1307* (London: Edward Arnold, 1979), p. 20.

5 McDonald and Snooks, *Domesday Economy*.

6 Hallam, *Domesday Book*, pp. 47–51.

7 Darby, *Domesday England*, pp. 57–61.

8 *Report of the (Lindop) Committee on Data Protection*, British Parliamentary Papers PP 1978–79, V.

9 *The Independent*, 10 May 1999. But for a rather jaundiced evaluation of the technical deficiencies of such OCR (optical character recognition) traffic systems see Barry Fox, 'More money than sense', *Personal Computer World* (November 2002), p. 35.

10 The term is taken from Michael Mann, *States, War and Capitalism: Studies in Political Sociology* (Oxford: Blackwell, 1988), p. 5.

11 David Martin Luebke and Sybil Milton, 'Locating the victim: an overview of census-taking, tabulation technology, and persecution in Nazi Germany', *IEEE Annals of the History of Computing*, 16 (1994), pp. 25–39; Edwin Black, *IBM and the Holocaust* (London: Little, Brown, 2001); Timothy Longman, 'Identity cards, ethnic self-perception, and genocide in Rwanda', in Jane Caplan and John Torpey (eds), *Documenting Individual Identity: The Development of State Practices in the Modern World* (Princeton, NJ: Princeton University Press, 2001), pp. 345–57.

12 See, for example, Peter Townsend, Nick Davidson and Margaret Whitehead (eds), *Inequalities in Health: The Black Report* (London: Penguin, 1988), pp. 2–3.

13 Michel Foucault, 'The subject and power', in Hubert L. Dreyfus and Paul Rabinow (eds), *Michel Foucault: Beyond Structuralism and Hermeneutics, with an Afterword by Michel Foucault* (Brighton: Harvester, 1982), pp. 208–26.

2 Some models of state information gathering

1 Michael Mann, *The Sources of Social Power,* vol. I: *A History of Power from the Beginning to AD1760* (Cambridge: Cambridge University Press, 1986), pp. 31–2.
2 Anthony Giddens, *A Contemporary Critique of Historical Materialism* (London: Macmillan, 1995), p. 218; Anthony Giddens, *The Nation-State and Violence: Volume Two of a Contemporary Critique of Historical Materialism* (Cambridge: Polity Press, 1987), pp. 179–81.
3 Giddens, *A Contemporary Critique*, pp. 174–5, 218; Giddens, *The Nation-State*, pp. 179–80.
4 David Eastwood, '"Amplifying the province of the Legislature": The flow of information and the English State in the early nineteenth century', *Historical Research* LXII (1989), pp. 276–94.
5 Christopher Dandeker, *Surveillance, Power and Modernity. Bureaucracy and Discipline from 1700 to the Present Day* (Cambridge: Polity, 1990), pp. 12, 110, 117.
6 James B. Rule, *Private Lives and Public Surveillance* (London: Allen Lane, 1973), pp. 27–31.
7 Michel Foucault, 'The subject and power', in Hubert L. Dreyfus and Paul Rabinow (eds), *Michel Foucault: Beyond Structuralism and Hermeneutics, with an Afterword by Michel Foucault* (Brighton: Harvester, 1982), pp. 208–26; Michel Foucault, 'Governmentality', in Graham Burchell, Colin Gordon and Peter Miller (eds), *The Foucault Effect: Studies in Governmentality* (London: Harvester Wheatsheaf, 1991), pp. 87–104.
8 Jane Caplan and John Torpey, 'Introduction', in Jane Caplan and John Torpey (eds), *Documenting Individual Identity: The Development of State Practices in the Modern World* (Princeton, NJ: Princeton University Press, 2001), p. 7.
9 David Lyon, *The Electronic Eye: The Rise of the Surveillance Society* (Cambridge: Polity, 1994), p. 24.
10 Rule, *Private Lives*, pp. 30–1.
11 Hans Joas, *G. H. Mead: A Contemporary Re-examination of His Thought* (Cambridge: Polity Press, 1985); Jürgen Habermas, *The Theory of Communicative Action: The Critique of Functionalist Reason,* vol. 2 (Cambridge: Polity, 1989), pp. 1–42; M. Janowitz, 'Sociological theory and social control', *American Journal of*

Sociology, 81 (1975), pp. 82–95; David J. Rothman, 'Social control: the uses and abuses of the concept in the history of incarceration', in Stanley Cohen and Andrew Scull (eds), *Social Control and the State: Historical and Comparative Essays* (Oxford: M. Robertson, 1983), p. 107; Colin Sumner, 'Social control: the history and politics of a central concept in Anglo-American sociology', in Roberto Bergalli and Colin Sumner (eds), *Social Control and Political Orders: European Perspectives at the End of the Century* (London: Sage, 1997), p. 5.

12 Talcott Parsons, *The Social System* (London: Routledge and Kegan Paul, 1951); Sumner, 'Social control', pp. 22–3.

13 Janowitz, 'Sociological theory', pp. 95–6; Rothman, 'Social control', pp. 109–10; Sumner, 'Social control', p. 30.

14 Philip Corrigan and Derek Sayer, *The Great Arch: English State Formation as Cultural Revolution* (Oxford: Blackwell, 1985), p. 187.

15 Steven Spitzer, 'The rationalization of crime control in capitalist society', in Stanley Cohen and Andrew Scull (eds), *Social Control and the State: Historical and Comparative Essays* (Oxford: M. Robertson, 1983), pp. 312–33.

16 A. P. Donajgrodzki, 'Introduction', in A. P. Donajgrodzki (ed.), *Social Control in Nineteenth Century Britain* (London: Croom Helm, 1977), pp. 9–26.

17 Giddens, *A Contemporary Critique*, p. 169; Dandeker, *Surveillance, Power and Modernity*, p. 37.

18 Giddens, *The Nation-State*, pp. 47, 179–86.

19 Dandeker, *Surveillance, Power and Modernity*, pp. 37, 42.

20 Rule, *Private Lives*, pp. 20–4.

21 Giddens, *A Contemporary Critique*, pp. 209–20; Dandeker, *Surveillance, Power and Modernity*, pp. 5–6; Michael Mann, *The Sources of Social Power*, vol. II: *The Rise of Classes and Nation-States* (Cambridge: Cambridge University Press, 1993), pp. 45–88.

22 Dandeker, *Surveillance, Power and Modernity*, pp. 66–101.

23 Theda Skocpol, *States and Social Revolutions: A Comparative Analysis of France, Russia and China* (Cambridge: Cambridge University Press, 1979), pp. 22–8.

24 Giddens, *A Contemporary Critique*, pp. 174–5; Rule, *Private Lives*, p. 19.

25 Dandeker, *Surveillance, Power and Modernity*, pp. 12, 24–7; Michael Foucault, *Discipline and Punish: The Birth of the Prison* (London: Allen Lane, 1977).

26 Dandeker, *Surveillance, Power and Modernity*, pp. 12, 24–7; Rule, *Private Lives*, pp. 13–14.

27 F. M. L. Thompson, 'Social control in Victorian Britain', *Economic History Review, Second Series* XXXIV (1981), pp. 189–208; Martin J. Wiener's review of A. P. Donajgrodzki (ed.), *Social Control in*

Nineteenth Century Britain in *The Journal of Social History* 12 (1978), pp. 314–20. See also, John A. Mayer, 'Notes towards a working definition of social control in historical analysis', in Stanley Cohen and Andrew Scull (eds), *Social Control and the State: Historical and Comparative Essays* (Oxford: M. Robertson, 1983), pp. 17–38. For an effective debunking of the vague notion of social control as ideological control see Gareth Stedman Jones, 'Class expression versus social control? A critique of recent trends in the social history of "leisure"', *History Workshop Journal* 4 (1977), pp. 162–70.

28 Caplan and Torpey, 'Introduction', pp. 1–12.
29 Giddens, *The Nation-State*, pp. 200–6.
30 This has been noted by David Lyon: Lyon, *The Electronic Eye*, p. 36.
31 T. H. Marshall, 'Citizenship and social class', in Bryan S. Turner and Peter Hamilton (eds), *Citizenship: Critical Concepts,* vol. II (London: Routledge, 1994), pp. 5–44.
32 Giddens, *The Nation-State*, p. 309.
33 Mann, *The Sources of Social Power*, vol. II, pp. 82–8.
34 Charles Taylor, *Sources of the Self: The Making of Modern Identity* (Cambridge: Cambridge University Press, 1989).
35 Rule, *Private Lives*, pp. 123, 274–338; Giddens, *The Nation-State*, p. 309; Anthony Giddens, *The Consequences of Modernity* (Cambridge: Polity Press, 1991), pp. 167–8.
36 Rule, *Private Lives*, p. 340.
37 Dandeker, *Surveillance, Power and Modernity*, pp. 202–3.
38 Anthony Giddens, *The Third Way: The Renewal of Social Democracy* (Cambridge: Polity Press, 1998), pp. 47, 71.
39 Benedict Anderson, *Imagined Communities: Reflections on the Origin and Spread of Nationalism* (London: Verso, 1983).
40 Philip Kreager, 'Quand une population est-elle un nation? Quand une nation est-elle un état? La démographie et l'emergence d'un dilemme moderne, 1770–1870', *Population*, 6 (1992), pp. 1639–56.
41 Ibid., *passim*; Nico Randeraad, 'Nineteenth-century population registers as statistical source and instrument of social control (Belgium, Italy and the Netherlands)', *Tijdschrift voor sociale geschiedenis* 21 (1995), pp. 319–42.
42 Foucault, 'The subject and power', pp. 208–26; Foucault, 'Governmentality', pp. 87–104.
43 Bruce Curtis, *The Politics of Population: State Formation, Statistics and the Census of Canada, 1840–1875* (Toronto: University of Toronto Press, 2001), p. 26.
44 Jean-Claude Perrot and Stuart J. Woolf, *State and Statistics in France, 1789–1815* (New York: Harwood Academic Publishers, 1984), p. 89. See also, Alain Desrosières, *La politique des grands*

nombres: histoire de la raison statistique (Paris: Éditions la Découverte, 1993), pp. 47–8.

45 Ignace Th. M. Snellen, 'From societal scanning to policy feedback: two hundred years of government information processing in the Netherlands', *Yearbook of European Administrative History 9* (Baden-Baden: Nomos Verlagsgesellschaft, 1997), pp. 198–9.

46 Silvana Patriarca, *Numbers and Nationhood: Writing Statistics in Nineteenth-century Italy* (Cambridge: Cambridge University Press, 1996).

47 Michael Ignatieff, *A Just Measure of Pain: The Penitentiary in the Industrial Revolution, 1750–1850* (London: Macmillan, 1978), p. 29.

48 Frank Webster, *Theories of the Information Society* (London: Routledge, 1995), pp. 55–7.

49 Dandeker, *Surveillance, Power and Modernity*, pp. 110–17; Rule, *Private Lives*, pp. 27–8.

50 Ferdinand Tönnies, *Community and Civil Society (Gemeinschaft und Gesellschaft)* (Cambridge: Cambridge University Press, 2001).

51 For a critique of such utopianism, see Stanley Cohen, *Visions of Social Control: Crime, Punishment and Classification* (Cambridge: Polity Press, 1985), p. 118.

52 José Harris, 'General introduction', in Ferdinand Tönnies, *Community and Civil Society (Gemeinschaft und Gesellschaft)* (Cambridge: Cambridge University Press, 2001), pp. ix–xl.

53 Michael Ignatieff, 'State, civil society and total institutions: a critique of recent social histories of punishment', in Stanley Cohen and Andrew Scull (eds), *Social Control and the State: Historical and Comparative Essays* (Oxford: M. Robertson, 1983), p. 98.

54 Giddens, *The Third Way*, pp. 86–7.

55 Giddens, *The Nation-State, passim*; Rule, *Private Lives*, pp. 21–8.

56 See also Mann, *States, War and Capitalism*, pp. 4, 74.

57 Giddens, *The Nation-State*, pp. 61–171.

58 Dandeker, *Surveillance, Power and Modernity*, pp. 45–9.

59 Giddens, *The Nation-State*, pp. 82–5.

60 Dandeker, *Surveillance, Power and Modernity*, pp. 55–6; Rule, *Private Lives*, p. 25.

61 Dandeker, *Surveillance, Power and Modernity*, p. 121.

62 Mann, *The Sources of Social Power*, vol. II, pp. 96–7, 112, 268; Mann, *States, War and Capitalism*, pp. 85–6, 140, 392.

63 J. A. Hall, 'Capstones and organisms: political forms and the triumph of capitalism', *Sociology* 19 (1985), pp. 173–92; John A. Hall, *Powers and Liberties: The Causes and Consequences of the Rise of the West* (Oxford: Basil Blackwell, 1985).

64 Niklas Luhmann, *Social Systems* (Stanford, CA: Stanford University Press, 1995), pp. 462–3.

3 State information gathering in early modern England

1 Alan Macfarlane, *Reconstructing Historical Communities* (Cambridge: Cambridge University Press, 1977), p. 1; Alan Macfarlane, *The Origins of English Individualism* (Oxford: Blackwell, 1978), p. 5. See also, Keith Wrightson, 'The politics of the parish', in P. Griffiths, Adam Fox and Steve Hindle (eds), *The Experience of Authority in Early Modern England* (Basingstoke: Palgrave Macmillan, 1996), pp. 10–46.
2 Macfarlane, *The Origins of English Individualism*, pp. 82–3.
3 Ibid., pp. 68, 148–9.
4 E. A. Wrigley and R. S. Schofield, *The Population History of England, 1541–1871* (London: Edward Arnold, 1981), pp. 207–9.
5 Steve Hindle, *The State and Social Change in Early Modern England, c.1550–1640* (Basingstoke: Palgrave Macmillan, 2000), pp. 39–40.
6 Keith Wrightson, *English Society, 1580–1680* (London: Hutchinson, 1982), p. 42.
7 Macfarlane, *Reconstructing Historical Communities*, p. 9.
8 Hindle, *The State and Social Change*, pp. 41–8, 51.
9 Wrightson, *English Society*, pp. 24, 65.
10 Keith Wrightson, 'The social order of early modern England: Three approaches', in Lloyd Bonfield, Richard M. Smith and Keith Wrightson (eds), *The World We have Gained: Histories of Population and Social Structure. Essays Presented to Peter Laslett on His Seventieth Birthday* (Oxford: Blackwell, 1986), p. 191.
11 Wrightson, *English Society*, pp. 170, 181, 227; J. A. Sharpe, *Crime in Early Modern England, 1550–1750* (London: Longman, 1984), pp. 75–6.
12 Paul Slack, *Poverty and Policy in Tudor and Stuart England* (London: Longman, 1988), p. 26.
13 F. M. Stenton, *Anglo Saxon England* (Oxford: Oxford University Press, 1971), pp. 644–8.
14 Slack, *Poverty and Policy, passim.*
15 David Crook, *Records of the General Eyre* (London: HMSO, 1982), p. 2.
16 David Eastwood, *Government and Community in the English Provinces, 1700–1870* (London: Macmillan Press, 1997), p. 10; Gerald Harriss, 'Political society and the growth of government in late medieval England', *Past and Present* 138 (1993), pp. 28–57.
17 G. R. Elton, *Policy and Police: The Enforcement of the Reformation in the Age of Thomas Cromwell* (Cambridge: Cambridge University Press, 1972), pp. 259–60.
18 Public Record Office, *Guide to the Contents of the Public Record Office*, vol. 1: *Legal Records, etc.* (London: HMSO, 1963), pp. 135–6.

19 Michael Clanchy, *From Memory to Written Record: England, 1066–1307* (London: Edward Arnold, 1979), p. 33.
20 Michael J. Braddick, *State Formation in Early Modern England, c.1550–1700* (Cambridge: Cambridge University Press, 2000), pp. 11–18.
21 Niklas Luhmann, *Social Systems* (Stanford, CA: Stanford University Press, 1995), pp. 20–3.
22 Hindle, *The State and Social Change*, pp. 20–3. For similar arguments see: M. J. Braddick, 'State formation and social change in early modern England: a problem stated and approaches suggested', *Social History* 16 (1991), pp. 1–17; M. J. Braddick, *Parliamentary Taxation in Seventeenth-century England: Local Administration and Response* (Woodbridge: Boydell Press, 1994), p. 17; Paul Griffiths, Adam Fox and Steve Hindle, 'Introduction', in Paul Griffiths, Adam Fox and Steve Hindle (eds), *The Experience of Authority in Early Modern England* (Basingstoke: Palgrave Macmillan, 1996), pp. 2, 5.
23 Braddick, *State Formation*, pp. 24–46, 90.
24 Mark Goldie, 'The unacknowledged republic: officeholding in early modern England', in Tim Harris (ed.), *The Politics of the Excluded, c.1500–1850* (Basingstoke: Palgrave Macmillan, 2001), p. 154. For a general discussion of the nature of the pre-modern state, see Discussion Group on the State, 'When and what was the State? St Peter's Oxford, 29–31 March, 2001', *Journal of Historical Sociology* 15(1) (March 2002), pp. 59–165.
25 H. R. French, 'Social status, localism and the "middle sort of people" in England, 1620–1750', *Past and Present* 166 (2000), pp. 66–99.
26 A. J. Musson, 'Sub-keepers and constables: the role of local officers in keeping the peace in fourteenth-century England', *English Historical Review* CXVII, 470 (2002), pp. 1–24.
27 Braddick, *State Formation*, pp. 17–18.
28 Anthony Fletcher, *Reform in the Provinces: The Government of Stuart England* (London: Yale University Press, 1986), pp. 24–5.
29 J. A. Hall, 'Capstones and organisms: political forms and the triumph of capitalism', *Sociology*, 19 (1985) pp. 173–92; R. M. Smith, ' "Modernisation" and the corporate medieval community in England: some sceptical reflections', in A. H. R. Baker and D. Gregory (eds), *Explorations in Historical Geography* (Cambridge: Cambridge University Press, 1984), pp. 140–79.
30 Michel Rouche, 'Autopsy of the West: the early fifth century', in Robert Fossier (ed.), *The Cambridge Illustrated History of the Middle Ages, 350–950* (Cambridge: Cambridge University Press, 1997), pp. 17–51.
31 John King Fairbank, *China: A New History* (London: Harvard University Press, 1992), p. 428.

32 Harriss, 'Political society', p. 56.

33 Wrightson, *English Society*, p. 26.

34 Martin Daunton, 'Introduction', in Martin Daunton (ed.), *Charity, Self-interest and Welfare in the English Past* (London: UCL Press, 1996), pp. 5–6.

35 Marjorie Keniston McIntosh, *Controlling Misbehaviour in England, 1370–1600* (Cambridge: Cambridge University Press, 1998).

36 Ibid., p. 83.

37 Steve Hindle, 'The keeping of the public peace', in Paul Griffiths, Adam Fox and Steve Hindle (eds), *The Experience of Authority in Early Modern England* (Basingstoke: Palgrave Macmillan, 1996), pp. 213–48; Braddick, 'State formation and social change in early modern England', p. 7; Joan R. Kent, 'The centre and the localities: state formation and parish government in England, circa 1640–1740', *Historical Journal* 38 (1995), pp. 391–401.

38 John Brewer, *The Sinews of Power: War, Money and the English State, 1688–1783* (London: Unwin Hyman, 1989), p. 89; Patrick K. O'Brien, 'The political economy of British taxation, 1660–1815', *Economic History Review*, 2nd sev., XLI (1988), pp. 1–32.

39 Alexis de Tocqueville, *The Old Regime and the French Revolution* (New York: Doubleday, 1955), p. 98.

40 W. E. Tate, *The Parish Chest: A Study of the Records of Parochial Administration in England* (Cambridge: Cambridge University Press, 1951).

41 Goldie, 'The unacknowledged republic', pp. 160–3.

42 Kent, 'The centre and the localities', pp. 376–91.

43 Hindle, *The State and Social Change*, p. 10.

44 Wrightson, *English Society*, p. 152.

45 Keith Wrightson, 'Two concepts of order: justices, constables and jurymen in seventeenth-century England', in John Brewer and John Styles (eds), *An Ungovernable People: The English and Their Law in the Seventeenth and Eighteenth Centuries* (London: Hutchinson, 1980), pp. 21–46; Fletcher, *Reform in the Provinces*, pp. 43–62; Goldie, 'The unacknowledged republic', p. 166; David Eastwood, *Governing Rural England: Tradition and Transformation in Local Government, 1780–1840* (Oxford: Oxford University Press, 1994), p. 50.

46 Sharpe, *Crime in Early Modern England*, p. 21.

47 Hindle, *The State and Social Change*, p. 85.

48 Martin Ingram, *Church Courts, Sex and Marriages in England, 1570–1640* (Cambridge: Cambridge University Press, 1990), pp. 2–3.

49 Braddick, *State Formation*, pp. 291–333.

50 Ibid., pp. 44–5; Johann P. Somerville, *Thomas Hobbes: Political Ideas in Historical Context* (Basingstoke: Palgrave Macmillan, 1992), p. 120.

51 Ingram, *Church Courts*, pp. 2–3.
52 Ralph A. Houlbrooke, *Church Courts and the People During the English Reformation, 1520–1570* (Oxford: Oxford University Press, 1979), p. 46.
53 Ibid., pp. 44, 47; Ingram, *Church Courts*, p. 367.
54 Quoted in Elton, *Policy and Police*, pp. 259–60.
55 Christopher Hill, *Liberty against the Law: Some Seventeenth-century Controversies* (London: Allen Lane, 1996), p. 202.
56 Sharpe, *Crime in Early Modern England*, p. 28.
57 Houlbrooke, *Church Courts*, p. 77.
58 Arthur Warne, *Church and Society in Eighteenth-century Devon* (Newton Abbot: David & Charles, 1969), p. 84.
59 Goldie, 'The unacknowledged republic', pp. 153–94.
60 Slack, *Poverty and Policy*, p. 26.
61 K. D. M. Snell, *Annals of the Labouring Poor: Social Change and Agrarian England, 1660–1900* (Cambridge: Cambridge University Press, 1987), pp. 104–37.
62 Ibid., pp. 65–75, 180.
63 N. Landau, 'Laws of settlement and surveillance of immigration in eighteenth-century Kent', *Continuity and Change* 3 (1988), pp. 391–420. But for a contrary view see, K. D. M. Snell, 'Pauper settlement and the right to relief in England and Wales', *Continuity and Change* 6 (1991), pp. 375–415.
64 Slack, *Poverty and Policy*, pp. 92, 118–25.
65 Ibid., p. 118.
66 David Hey, *The Oxford Companion to Local and Family History* (Oxford: Oxford University Press, 1998), p. 32.
67 Slack, *Poverty and Policy*, pp. 97, 118.
68 Pat Thane, 'Old people and their families in the English past', in Martin Daunton (ed.), *Charity, Self-interest and Welfare in the English Past* (London: UCL Press, 1996), p. 120.
69 Slack, *Poverty and Policy*, p. 84.
70 Quoted in Roger Lonsdale (ed.), *Eighteenth Century Verse* (Oxford: Oxford University Press, 1987), p. 63.
71 Michael Mann, *States, War and Capitalism: Studies in Political Sociology* (Oxford: Blackwell, 1988), pp. xi, 73–123.
72 Ibid., pp. 112–13.
73 N. A. M. Rodger, *The Wooden World: An Anatomy of the Georgian Navy* (London: Collins, 1986), pp. 256–8.
74 Carola Oman, *Nelson* (London: Hodder and Stroughton, 1967), pp. 546–50.
75 Roy Douglas, *Taxation in Britain since 1660* (Basingstoke: Palgrave Macmillan, 1999), pp. 2–3.
76 Brewer, *The Sinews of Power*, pp. 155–6.

77 Ibid., p. 42.
78 Philp Harling, *The Modern British State: An Historical Introduction* (Cambridge: Polity, 2001), p. 42.
79 M. J. Braddick, *The Nerves of State: Taxation and the Finance of the English State, 1558–1714* (Manchester: Manchester University Press, 1996), p. 191.
80 Brewer, *The Sinews of Power*, pp. 31–2.
81 Harling, *The Modern British State*, p. 21.
82 M. Jurkowski, C. Smith and D. Crook, *Lay Taxes in England and Wales, 1188–1688* (London: Public Record Office, 1998).
83 M. W. Beresford, 'The poll taxes of 1377, 1379 and 1381', *The Amateur Historian* 3 (1958), pp. 271–78.
84 W. R. Ward, *The English Land Tax in the Eighteenth Century* (Oxford: Oxford University Press, 1953), pp. 4–5.
85 Ibid.
86 Ibid., pp. 10–11.
87 Braddick, *The Nerves of State*, pp. 92–3; Braddick, *Parliamentary Taxation*, p. 31.
88 Ward, *The English Land Tax*, p. 37; Braddick, *The Nerves of State*, pp. 166–7; Braddick, *Parliamentary Taxation*, p. 281.
89 Ward, *The English Land Tax*, p. 35; Braddick, *The Nerves of State*, p. 97; Braddick, *Parliamentary Taxation*, p. 290.
90 Brewer, *The Sinews of Power*, pp. 101–2.
91 Public Record Office, *Guide to the Contents of the Public Record Office*, vol. 1, pp. 27–8.
92 David Ogg, *England in the Reign of Charles II* (Oxford: Oxford University Press, 1934), pp. 159–61.
93 Public Record Office, Military Records Information 2, Public Record Office website, http://www.pro.gov.uk/leaflets/ri2002.htm (July 2001).
94 Braddick, *State Formation*, pp. 181–96.
95 Ibid., pp. 202–26.
96 N. A. M. Rodger, *The Admiralty* (Lavenham: Terence Dalton, 1979), p. 117; N. A. M. Rodger, *The Wooden World An Anatomy of the Georgian Navy* (London: Fontana, 1988), p. 147.
97 Rodger, *The Wooden World*, pp. 164–82.
98 Ibid., pp. 124–37; N. A. M. Rodger, *Naval Records for Genealogists* (London: PRO Publications, 1988), p. 45.
99 Public Record Office, *Guide to the Contents of the Public Record Office*, vol. II: *State Papers and Departmental Records.* (London: HMSO, 1963), p. 18.
100 Rodger, *Naval Records for Genealogists*, p. 33.
101 P. G. Parkhurst, *Ships of Peace* (New Malden: P. G. Parkhurst, 1962), p. 173.

102 Ibid., p. 174.
103 Public Record Office, *Current Guide* (London: Public Record Office, n.d.), section 703/6/5.
104 Ibid.; Public Record Office, *Current Guide*, section 606/1/1.
105 Public Record Office, *Guide to the Contents of the Public Record Office*, vol. II, pp. 308–13; Simon Fowler and William Spencer, *Army Records for Family Historians* (London: PRO Publications, 1998), pp. 38–9.
106 Curtis C. Breight, *Surveillance, Militarism and Drama in the Elizabethan Era* (London: Macmillan, 1996), pp. 47–52.
107 Richard Deacon, *British Secret Service* (London: Grafton, 1991), pp. 67–76.
108 E. P. Thompson, *The Making of the English Working Class* (Harmondsworth: Penguin Books, 1968), pp. 532–3.
109 Public Record Office, *Guide to the Contents of the Public Record Office*, vol. II, pp. 1–3.
110 Wallace MacCaffrey, *Elizabeth I* (London: Edward Arnold, 1993), pp. 376–7.
111 See, for example, Mann, *States, War and Capitalism*, p. 74.
112 Quoted in Norbert Elias, *The Civilizing Process* (Oxford: Basil Blackwell, 2000), p. 341.
113 Ibid.
114 David Martin Jones, *Conscience and Allegiance in Seventeenth-century England: The Political Significance of Oaths and Engagements* (New York: University of Rochester Press, 1999).
115 Public Record Office, *Guide to the Contents of the Public Record Office*, vol. I, p. 39.
116 Ibid.
117 Elton, *Policy and Police*, pp. 259–60: M. L. Bush, *The Government Policy of Protector Somerset* (London: Edward Arnold, 1975), pp. 40–83.
118 Matthew Woollard, 'The natural philosophers' (paper in the author's possession, [2000]), pp. 1–10.
119 Joan Thirsk and J. P. Cooper, *Seventeenth Century Economic Documents* (Oxford: Oxford University Press, 1972), pp. 770–90, 798–811.
120 D. V. Glass, 'Two papers on Gregory King', in D. V. Glass and D. E. C. Eversley (eds), *Population in History: Essays in Historical Demography* (London: Edward Arnold, 1965), pp. 159–220.
121 Peter Laslett, 'Gregory King, Thomas Malthus and the origins of English social realism', *Population Studies* 39 (1985), pp. 351–62; Peter Laslett, 'Natural and political observations on the population of the late seventeenth-century England: reflections on the work of Gregory King and John Graunt', in Kevin Schürer and Tom Arkell

(eds), *Surveying the People: The Interpretation and Use of Document Sources for the Study of Population in the Later Seventeenth Century* (Oxford: Leopard's Head Press, 1992), pp. 6–30.

122 G. S. Holmes, 'Gregory King and the social structure of pre-industrial England', *Transactions of the Royal Historical Society* Fifth series, 27 (1977), pp. 41–68.

123 Glass, 'Two papers on Gregory King', p. 165.

124 PRO: Board of Inland Revenue: Statistics and Intelligence Division: Correspondence and Papers [IR 64]: IR 64/532 Notes on the development of the Inland Revenue statistics.

125 The subsequent section is based on material to be found in the Records of Earls Colne website: http://linux02.lib.cam.ac.uk/earlsecolne/.

126 For an attempt to use similar material to reconstruct some aspects of a past community, see: Keith Wrightson and David Levine, *Poverty and Piety in an English Village, Terling, 1525–1700* (London: Academic Press, 1979).

127 Bruce Curtis, *The Politics of Population: State Formation, Statistics and the Census of Canada, 1840–1875* (Toronto: University of Toronto Press, 2001), p. 44.

4 State information gathering in the classic Liberal State

1 A. V. Dicey, *Lectures on the Relation between Law and Public Opinion in England during the Nineteenth Century* (London: Macmillan, 1905).

2 Pat Thane, 'Government and society in England and Wales, 1750–1914', in F. M. L. Thompson (ed.), *The Cambridge Social History of Britain, 1750–1950*, vol. 3: *Social Agencies and Institutions* (Cambridge: Cambridge University Press, 1990), p. 11; Philip Harling, 'The politics of administrative change in Britain, 1780–1850', *Yearbook of European Administrative History 8* (Baden-Baden: Nomos Verlagsgesellschaft, 1996), pp. 191–212.

3 Michael Mann, *The Sources of Social Power*, vol. II: *The Rise of Classes and Nation-States* (Cambridge: Cambridge University Press, 1993), pp. 366–7.

4 Chris Cook and Brendan Keith, *British Historical Facts, 1830–1900* (New York: St Martin's Press, 1975), p. 150.

5 Philip Corrigan and Derek Sayer, *The Great Arch: English State Formation as Cultural Revolution* (Oxford: Blackwell, 1985), pp. 125–35.

6 Philip Harling, *The Modern British State: An Historical Introduction* (Cambridge: Polity Press, 2001), pp. 88–111.

7 Theda Skocpol and Dietrich Rueschemeyer, 'Introduction', in Dietrich Rueschemeyer and Theda Skocpol (eds), *States, Social Knowledge, and the Origins of Modern Social Policy* (Princeton, NJ: Princeton University Press, 1996), pp. 5–6.

8 Harold Perkin, *The Rise of Professional Society: England since 1880* (London: Routledge, 1989). For the powerful role of the professions in the early nineteenth century, see Penelope J. Corfield, *Power and the Professions in Britain, 1700–1850* (London: Routledge, 1995).

9 Harling, *The Modern British State*, pp. 78–87.

10 Oliver MacDonagh, 'The nineteenth-century revolution in government: a reappraisal', *The Historical Journal* I (1958), pp. 52–67; Oliver MacDonagh, *A Pattern of Government Growth: The Passenger Acts and Their Enforcement, 1800–1860* (London: MacGibbon and Kee, 1961); Oliver MacDonagh, *Early Victorian Government, 1830–1870* (London Weidenfeld and Nicolson, 1977).

11 E. P. Hennock, *Fit and Proper Persons: Ideal and Reality in Nineteenth-century Urban Government* (London: Edward Arnold, 1973).

12 K. Theodore Hoppen, *The Mid-Victorian Generation, 1846–1886* (Oxford: Oxford University Press, 1998), p. 123.

13 See, for example: R. J. Morris, *Class, Sect and Party: The Making of the British Middle Class: Leeds, 1820–1850* (Manchester: Manchester University Press, 1990); Patrick Joyce, *Visions of the People: Industrial England and the Question of Class, 1840–1914* (Cambridge: Cambridge University Press, 1991).

14 Michael Anderson, *Family Structure in Nineteenth Century Lancashire* (Cambridge: Cambridge University Press, 1971).

15 John Foster, *Class Struggle and the Industrial Revolution: Early Industrial Capitalism in Three English Towns* (London: Methuen, 1974).

16 S. E. Finer, *The Life and Times of Sir Edwin Chadwick* (London: Methuen, 1952), pp. 453–74; Anthony Brundage, *England's 'Prussian Minister': Edwin Chadwick and the Politics of Government Growth, 1832–1854* (University Park, PA: Pennsylvania State University Press, 1988), pp. 133–56.

17 Christine Bellamy, *Administering Central–Local Relations, 1871–1919: The Local Government Board in its Fiscal and Cultural Context* (Manchester: Manchester University Press, 1988); Alan Kidd, 'The 'Liberal State' civil society and social welfare in nineteenth-century England', *Historical Sociology* 15 (2002), pp. 114–19.

18 Alexis de Tocqueville, *Journeys to England and Ireland* (London: Faber and Faber, 1958), pp. 61–2.

19 David Eastwood, '"Amplifying the province of the Legislature": The flow of information and the English state in the early nineteenth century', *Historical Research* LXII (1989), pp. 276–94.

20 John Stuart Mill, 'Considerations on representative government', in *Utilitarianism, On Liberty, Considerations on Representative Government* (London: J. M. Dent, 1993), pp. 388–9.

21 Brian Harrison, *The Transformation of British Politics, 1860–1995* (Oxford: Oxford University Press, 1996), p. 310.

22 Eugenio F. Biagini, 'Liberalism and direct democracy: John Stuart Mill and the model of ancient Athens', in Eugenio F. Biagini (ed.), *Citizenship and Community: Liberals, Radicals and Collective Identities in the British Isles, 1865–1931* (Cambridge: Cambridge University Press, 1996), pp. 21–44.

23 Philip Harling, 'The power of persuasion: central authority, local bureaucracy and the New Poor Law', *English Historical Review* 107 (1992), pp. 30–53.

24 Philip Abrams, *The Origins of British Sociology: 1834–1914* (Chicago, IL: University of Chicago, 1968), pp. 37–8; Thane, 'Government and society', p. 17; Martin J. Wiener, *Reconstructing the Criminal: Culture, Law and Policing in England, 1830–1914* (Cambridge: Cambridge University Press, 1990), pp. 14–156; Harrison, *The Transformation of British Politics*, pp. 74–5; Alan Kidd, *State, Society and the Poor in Nineteenth-century England* (Basingstoke: Palgrave Macmillan, 1999), p. 4.

25 Edwin Chadwick, *Report on the Sanitary Condition of the Labouring Population of Gt. Britain* (Edinburgh: Edinburgh University Press, 1965) pp. 198–9. See also, Anna La Berge, 'Edwin Chadwick and the French connection', *Bulletin of the History of Medicine* 62 (1988), pp. 23–41.

26 Clive Emsley, *The English Police: A Political and Social History* (Hemel Hempstead: Harvester Wheatsheaf, 1991), pp. 49–68; Wiener, *Reconstructing the Criminal*, pp. 101–22.

27 Corrigan and Sayer, *The Great Arch*, pp. 116–28.

28 E. A. Wrigley and R. S. Schofield, *The Population History of England, 1541–1871* (London: Edward Arnold, 1981), pp. 402–53.

29 E. Hopkins, *Working-class Self Help in Nineteenth Century England: Responses to Industrialisation* (London: University College London Press, 1995); George Finlayson, *Citizen, State and Social Welfare in Britain, 1830–1990* (Oxford: Oxford University Press, 1994), pp. 24–34.

30 Kidd, *State, Society and the Poor*, p. 169.

31 Edward Higgs, *Making Sense of the Census: The Manuscript Returns for England and Wales, 1801–1901* (London: HMSO, 1989), pp. 4–7.

32 Ibid.
33 Daniel Headrick, *When Information Came of Age: Technologies of Knowledge in the Age of Reason and Revolution, 1700–1850* (New York: Oxford University Press, 2000), pp. 66–8.
34 D. V. Glass, *Numbering the People* (London: Gordon and Cremonesi, 1978), pp. 11–89.
35 William Cobbett, *Rural Rides* (Harmondsworth: Penguin, 1983), p. 81.
36 Higgs, *Making Sense*, p. 7.
37 Michael J. Cullen, *The Statistical Movement in Early Victorian Britain* (Hassocks: Harvester Press, 1975).
38 Higgs, *Making Sense*, pp. 5–7.
39 Ibid., pp. 7–10.
40 PRO: GRO: Census Returns: Specimens of Forms and Documents (RG 27): RG 27/1 History of the Census of 1841, p. 5.
41 Nico Randeraad, 'Nineteenth-century population registers as statistical source and instrument of social control (Belgium, Italy and the Netherlands)', *Tijdschrift voor sociale geschiedenis* 21 (1995), pp. 319–42.
42 Higgs, *Making Sense*, pp. 19–20.
43 Edward Higgs, *A Clearer Sense of the Census: The Victorian Censuses and Historical Research* (London: HMSO, 1996), pp. 155–6.
44 PRO: GRO: Letter Books (RG 29): RG 29/1, p. 311.
45 PRO: RG 29/2, p 129; *Report of the Treasury Committee on the Census*, PP 1890 LVIII, QQ 2265–6, 2480–2; Greater London Record Office: London School Board Statistical Committee (SBL 908): SBL 908/Minutes of 3 April 1871, 15 May 1871 and 6 July 1871.
46 Muriel Nissel, *People Count: A History of the General Register Office* (London: HMSO, 1996), pp. 12–24.
47 Paul Johnson, 'The role of the State in twentieth-century Britain', in Paul Johnson (ed.), *Twentieth-century Britain: Economic, Social and Cultural Change* (Harlow: Longman, 1994), pp. 482–3.
48 E.g. 1891 Factory and Workshop Act (54 & 55 Vict., c. 75), s. 20; 1901 Factory and Workshop Act (1 Edw 7, c. 22), s. 134.
49 J. S. Hurt, *Elementary Schooling and the Working Classes, 1860–1918* (London: Routledge and Kegan Paul, 1979), pp. 155–213; Anna Davin, 'Working or helping? London working-class children in the domestic economy', in J. Smith, I. Wallerstein and H. Evers (eds), *Households and the World Economy* (London: Sage 1984), pp. 215–32; Pamela Horn, 'Child workers in the Victorian countryside: the case of Northamptonshire', *Northamptonshire Past and Present* VII (1985–6), p. 177; Anna Davin, *Growing up Poor: Home, School and Street in London, 1870–1914* (London: Rivers Oram Press, 1996), pp. 84–153.

50 Ursula R. Q. Henriques, *The Early Factory Acts and Their Enforcement* (London: Historical Association, 1971), pp. 12–15.

51 Albert Fried and Richard M. Elman, *Charles Booth's London: A Portrait of the Poor at the Turn of the Century* (London: Hutchinson, 1969), pp. 3–4.

52 R. M. MacLeod, 'Law, medicine and public opinion: the resistance to compulsory health legislation, 1870–1907. Part I and II', *Public Law* (1967), pp. 107–28, 189–211; Naomi Williams, 'The implementation of compulsory health legislation: infant smallpox vaccination in England and Wales, 1840–1890', *Journal of Historical Geography* 20 (1994), pp. 396–412: Nadja Durbach, '"They might as well brand us": working-class resistance to compulsory vaccination in Victorian England', *Social History of Medicine* 13 (2000), pp. 45–62.

53 J. Walkowitz, *Prostitution and Victorian Society: Women, Class and State* (Cambridge: Cambridge University Press, 1980); Paul McHugh, *Prostitution and Victorian Social Reform* (London: Croom Helm, 1980); Frank Mort, *Dangerous Sexualities: Medico-moral Politics in England since 1830* (London: Routledge and Kegan Paul, 1987); Patrick Joyce, *Visions of the People: Industrial England and the Question of Class, 1848–1914* (Cambridge: Cambridge University Press, 1991), pp. 70–2.

54 Glass, *Numbering the People*, p. 181; Anne Hardy, '"Death is the cure of all diseases": using the General Register Office cause of death statistics for 1837–1920', *Social History of Medicine* 7 (1994), pp. 474–5; *Second Report of the Royal Sanitary Commission*, vol. 1, PP 1871 XXXV, p. 58.

55 *Hansard*, 3rd series, vol. CCXIX, cols. 275, 281–2.

56 R. J. Lambert, 'A Victorian National Health Service: state vaccination, 1855–1871', *The Historical Journal* V (1962), pp. 1–18.

57 E. P. Hennock, 'Vaccination policy against smallpox, 1835–1914: a comparison of England with Prussia and Imperial Germany', *Social History of Medicine* 11 (1998), pp. 60–5.

58 F. B. Smith, 'The Contagious Diseases Acts reconsidered', *Social History of Medicine* 3 (1990), 197–217.

59 Michael J. Cullen, 'The making of the Civil Registration Act of 1836', *Journal of Ecclesiastical History* 25 (1974), pp. 39–59.

60 Edward Higgs, 'A cuckoo in the nest? The origins of civil registration and state medical statistics in England and Wales', *Continuity and Change* 11 (1996), pp. 115–20.

61 Ibid., pp. 120–1.

62 Michael Drake, *Population and Society in Norway, 1735–1865* (Cambridge: Cambridge University Press, 1969), pp. 1–18.

63 General Register Office, *22nd Annual Report of the Registrar General of Births, Marriages and Deaths for England and Wales* [hereafter ARRG] *for 1859* (London: HMSO, 1861), pp. xliv–xlv.

64 Gerald J. Postema, *Bentham and the Common Law Tradition* (Oxford: Oxford University Press, 1986).

65 John Stuart Mill, 'Bentham', in John Stuart Mill and Jeremy Bentham, *Utilitarianism and Other Essays* (London: Penguin, 1987), pp. 158–61.

66 A. H. Manchester, *A Modern Legal History of England and Wales, 1750–1950* (London: Butterworths, 1980); Sir William Holdsworth, *A History of English Law*, vol. 13 (London: Sweet and Maxwell, 1952), pp. 1–307; Robert Mackenzie Stewart, *Henry Brougham, 1778–1868: His Public Career* (London: Bodley Head, 1986).

67 *Hansard*, 3rd series, vol. 31, 12 February 1836, col. 371.

68 Glass, *Numbering the People*, pp. 181–4.

69 Jürgen Habermas, *The Structural Transformation of the Public Sphere: An Inquiry into a Category of Bourgeois Society* (Cambridge: Polity Press, 1992).

70 *General Report of the Commissioners on the Public Records*, PP 1837 XXXIV Pt 1, p. 10.

71 Public Record Office, *Current Guide*, section 125; Public Record Office, *Guide to the Contents of the Public Record Office*, vol. 1, p. 2; Aidan Lawes, *Chancery Lane, 1377–1977: The Strong Box of the Empire* (Kew: PRO Publications, 1996), pp. 21–2.

72 Public Record Office, *Current Guide*, section 602; *British Imperial Calendar for 1877* (London: HMSO, 1877), p. 283.

73 *British Imperial Calendar for 1863* (London: HMSO, 1863), p. 279.

74 Public Record Office, *Current Guide*, section 602; *British Imperial Calendar for 1876* (London: HMSO, 1876), p. 283.

75 Public Record Office, *Current Guide*, section 347.

76 *British Imperial Calendar for 1875* (London: HMSO, 1875), p. 286.

77 Gerard Noiriel, 'The identification of the citizen: the birth of republican civil status in France', in Jane Caplan and John Torpey (eds), *Documenting Individual Identity: The Development of State Practices in the Modern World* (Princeton, NJ: Princeton University Press, 2001), pp. 28–48.

78 Jane Caplan, ' "This or that person": protocols of identification in nineteenth-century Europe', in Jane Caplan and John Torpey (eds), *Documenting Individual Identity: The Development of State Practices in the Modern World* (Princeton, NJ: Princeton University Press, 2001), pp. 49–66.

79 Ivan Waddington, *The Medical Profession in the Industrial Revolution* (Dublin: Gill and Macmillan, 1984), pp. 96–152.

80 Irvine Loudon, *Medical Care and the General Practitioner, 1750–1850* (Oxford: Oxford University Press, 1986), pp. 297–301.

81 Ann Digby, *Making a Medical Living: Doctors and Patients in the English Market for Medicine, 1720–1911* (Cambridge: Cambridge University Press, 1994), pp. 28–38, 135–69.

82 1868 Pharmacy Act (31 & 32 Vict., c.121), 1878 Dentists Act (41 & 42 Vict., c.33), 1881 Veterinary Surgeons Act (44 & 45 Vict., c.62).

83 PRO: General Register Office Establishment and Accounts Division: Correspondence and Papers (RG 20): RG 20/80 Organisation and staffing, 1920. Tables showing the number of parliamentary and local electors also began to be published by the GRO: see General Register Office, *Registrar General's Statistical Review for 1921* (London: HMSO, 1923), pp. 116–19.

84 Margo Anderson, *The American Census: A Social History* (New Haven, CT: Yale University Press, 1988).

85 Edward Higgs, '*The Annual Report of the Registrar General*, 1839–1920: a textual history', in Eileen Magnello and Anne Hardy (eds), *The Road to Medical Statistics* (Amsterdam: Rodopi, 2002), pp. 55–76.

86 For the statistical congresses, see Harald Westergaard, *Contributions to the History of Statistics* (London: P. S. King, 1932), pp. 172–90; Jacques and Michel Dupâquier, *Histoire de la démographie: La statistique de la population des origines à 1914* (Paris: Libr. Academique Perrin, 1985), pp. 299–320.

87 For the development of statistics in this period, see Ian Hacking, *The Emergence of Probability* (Cambridge: Cambridge University Press, 1975); Theodore M. Porter, *The Rise of Statistical Thinking, 1820–1900* (Princeton, NJ: Princeton University Press, 1986); Ian Hacking, *The Taming of Chance* (Cambridge: Cambridge University Press, 1990).

88 PRO: Treasury: Treasury Board Papers (T 1): T 1/5828B/20825.

89 General Register Office, *16th ARRG for 1853* (London: HMSO, 1856), p. 116–25.

90 General Register Office, *Supplement to the 35th ARRG. Letter to the Registrar General on the mortality in the registration districts of England during the 10 years 1861–70, by Wm Farr* (London: HMSO, 1875), p. iv.

91 General Register Office, *25th ARRG for 1862* (London: HMSO, 1864), pp. xlvi–xlix.

92 General Register Office, *34th ARRG for 1871* (London: HMSO, 1873), p. xxvi.

93 See William Farr's commentary on the human resources of the Great Powers: General Register Office, *16th ARRG for 1853*, pp. 116–25.

94 Hew Strachan, *European Armies and the Conduct of War* (London: George Allen & Unwin, 1983), pp. 108–11; Alessandro Stanziani, 'Les sources démographiques entre contrôle policier et utopies technocratiques: le cas russe, 1870–1926', *Cahiers du monde russe* 38 (1997), pp. 457–88.

95 Edward Higgs, 'Diseases, febrile poisons, and statistics: the census as a medical survey', *Social History of Medicine* 4 (1991), p. 467.

96 Higgs, *A Clearer Sense*, p. 158.
97 Simon Szreter, *Fertility, Class and Gender in Britain, 1860–1940* (Cambridge: Cambridge University Press, 1996), pp. 114–20.
98 Higgs, 'A cuckoo in the nest?', pp. 124–8.
99 John M. Eyler, *Victorian Social Medicine: The Ideas and Methods of William Farr* (London: Johns Hopkins University Press, 1979), *passim*.
100 Simon Szreter, 'The GRO and the public health movement in Britain, 1837–1914', *Social History of Medicine* 4 (1991), pp. 435–64.
101 General Register Office, *16th ARRG for 1853*, p. 38.
102 Higgs, 'Diseases, febrile poisons, and statistics', pp. 471–5.
103 Ibid., pp. 467–9.
104 C. Hamlin, *Public Health and Social Justice in the Age of Chadwick: Britain, 1800–1854* (Cambridge: Cambridge University Press, 1998), *passim*.
105 Ibid., pp. 143–6; C. Hamlin, 'Could you starve to death in England in 1839? The Chadwick–Farr controversy and the loss of the "social" in public health', *American Journal of Public Health* 85 (1995), pp. 856–66.
106 Gerry Kearns, 'Private property and public health reform, 1830–70', *Social Science & Medicine* 26 (1988) pp. 187–99; Perkin, *The Rise of Professional Society*, p. 385.
107 Quoted in Perkin, *The Rise of Professional Society*, p. 121.
108 PRO RG 29/1, p. 551.
109 Edward Higgs, *'The Annual Report of the Registrar General, 1839–1920'*, *passim*.
110 See, for example, Emsley, *The English Police*, pp. 23–4, 49–57; David Philips, ' "A new engine of power and authority": the institutionalization of law-enforcing in England, 1780–1830', in V. Gatrell, B. Lenman, and G. Parker (eds) *Crime and the Law: The Social History of Crime in Western Europe since 1500* (London: Europa Publications, 1980), pp. 155–89; V. A. C. Gatrell, 'Crime, authority and the policeman state', in F. M. L. Thompson (ed.), *The Cambridge Social History of Britain, 1750–1950*, vol. 3: *Social Agencies and Institutions* (Cambridge: Cambridge University Press, 1990), pp. 243–310.
111 David Philips, *Crime and Authority in Victorian England: The Black Country, 1835–1860* (London: Croom Helm, 1977), pp. 76–7.
112 Roger Geary, *Policing Industrial Disputes: 1893 to 1985* (Cambridge: Cambridge University Press, 1985).
113 V. A. C. Gatrell and T. B. Hadden, 'Criminal statistics and their interpretation', in E. A. Wrigley (ed.), *Nineteenth-century Society. Essays in the Use of Quantitative Methods for the Study of Social Data* (Cambridge: Cambridge University Press, 1972), pp. 336–96.

114 A. P. Donajgrodzki, ' "Social police" and the bureaucratic elite: a vision of order in the age of reform', in A. P. Donajgrodzki (ed.), *Social Control in Nineteenth Century Britain* (London: Croom Helm, 1977), pp. 51–76.

115 T. A. Critchley, *A History of Police in England and Wales* (London: Constable, 1978), pp. 209–10; Clive Emsley, *Crime and Society in England, 1750–1900* (London: Longman, 1987), p. 176.

116 Stanziani, 'Les sources démographiques entre contrôle policier et utopies technocratiques', p. 466; Charles Steinwedel, 'Making social groups, one person at a time: the identification of individuals by estate, religious confession, and ethnicity in late Imperial Russia', in Jane Caplan and John Torpey (eds), *Documenting Individual Identity: The Development of State Practices in the Modern World* (Princeton, NJ: Princeton University Press, 2001), pp. 73–78; Andrea Geselle, 'Domenica Saba takes to the road: origins and development of a modern passport system in Lombardy-Veneto', in ibid., pp. 199–217; Leo Lucassen, 'A many-headed monster: the evolution of the passport system in the Netherlands and Germany in the long nineteenth century', in ibid., pp. 235–55.

117 Howard Taylor, 'Rationing crime: the political economy of criminal statistics since the 1850s', *Economic History Review* LI (1998), pp. 569–90.

118 PRO: Home Office: Domestic Correspondence from 1773 to 1861 (HO 44): HO 44/58 Plan for New Police Gazette to replace Hue and Cry, f. 2; PRO: Home Office: Registered Papers (HO 45): HO 45/9618/A14252 The Police Gazette, p. 5.

119 Victor Bailey, 'Introduction', in Victor Bailey (ed.), *Policing and Punishment in Nineteenth Century Britain* (London: Croom Helm, 1981), pp. 14–15.

120 Emsley, *The English Police*, p. 208.

121 Ibid., p. 24.

122 Robert Baldwin and Richard Kinsey, *Police Powers and Politics* (London: Quartet Books, 1982), pp. 9–11.

123 Geary, *Policing Industrial Disputes*, pp. 20–1; Emsley, *The English Police*, pp. 98–9; Bernard Porter, *The Origins of the Vigilant State: The London Metropolitan Police Special Branch before the First World War* (London: Weidenfeld and Nicolson, 1987), pp. 9–10.

124 Peter W. J. Bartrip, 'Public opinion and law enforcement: the ticket-of-leave scares in mid-Victorian Britain', in Victor Bailey (ed.), *Policing and Punishment in Nineteenth Century Britain* (London: Croom Helm, 1981), pp. 152–4.

125 Michel Foucault, *Discipline and Punish: The Birth of the Prison* (London: Allen Lane, 1977), *passim*.

126 Wiener, *Reconstructing the Criminal*, pp. 149–50; *Report of a Committee Appointed by the Secretary of State to Inquire into the Best Means Available for Identifying Habitual Criminals...*, PP 1893–94 LXXII, pp. 6–7.

127 Ibid., pp. 215–16; PRO: Metropolitan Police; Criminal Record Office: Habitual Criminals Registers and Miscellaneous Papers (MEPO 6): MEPO 6/90 Pt 2; Registry of Criminal, p. 8; PRO: Home Office Registered Papers, Supplementary (HO 144): HO 144/184/A45507, p. 4.

128 PRO: HO 45/9320/16629C, Prisons and Prisoners: (4) Other: Prevention of Crimes Act, 1871. Regulations for photographing prisoners; *Report ... into ... Identifying Habitual Criminals*, pp. 12–19; PRO: HO 144/530/A6508(14). Original photographs can be found in PRO: Home Office and Prison Commission: Prisons Records, Series I (PCOM 2).

129 Martine Kaluszynski, 'Republican identity: Bertillonage as government technique', in Jane Caplan and John Torpey (eds), *Documenting Individual Identity: The Development of State Practices in the Modern World* (Princeton, NJ: Princeton University Press, 2001), p. 124; Peter Becker, 'The standardised gaze: the standardization of the search warrant in nineteenth-century Germany', in ibid., pp. 153–63.

130 *Report ... into ... Identifying Habitual Criminals*, p. 219.

131 Ibid., p. 217; PRO: HO 144/184/A45507, pp. 8–17.

132 PRO: HO 45/9675/A46826 Request for increase in staff of Convict Supervision Office; *Report ... into ... Identifying Habitual Criminals*, p. 226.

5 The New Liberal State and information gathering

1 G. R. Searle, *The Quest for National Efficiency: A Study in British Politics and Political Thought, 1899–1914* (Oxford: Basil Blackwell, 1971), pp. 6–12.

2 Roger Davidson, *Whitehall and the Labour Problem in Late-Victorian and Edwardian Britain* (London: Croom Helm, 1985), pp. 36–7; Harold Perkin, *The Rise of Professional Society: England since 1880* (London: Routledge, 1989), pp. 36–7.

3 Searle, *The Quest for National Efficiency*, pp. 6–11.

4 Asa Briggs, *Social Thought and Social Action: A Study of the Work of Seebohm Rowntree, 1871–1954* (London: Longman, 1961), pp. 42–3.

5 Searle, *The Quest for National Efficiency*, pp. 60–4.

6 E. P. Hennock, 'Poverty and social theory in England: the experience of the eighteen-eighties', *Social History* 1(1976), p. 73.

7 Seebohm Rowntree, *Poverty: A Study of Town Life* (London: Macmillan, 1902), p. 117.

8 Philip Harling, *The Modern British State: An Historical Introduction* (Cambridge: Polity Press, 2001), p. 115.

9 Searle, *The Quest for National Efficiency*, pp. 54–97.

10 Michael Mann, *The Sources of Social Power*, vol. II (Cambridge: Cambridge University Press, 1993), pp. 492–5. But see Jan Palmowski, 'Liberalism and local government in late nineteenth-century Germany and England', *Historical Journal* 45 (2002), 381–410.

11 See, for example, Patrick O'Farrell, *Ireland's English Question* (London: B.T. Batsford, 1971), pp. 161–279.

12 Davidson, *Whitehall and the Labour Problem*, pp. 35–42.

13 Gareth Stedman Jones, *Outcast London: A Study in the Relationship between Classes in Victorian Society* (Harmondsworth: Penguin, 1984), pp. 239–336.

14 The discussion in support and against such ideas has been voluminous. See, for example: J. R. Hay, 'Employers' attitudes to social policy and the concept of 'social control', 1900–1920', in Pat Thane (ed.), *The Origins of British Social Policy* (London: Croom Helm, 1978), pp. 107–25; Stuart Hall and Bill Schwarz, 'State and society, 1880–1930', in Mary Langan and Bill Schwarz (eds), *Crises in the British State, 1880–1930* (London: Hutchinson, 1985), pp. 7–32; Mann, *The Sources of Social Power*, vol. II, pp. 405, 481–4; E. P. Hennock, 'Poverty and social reforms', in Paul Johnson (ed.), *Twentieth-century Britain: Economic, Social and Cultural Change* (London: Longman, 1994), pp. 79–93; Pat Thane, 'The working class and state "welfare" in Britain, 1880–1914', in David Gladstone, *Before Beveridge: Welfare before the Welfare State* (London: IEA Health and Welfare Unit, 1999), pp. 86–112.

15 Victor Bailey, 'The Metropolitan Police, the Home Office and the threat of Outcast London', in Victor Bailey (ed.), *Policing and Punishment in Nineteenth Century Britain* (London: Croom Helm, 1981), pp. 96–7; José Harris, *Unemployment and Politics: A Study in English Social Policy, 1886–1914* (Oxford: Oxford University Press, 1984), p. 56.

16 Catherine Hall, Keith McClelland and Jane Rendall, *Defining the Victorian Nation: Class, Race, Gender and the British Reform Act of 1867* (Cambridge: Cambridge University Press, 2000).

17 Perkin, *The Rise of Professional Society*, p. 139; Harris, *Unemployment and Politics*, pp. 213–15; David Vincent, *Poor Citizens: The State and the Poor in Twentieth-century Britain* (London: Longman, 1991) pp. 30–1; Martin Pugh, 'Working-class experience and state social welfare, 1908–1914: old age pensions reconsidered', *Historical Journal* 45 (2002), pp. 775–97.

18 José Harris, *Private Lives, Public Spirit: A Social History of Britain, 1870–1914* (London: Penguin, 1994), p. 202.

19 Peter Clarke, 'The end of laissez faire and the politics of cotton', *Historical Journal* 15 (1972), 493–512; H. V. Emy, *Liberals, Radicals and Social Politics, 1892–1914* (Cambridge: Cambridge University Press, 1973).

20 Hall and Schwarz, 'State and society', p. 25.

21 Perkin, *The Rise of Professional Society*, pp. 158–60.

22 Alan Kidd, *State, Society and the Poor in Nineteenth-century England* (Basingstoke: Palgrave Macmillan, 1999), p. 62.

23 Cited in Briggs, *Social Thought*, p. 35.

24 Cited in Pauline M. H. Mazumdar, *Eugenics, Human Genetics and Human Failings: The Eugenics Society, Its Sources and Its Critics in Britain* (London: Routledge, 1992), p. 85.

25 Simon Szreter, *Fertility, Class and Gender in Britain, 1860–1940* (Cambridge: Cambridge University Press, 1996), pp. 212–16.

26 Greta Jones, *Social Hygiene in Twentieth Century Britain* (London: Croom Helm, 1986).

27 Martin J. Wiener, *Reconstructing the Criminal: Culture, Law and Policing in England 1830–1914* (Cambridge: Cambridge University Press, 1990), pp. 159–84.

28 Harris, *Private Lives, Public Spirit*, pp. 200–1; Harling, *The Modern British State*, pp. 123–4.

29 Brian Harrison, *The Transformation of British Politics, 1860–1995* (Oxford: Oxford University Press, 1996), p. 81.

30 Harris, *Private Lives, Public Spirit*, pp. 20–1.

31 Perkin, *The Rise of Professional Society*, pp. 266–7.

32 Harris, *Private Lives, Public Spirit*, pp. 20, 200.

33 Bernard Porter, *The Origins of the Vigilant State: The London Metropolitan Police Special Branch before the First World War* (London: Weidenfeld and Nicolson, 1987), p. 8.

34 Michael Smith, *New Cloak, Old Dagger: How Britain's Spies Came in from the Cold* (London: Victor Gollancz, 1996), p. 34.

35 Porter, *The Origins of the Vigilant State*, pp. 45–165.

36 Richard Deacon, *British Secret Service* (London: Grafton, 1991), p. 147.

37 PRO: Committee of Imperial Defence: Ad-Hoc Sub-Committees: Minutes, Memoranda and Reports (CAB 16): CAB 16/8 Report of a subcommittee of the Committee of Imperial defence to consider foreign espionage in the UK, July 1909, p. iv.

38 PRO: Security Services: First World War Historical Reports and Other Papers (KV 1): KV 1/1 Organisation of secret service: note prepared for the DMO.

39 Deacon, *British Secret Service*, pp. 147–50, 172–3.

40 A. W. Brian Simpson, *In the Highest Degree Odious: Detention Without Trial in Wartime Britain* (Oxford: Oxford University Press, 1992), p. 11.
41 PRO: KV 1/6 CID meeting: Kell's presentation of the work and records of the Bureau.
42 Smith, *New Cloak, Old Dagger*, p. 45.
43 John Curry, 'The Security Service: its problems and organisational adjustments, 1908–1945', in Christopher Andrew (ed.), *The Security Service: The Official History* (London: Public Record Office, 1999), p. 69.
44 Smith, *New Cloak, Old Dagger*, p. 50.
45 Porter, *The Origins of the Vigilant State*, pp. 72, 96.
46 Ibid., pp. 179–80; Richard Thurlow, *The Secret State: British Internal Security in the Twentieth Century* (Oxford: Blackwell, 1994), p. 49.
47 Daniel R. Headrick, *The Invisible Weapon: Telecommunications and International Politics, 1851–1945* (Oxford: Oxford University Press, 1991), pp. 118, 126.
48 *Hansard, Fourth Series*, 140, 10 August to 15 August 1904, col. 513. See also, *Memorandum Explanatory of the Wireless Telegraphy Bill*, PP 1904 LXXIX [271.]
49 Headrick, *The Invisible Weapon*, p. 145.
50 Asa Briggs, *The History of Broadcasting in the United Kingdom*, vol. II: *The Golden Age of Wireless* (London: Oxford University Press, 1965), p. 6; Paddy Scannell and David Cardiff, *A Social History of British Broadcasting*, vol. I: *1922–1939: Serving the Nation* (Oxford: Blackwell, 1991), pp. 5–6.
51 Public Record Office, *Current Guide*, section 606/1/1; W. J. Killingback, *The Work of the Registry of Shipping and Seamen and of the Mercantile Marine Office* (n/a: W. J. Killingback, 1945), Part I, 3.
52 Wiener, *Reconstructing the Criminal*, pp. 185–381.
53 Robert Baldwin and Richard Kinsey, *Police Powers and Politics* (London: Quartet Books, 1982), p. 11.
54 *Report ... into ... identifying habitual criminals ...*, pp. 5–35; Anne M. Joseph, 'Anthropometry, the police expert, and the Deptford Murders: the contested introduction of fingerprinting for the identification of criminals in late Victorian and Edwardian Britain', in Jane Caplan and John Torpey (eds), *Documenting Individual Identity: The Development of State Practices in the Modern World* (Princeton, NJ: Princeton University Press, 2001), pp. 164–71.
55 Martine Kaluszynski, 'Republican identity: Bertillonage as government technique', in Jane Caplan and John Torpey (eds), *Documenting Individual Identity: The Development of State Practices in the Modern World* (Princeton, NJ: Princeton University Press, 2001), pp. 123–8; Peter Becker, 'The standardized gaze: the standardization of the

search warrant in nineteenth-century Germany', in ibid., pp. 141–53; Armand Mattelart, *The Invention of Communication* (London: University of Minnesota Press, 1996), pp. 233–6; The Health of the Body Politic website: http://www.cimm.jcu.edu.au/hist/stats/bert/ (21/6/2002).

56 The Health of the Body Politic website.

57 Mattelart, *The Invention of Communication*, pp. 236–9; Francis Galton, *Finger Prints* (London: Macmillan, 1892); Colin Bevan, *Fingerprints: Murder and the Race to Uncover the Science of Identity* (London: Fourth Estate, 2002).

58 PRO: Treasury: Treasury Blue Notes (T 165); T 165/21 Police of England and Wales, 1904–5.

59 Joseph, 'Anthropometry', pp. 170–1.

60 PRO: HO 144/566/A62042 Report of the Committee to Inquire into the Method of Identification of Criminals 1900; Joseph, 'Anthropometry', pp. 171–4.

61 *Report of the (Desborough) Committee on the Police Service of England, Wales and Scotland. Minutes of Evidence*, PP 1920 XXII, p. 111, minute 1995.

62 See, for example, Clive Emsley, *The English Police: A Political and Social History* (Hemel Hempstead: Harvester Wheatsheaf, 1991), pp. 5–6; V. A. C. Gatrell, 'Crime, authority and the police-man state', in F. M. L. Thompson (ed.), *The Cambridge Social History of Britain, 1750–1950*, vol. 3: *Social Agencies and Institutions* (Cambridge: Cambridge University Press, 1990), pp. 243–310; Robert Reiner, *The Politics of the Police* (Oxford: Oxford University Press, 2000), p. 45.

63 For a general consideration of the genesis and significance of the Act, see Clive Emsley, ' "Mother, what *did* policemen do when there weren't any motors?" The law, the police and the regulation of motor traffic in England, 1900–1939', *Historical Journal*, 36 (1993), pp. 357–81.

64 Ibid., pp. 366–7.

65 PRO: Road Traffic and Safety Correspondence and Papers (MT 34): MT 34/39 Motor Car Act, 1903, Amending Motor Car (Registration and Licencing) Orders 1903.

66 *Hansard, Fourth Series* 122, 7 May to 26 May 1903, cols 1060–1; *Hansard, Fourth Series* 125, 8 July to 22 July 1903, cols 529–30; *Hansard, Fourth Series* 127, 6 August to 14 August 1903, col. 416.

67 *Hansard, Fourth Series* 125, 8 July to 22 July 1903, col. 977; *Hansard, Fourth Series* 127, 6 August to 14 August 1903, col. 471.

68 E. P. Thompson, *Whigs and Hunters: The Origin of the Black Act* (Harmondsworth: Penguin, 1977).

69 T. A. Critchley, *A History of Police in England and Wales* (London: Constable, 1978), p. 177; Clive Emsley, ' "Mother, what *did* policemen do?" ', pp. 369–71.

70 *Hansard, Fourth Series* 125, 8 July to 22 July 1903, col. 530; *Hansard, Fourth Series* 127, 6 August to 14 August 1903, col. 418.

71 *Hansard, Fourth Series* 125, 8 July to 22 July 1903, cols 530–1.

72 *Hansard, Fourth Series* 122, 7 May to 26 May 1903, col. 1055; *Hansard, Fourth Series 126*, 23 July to 5 August 1903, cols 1460–3, 1494.

73 Lois R. Kuznets, *Kenneth Grahame* (Boston: Twayne Publishers, 1987), Preface.

74 *Hansard, Fourth Series* 122, 7 May to 26 May 1903, col. 1060; *Hansard, Fourth Series* 125, 8 July to 22 July 1903, col. 537.

75 Bentley B. Gilbert, *British Social Policy, 1914–1939* (London: B.T. Batsford, 1970), pp. 53, 88; Noel Whiteside, 'Private provision and public welfare: health insurance between the wars', in David Gladstone (ed.), *Before Beveridge: Welfare before the Welfare State* (London: IEA Health and Welfare Unit, 1999), pp. 26–42.

76 W. R. Garside, *The Measurement of Unemployment: Methods and Sources in Great Britain, 1850–1979* (Oxford: Blackwell, 1980), p. 39.

77 Pat Thane, 'Non-contributory versus insurance pensions, 1878–1908', in Pat Thane (ed.), *The Origins of British Social Policy* (London: Croom Helm, 1978), p. 103.

78 John Brown, 'Social control and the modernisation of social policy, 1890–1929', in Pat Thane (ed.), *The Origins of British Social Policy* (London: Croom Helm, 1978), pp. 130–3.

79 Vincent, *Poor Citizens*, p. 40.

80 Thane, 'Non-contributory versus insurance pensions, 1878–1908', p. 104.

81 Vincent, *Poor Citizens*, p. 37.

82 Paul Johnson, 'Risk, redistribution and social welfare in Britain from the poor law to Beveridge', in Martin Daunton (ed.), *Charity, Self-interest and Welfare in the English Past* (London: UCL Press, 1996), p. 242.

83 Thane, 'The working class and state "welfare" ', p. 112; Pugh, 'Working-class experience', *passim*.

84 PRO: RG 29/8, p. 23.

85 PRO: RG 29/4, p. 107; PRO: RG 29/8, p. 51.

86 PRO: Ministry of National Insurance and Successors: Staff and Establishment, Registered Files (PIN 23): PIN 23/7 Organisation and initial complements outstational executive depts: Blackpool staff.

87 PRO: Department of Employment and Predecessors: Establishment Division and Predecessors: Registered Files (LAB 12): LAB 12/53 Committee appointed to consider sick leave at the Claims and Record Office, Kew.

88 Garside, *The Measurement of Unemployment*, pp. 27, 33–45.

89 Ministry of Labour, *Report on National Unemployment Insurance to July 1923* (London: HMSO, 1923), pp. 70–1.

90 PRO: LAB 12/53; *Estimates for Civil Services for the year ending 31 March 1926* PP 1924–25 XIX 35, Class VII, 3, p. 41.

91 Anthony Giddens, *The Constitution of Society* (Cambridge: Polity Press, 1986), pp. 64–73, 123–4.

92 Leslie Hannah, *The Rise of the Corporate Economy* (London: Methuen, 1976).

93 JoAnne Yates, *Control through Communication: The Rise of System in American Management* (Baltimore, MD: Johns Hopkins University Press, 1989), p. 271. See also: James R. Beniger, *The Control Revolution: Technology and the Economic Origins of the Information Society* (Cambridge, MA: Harvard University Press, 1986).

94 Daniel Nelson, *Frederick W. Taylor and the Rise of Scientific Management* (Madison, WI: University of Wisconsin Press, 1980); Frank Barkley Copley, *Frederick W. Taylor: Father of Scientific Management* (London: Routledge, 1993).

95 Yates, *Control through Communication*, pp. 10, 21–64. The period also saw the development of early systems of record/information management within organisations: Edward Higgs, 'From medieval erudition to information management: the evolution of the archival profession', *Archivum (Proceedings of the XIII International Congress on Archives, Beijing, 2–7 September 1996)* XLIII (1997), pp. 136–44.

96 Niklas Luhmann, *The Differentiation of Society* (New York: Columbia University Press, 1982), pp. 20–46.

97 Albert Fried and Richard Elman, *Charles Booth's London: A Portrait of the Poor at the Turn of the Century, Drawn from His 'Life and Labour of the People in London'* (London: Hutchinson, 1969), pp. 290–300.

98 The legend over the gates of the work camp at Auschwitz.

99 Davidson, *Whitehall and the Labour Problem, passim*.

100 Enclosure to PRO: T 1/8487B/9295.

101 Szreter, *Fertility, Class and Gender*, pp. 114–20.

102 PRO: Local Government Board: Correspondence and Papers (MH 19): MH 19/195, letters of 30 August, 8 September and 15 September 1890.

103 Kevin Schürer, 'The 1891 census and local population studies', *Local Population Studies* 47 (1991), pp. 16–29.

104 Edward Higgs, *A Clearer Sense of the Census: The Victorian Censuses and Historical Research* (London: HMSO, 1996), pp. 108–9.

105 Szreter, *Fertility, Class and Gender*, pp. 119–20.

106 Ellen F. Mappen, 'Strategists for change: social feminist approaches to the problems of women's work', in Angela V. John (ed.), *Unequal Opportunities: Women's Employment in England, 1800–1918* (Oxford: Basil Blackwell, 1986), p. 246.

107 PRO: RG 19/48B Departmental Committee on the Census of 1911, p. 103.

108 Rosalind Mitchison, *British Population Change since 1860* (London: Macmillan, 1977), p. 24.

109 General Register Office, *Supplement to the 65th Annual Report of the Registrar General. Letter to the Registrar General on the Mortality in the Registration Districts of England and Wales during the 10 years 1891–1900, by John Tatham* (London: HMSO, 1907), p. cv.

110 Muriel Nissel, *People Count: A History of the General Register Office* (London: HMSO, 1996), pp. 129–30. The infant mortality rate in fact improved in the Edwardian period, declining from 153 per thousand in 1891–1900 to 128 per thousand in 1901–10: General Register Office, *Supplement to the 75th Annual Report of the Registrar General: Part III Registration Summary Tables: Review of the Vital Statistics of England and Wales during the 10 years 1901–1911, by T. H. C. Stevenson* (London: HMSO, 1919), p. xxxiii.

111 Jane Lewis, *The Politics of Motherhood: Child and Maternal Welfare in England, 1900–1939* (London: Croom Helm, 1980); Deborah Dwork, *War is Good for Babies and Other Young Children* (London: Tavistock, 1987) ; Jeanne L. Brand, *Doctors and the State: The British Medical Profession and Government Action in Public Health, 1870–1912* (Baltimore, MD: Johns Hopkins University Press, 1965), pp. 177–83; Pat Thane, *The Foundations of the Welfare State* (London: Longman, 1982), pp. 60–1.

112 John Burns, 'Presidential address delivered to the First National Conference on Infantile Mortality on June 13, 1906', in G. F. McCleary, *The Early History of the Infant Welfare Movement* (London: H. K. Lewis & Co., 1933), pp. 151–68; National Conference on Infantile Mortality, *Report of the Proceedings of the National Conference on Infantile Mortality ... 23rd, 24th, and 25th March 1908* (London: P. S. King & Son, 1908), pp. 11–28.

113 General Register Office, *68th ARRG for 1905* (London: HMSO, 1907), pp. cxviii–cxxxiii. From 1889 onwards the GRO had published tables showing infant mortality in the first and second three-month

periods of life, and in the second six-month period: General Register Office, *51st ARRG for 1888* (London: HMSO, 1889), p. ix. For other innovations in this period with respect to infant and child mortality, see Szreter, *Fertility, Class and Gender*, pp. 247–8. See also David Armstrong, 'The invention of infant mortality', *Sociology of Health and Illness*, 8(3), (1986), pp. 211–32.

114 General Register Office, *67th ARRG for 1904* (London: HMSO, 1906), pp. xciii–xcviii; General Register Office, *Supplement to the 65th Annual Report of the Registrar General*, pp. cv–cxvi.

115 Szreter, *Fertility, Class and Gender*, pp. 129–282.

116 *Census of 1911. Vol. XIII. Fertility of Marriage Report, Part I*, PP 1917–18 XXXV; *Census of 1911. Vol. XIII. Fertility of Marriage Report, Part II*, PP 1923.

117 Edward Higgs, 'The statistical Big Bang of 1911: ideology, technological innovation and the production of medical statistics', *Social History of Medicine* 9(3) (1996), pp. 409–26.

118 Martin Campbell-Kelly, *ICL: A Business and Technical History* (Oxford: Oxford University Press, 1989), pp. 8–13.

119 Higgs, 'The statistical Big Bang', p. 421.

120 Bernard Mallet, 'The organisation of registration in its bearings on vital statistics', *Journal of the Royal Statistical Society* LXXX (1917), p. 8.

121 PRO: KV 1/65 Control of Aliens Including CID Sub-committees: MI5 Policy Matters, 1914–15.

122 B. E. V. Sabine, *A History of the Income Tax* (London: Allen & Unwin, 1966), p. 46.

123 Ibid., p. 62; *Hansard, Third Series* 67, 7 April to 2 May 1842, col. 658.

124 John Berger, *Ways of Seeing* (London: Penguin, 1972), pp. 106–8.

125 J. A. Banks, *Prosperity and Parenthood: A Study of Family Planning among the Victorian Middle Classes* (London: Routledge and Keegan Paul, 1954).

126 *Hansard, Third Series*, 279, 7 May to 7 June 1883, cols 489–90.

127 Ibid., cols 499–500.

128 Sabine, *A History of the Income Tax*, p. 120.

129 *Report of the Royal Commission on Income Tax*, PP 1920, XVIII, pp. 75–6.

130 Ibid., pp. 77–86.

131 Rupert C. Jarvis, 'Official trade and revenue statistics', *Economic History Review* XVII (1964–65), pp. 43–62; PRO: IR 64/532 Notes on the Development of the Inland Revenue Statistics, 1947–66. For the use of such material by historians, see, W. D. Rubinstein, *Men of Property: The Very Wealthy in Britain since the Industrial Revolution* (London: Croom Helm, 1981), pp. 16–17.

132 Bernard Mallet, *British Budgets, 1887–1913* (London: Macmillan, 1913).

133 Josiah Stamp, *British Incomes and Property: The Application of Official Statistics to Economic Problems* (London: P. S. King & Son, 1916).

134 Public Record Office, *Current Guide*, section 207/3/1.

6   The Information State in total war and total welfare

1 Harold Perkin, *The Rise of Professional Society: England since 1880* (London: Routledge, 1989), pp. 20–2.

2 Hew Strachan, *European Armies and the Conduct of War* (London: George Allen & Unwin, 1983), p. 70.

3 Ibid., p. 40.

4 Ibid., pp. 108–11.

5 Paul Guinn, *British Strategy and Politics, 1914 to 1918* (Oxford: Oxford University Press, 1965), pp. 85, 179–80; J. M. Winter, *The Great War and the British People* (London: Macmillan, 1986), pp. 25–48; David French, *British Strategy and War Aims, 1914–1916* (London: Allen & Unwin, 1986), pp. 116–31; Keith Grieves, *The Politics of Manpower, 1914–19* (Manchester: Manchester University Press, 1988), pp. 19–24.

6 PRO: GRO: National Registration: Correspondence and Papers (RG 28): RG 28/8 1915 National Registration (Jackson) Committee: minutes; first and second interim reports: first interim report (6 August 1915), p. 2; PRO: RG 28/9 1915 National Register (Landsdowne) Committee: minutes, reports and papers: interim report (3 September 1915), p. 2.

7 Name, place of residence, date of birth, nationality, marital status, profession or occupation, employer's name and business address, and information on previous service in HM Forces.

8 Jon Agar, 'Modern horrors: British identity and identity cards', in Jane Caplan and John Torpey (eds), *Documenting Individual Identity: The Development of State Practices in the Modern World* (Princeton, NJ: Princeton University Press, 2001), pp. 103–6.

9 PRO: RG 28/1 Preparations for, and administration of, the National Registration Act, 1915–18, Vol. I.

10 PRO: GRO: Registration of Births, Deaths and Marriages. Correspondence and Papers (RG 48): RG 48/585 1917–18 Duties in respect of rationing schemes: correspondence with Ministry of Food and Registrar General for Scotland.

11 General Register Office, *77th ARRG for 1914* (London: HMSO, 1916), p. viii.

12 PRO: KV 1/65.

13 For the role of citizenship in the age of total war, see Michael Mann, *States, War and Capitalism: Studies in Political Sociology* (Oxford: Blackwell, 1988), pp. 154–9.

14 For such a claim see, Frank Webster, *Theories of the Information Society* (London: Routledge, 1995), pp. 66–7.

15 PRO: RG 28/3 National Register 1915–19, Vol. III. Committee on National Registration 1917–18: Prt I Correspondence. Simon Szreter implies that the idea came from the Registrar-General, Sir Bernard Mallet: Simon Szreter, *Fertility, Class and Gender in Britain, 1860–1940* (Cambridge: Cambridge University Press, 1996) p. 267. This appears to be based on a claim made by Mallet in the 1920s but the idea appears to have originated with his subordinate. See also Sir Bernard Mallet, 'The organisation of registration in its bearings on vital statistics', *Journal of the Royal Statistical Society* LXXX (1917), pp. 22–3.

16 PRO: RG 28/3: letter from B. B. Cubitt of 2 July 1917.

17 Ibid., letter of 26 February 1918.

18 RG 28/6 Report of the sub-committee appointed to consider a system of general registration..., pp. 3–8.

19 Ibid., p. 9.

20 Ibid., pp. 14–15.

21 PRO: RG 28/3: Letter to Sir Bernard Mallet from Sir Robert Morant, dated 12 July 1919.

22 Ibid.

23 The report was signed by Mallet, Arthur Newsholme, Stevenson, Vivian and Beatrice Webb: PRO RG 28/6.

24 PRO: RG 28/7 Committee on National Registration 1917, and suggestions for the reorganisation of the Registration Service; undated, unsigned memorandum.

25 PRO: RG 28/3: letter from Beatrice Webb to Sir Bernard Mallet of 26 February 1919; letter from Sir Robert Morant to Sir Bernard Mallet of 12 July 1919.

26 Philip Harling, *The Modern British State: An Historical Introduction* (Cambridge: Polity Press, 2001), p. 142.

27 PRO: T 1/12181/15387: System of identifying discharged soldiers, etc. by means of fingerprints; T 1/12500/10570 Pensions Ministry. Identification of pensioners. Observations on proposals; T 1/12181/18165 War Office. Identification by means of fingerprinting in case of discharged men.

28 PRO: T 1/12181/15387.

29 Pamela Sankar, 'DNA-typing: Galton's eugenic dream realized?', in Jane Caplan and John Torpey (eds), *Documenting Individual Identity: The Development of State Practices in the Modern World* (Princeton, NJ: Princeton University Press, 2001), pp. 277–9.

30　Armand Mattelart, *The Invention of Communication* (London: University of Minnesota Press, 1996), p. 238; Kristin Ruggiero, 'Fingerprinting and the Argentine plan for universal identification in the late nineteenth and early twentieth centuries', in Jane Caplan and John Torpey (eds), *Documenting Individual Identity: The Development of State Practices in the Modern World* (Princeton, NJ: Princeton University Press, 2001), pp. 192–6.

31　UK Passport Service website: http://www.ukpa.gov.uk/_history/history_03.htm (7 May 2002).

32　John Torpey, 'The Great War and the birth of the modern passport system', in Jane Caplan and John Torpey (eds), *Documenting Individual Identity: The Development of State Practices in the Modern World* (Princeton, NJ: Princeton University Press, 2001), pp. 256–70.

33　H. M. D. Parker, *Manpower: A Study of War-time Policy and Administration* (London: HMSO, 1957), p. 41.

34　PRO: RG 28/31 Committee of Imperial Defence: Registrar General's sub-committee on National Registration: correspondence and papers 1935–39; letter of Vivian to E. A. Armstrong, 17 December 1935.

35　Ibid.: memorandum on 'Draft Bills in Appendix C and Appendix E to document 350-B'. Both the official *Guide to Census Reports*, and Nissel, mistakenly give the impression that the preparations for the national registration system only began in 1938: Office of Population Censuses and Surveys and the General Register Office, Edinburgh, *Guide to Census Reports, Great Britain 1801–1966* (London: HMSO, 1977), p. 26; Muriel Nissel, *People Count: A History of the General Register Office* (London: HMSO, 1996), p. 75.

36　PRO: RG 28/31; undated memorandum 'Enumeration timetable'.

37　PRO: GRO: Population and Medical Statistics: Correspondence and Papers (RG 26): RG 26/6 National Register 1939: preparation in the event of war…1938–41; draft circular to clerks of local authorities, 1940; General Register Office, *National Registration. Statistics of Population on 29 September 1939 by Age, Sex and Marital Condition: Report and Tables* (London: HMSO, 1944).

38　Neil Stammers, *Civil Liberties in Britain during the 2nd World War* (London: Croom Helm, 1983), p. 174.

39　W. J. Killingback, *The Work of the Registry of Shipping and Seamen and of the Mercantile Marine Office* (n/a: W. J. Killingback, 1945), Part II, 1.

40　PRO, *Current Guide*, Section 606/1/1.

41　Agar, 'Modern horrors', pp. 106–11.

42　PRO: Cabinet Office: Miscellaneous Committees: Minutes and Papers (General Series) (CAB 134): CAB 134/907 Home Affairs Committee Memorandum H.A.(51)23.

43 Ibid.
44 PRO: RG 28/201 Discontinuance of the National Registration Act, 1939: proceedings in Parliament.
45 Ibid.
46 *Fifth Report of the Data Protection Registrar, June 1989*, PP 1988–89, 472, p. 34; Agar, 'Modern horrors', pp. 110–11.
47 Mattelart, *The Invention of Communication*, p. 238.
48 Marc Garcelon, 'Colonizing the subject: the genealogy and legacy of the Soviet internal passport', in Jane Caplan and John Torpey (eds), *Documenting Individual Identity: The Development of State Practices in the Modern World* (Princeton, NJ: Princeton University Press, 2001), pp. 83–100.
49 Nissel, *People Count*, pp. 75–7.
50 PRO: RG 20/50 Staff Organisation Charts 1951.
51 PRO: CAB 134/907.
52 Bernard Porter, *The Origins of the Vigilant State: The London Metropolitan Police Special Branch before the First World War* (London: Weidenfeld and Nicolson, 1987), pp. 179–80.
53 Richard Thurlow, *The Secret State: British Internal Security in the Twentieth Century* (Oxford: Blackwell, 1994), pp. 54–9.
54 John Curry, 'The Security service', in Christopher Andrew (ed.), *The Security Service: The Official History* (London: Public Record Office, 1999), p. 86.
55 PRO, KV 1/55 Work of the Registry (MI5 H.2) 1917.
56 T. A. Critchley, *A History of Police in England and Wales* (London: Constable, 1978), p. 183; Clive Emsley, *The English Police: A Political and Social History* (Hemel Hempstead: Harvester Wheatsheaf, 1991), pp. 118–22.
57 Christopher Andrew, 'Introduction', in Christopher Andrew (ed.), *The Security Service: The Official History* (London: Public Record Office, 1999), pp. 3–10; Curry, 'The Security service', p. 101; Thurlow, *The Secret State*, pp. 112–13, 141.
58 Andrews, 'Introduction', pp. 3–10; Curry, 'The Security service', p. 86; A. W. Brian Simpson, *In the Highest Degree Odious* (Oxford: Oxford University Press, 1992), *passim*; Stammers, *Civil Liberties in Britain*, pp. 29, 55–6, 114, 120.
59 PRO: Security Service: Policy (POL F Series) Files (KV 4): KV 4/21 Report on the workings of the Security Service Registry 1945; Andrew, 'Introduction', p. 15; Curry, 'The Security service', pp. 157, 376–7; Alistair Black and Rodney Brunt, 'Information management in MI5 before the age of the computer', *Intelligence and National Security* 16(2), Summer 2001, pp. 158–65.
60 Emsley, *The English Police*, p. 138.
61 Critchley, *A History of Police*, pp. 232–3.

62 Quoted in Critchley, *A History of Police*, p. 228.

63 Ibid., pp. 231, 294.

64 Peter Hennessy, *The Secret State: Whitehall and the Cold War* (London: Penguin, 2002), pp. 77–119.

65 Richard Deacon, *British Secret Service* (London: Grafton, 1991), p. 384; the MI5 website: http://www.mi5.gov.uk/facts.htm (17 June 2001).

66 Duncan Campbell and Steve Connor, *On the Record: Surveillance, Computers and Privacy – the Inside Story* (London: Michael Joseph, 1986), p. 258.

67 Metropolitan Police website: http://www.met.police.uk/about/fact2 (17 July 2001).

68 Peter Gill, *Policing Politics: Security Intelligence and the Liberal Democratic State* (London: Frank Cass, 1994), pp. 186–7.

69 MI5 website: http://www.mi5.gov.uk/facts.htm (17 June 2001).

70 MI5 website: http://www.mi5.gov.uk/threat.htm (28 August 2001).

71 David Vincent, *Poor Citizens: The State and the Poor in Twentieth-Century Britain* (London: Longman, 1991), pp. 120–1: José Harris, *William Beveridge: A Biography* (Oxford: Oxford University Press, 1977), pp. 388–95.

72 José Harris, 'Political thought and the Welfare State 1870–1940: an intellectual framework for British social policy', in David Gladstone (ed.), *Before Beveridge: Welfare before the Welfare State* (London: IEA Health and Welfare Unit, 1999), p. 44.

73 Perkin, *The Rise of Professional Society*, p. 360.

74 Rodney Lowe, *Adjusting to Democracy: The Role of the Ministry of Labour in British Politics, 1916–1939* (Oxford: Oxford University Press, 1986), p. 245.

75 General Register Office, *77th ARRG for 1914*, p. lv; Pat Thane, *The Foundations of the Welfare State* (London: Longman, 1982), pp. 127–8.

76 General Register Office, *77th ARRG for 1914*, p. lv; PRO: RG 20/76 Search Room: organisation and staffing 1919–20.

77 Susan Pedersen, *Family, Dependence, and the Origins of the Welfare State* (Cambridge: Cambridge University Press, 1993), pp. 107–13.

78 Charles Webster, 'Healthy or hungry thirties', *History Workshop Journal* XIII (1982), pp. 110–29.

79 Vincent, *Poor Citizens*, p. 71.

80 Bentley B. Gilbert, *British Social Policy, 1914–1939* (London: B. T. Batsford, 1970), pp. 251–2.

81 Lowe, *Adjusting to Democracy*, pp. 134–9, 155.

82 David Vincent, *The Culture of Secrecy: Britain, 1832–1998* (Oxford: Oxford University Press, 1998), pp. 151–2.

83 A. T. Peacock and Jack Wiseman, *The Growth of Public Expenditure in the United Kingdom* (London: Allen and Unwin, 1967), pp. 106–8; Lowe, *Adjusting to Democracy*, p. 8.

84 Noel Whiteside, 'Private provision and public welfare: health insurance between the wars', in David Gladstone (ed.), *Before Beveridge: Welfare before the Welfare State* (London: IEA Health and Welfare Unit, 1999), pp. 26–42.

85 José Harris, 'Society and the state in twentieth-century Britain', in F. M. L. Thompson (ed.), *The Cambridge Social History of Britain, 1750–1950. Volume 3: Social Agencies and Institutions* (Cambridge: Cambridge University Press, 1990), p. 90.

86 David Gladstone, *The Twentieth-century Welfare State* (Basingstoke: Palgrave Macmillan, 1999), pp. 70–91.

87 Paul Johnson, 'The role of the State in twentieth-century Britain', in Paul Johnson (ed.), *Twentieth-century Britain: Economic, Social and Cultural Change* (Harlow: Longman, 1994), p. 479.

88 Sir Geoffrey S. King, *The Ministry of Pensions and National Insurance* (London: Allen & Unwin, 1958), pp. 113–14; James B. Rule, *Private Lives and Public Surveillance* (London: Allen Lane, 1973), p. 122.

89 Department of Social Security website: Press Release 00/039, http://www.dss.gov.uk/mediacentre/pressreleases/2000/feb/000 39.pdf (24 July 2001).

90 PRO: Board of Inland Revenue: Private Office Papers: Memoranda (IR 74): IR 74/108 Numbers of taxpayers and non-taxpayers and income of the UK. Statistics by J. E. Chapman, 1901.

91 Roy Douglas, *Taxation in Britain since 1660* (Basingstoke: Palgrave Macmillan, 1999) pp. 109, 113.

92 PRO: Board of Inland Revenue: Commissioners of Inland Revenue: Reports (IR 15): IR 15/93 93rd Report of the commissioners of HM Inland Revenue for the year ended 31 March 1950, p. 34; IR 15/169 132nd Report of the Board of Inland Revenue for the year ending 31 March 1990, p. 62.

93 Inland Revenue, *Employer's Annual Pack 2001*.

94 Confederation of British Industry website: News release: CBI throws down red tape election challenge as new report highlights administrative burden: http://www.cbi.org.uk/80256716004baae5/ 33a87f2eee41b54e80256803004f04e4/db11d81feba3eff9802569 8400488630?OpenDocument (11/9/2001).

95 Inland Revenue website: *Inland Revenue Annual Report for the Year Ending 31st March 2000*, p. 11, http://www.inlandrevenue.gov.uk/ pdfs/report2000.pdf (10 July 2001).

96 General Register Office, *59th ARRG for 1896* (London: HMSO, 1897), p. xxxvi; PRO: RG 29/1–16.

97 PRO: GRO: Census Returns: Correspondence and Papers (RG 19): RG 19/49 Legislation: correspondence; memoranda; draft Census Bills, 1919–20, memo of Vivian to Morant 6 January 1920, ff.15, 20, 56.

98 For the events surrounding the passage of the Act, see Richard A. Soloway, *Demography and Degeneration: Eugenics and the Declining Birthrate in Twentieth-century Britain* (London: University of North Carolina Press, 1990), pp. 226–58.

99 General Register Office, *Registrar General's Statistical Review for 1938*: Civil tables (London: HMSO, 1944), pp. 108–207.

100 General Register Office, *Registrar General's Statistical Review for 1938 and 1939* (London: HMSO, 1947), p. 179. For the events leading up to the appointment of the Commission, see Soloway, *Demography and Degeneration*, pp. 312–43.

101 The GRO's own records on the Commission comprise a whole class of its records at the PRO: GRO: Royal Commission on Population, 1944–9 (RG 24).

102 PRO: Government Social Survey Department: Social Surveys: Reports and Papers (RG 23): RG 23/6 Foundation garments: a study by occupational groups, for the Board of Trade, November 1941.

103 For the history of the Government Social Survey, see Frank Whitehead, 'The Government Social Survey', in Martin Bulmer (ed.), *Essays in the History of British Sociological Research* (Cambridge: Cambridge University Press, 1985), pp. 83–100; Louis Moss, *The Government Social Survey: A History* (London: HMSO, 1991).

104 C. L. Dunn (ed.), *The Emergency Medical Services* (London: HMSO, 1952–3).

105 PRO: RG 26/83 Hospital in-patients summary: policy 1947–1951; 'Explanatory memorandum on the use of hospital in-patient summary'.

106 PRO: RG 26/24 Sample Survey of Sickness 1943–45 conducted by the Wartime Social Survey: initial planning and development; letter from Taylor to Stocks of 24 July 1943.

107 Ibid.; memorandum on 'MRC classification of diseases and injuries'.

108 Ibid.; letter from Stocks to Wilson of 31 January 1944.

109 Ibid.; memorandum from Stocks to the chief medical officer of 3 July 1944.

110 The Survey revealed that the only notifiable diseases for which notification could be regarded as fairly complete were acute poliomyelitis, cerebro-spinal fever, diptheria and scarlet fever. Respiratory tuberculosis came next with probably nine-tenths of active cases notified: General Register Office, *Registrar General's Statistical Review for 1946–1947: Medical* (London: HMSO, 1949), p. 3.

111 Nissel, *People Count*, pp. 87–9, 117; W. P. D. Logan and Eileen M. Brooke, *The Survey of Sickness, 1943 to 1952. General Register Office Studies on Medical and Population Subjects, no. 12* (London: HMSO, 1952).

112 General Register Office, *Registrar General's Statistical Review for 1951: Text* (London: HMSO, 1954), p. 4.

113 International Development Research Centre website: the Tanzania Essential Health Interventions Project: http://www.idrc.ca/reports/read_article_english.cfm?article_num=701 (21/8/2002); *Economist*, 17–23 August 2002, pp. 20–2.

114 General Register Office, *Registrar General's Statistical Review for 1946–1947: Medical*, pp. 1–2.

115 PRO: RG 26/83; memorandum of 14 April 1947 entitled 'Information to be obtained from National Statistics of Hospital Inpatients'.

116 *Registrar General's Statistical Review for 1946–1947: Medical*, p. 2.

117 Nissel, *People Count*, p. 116.

118 Charlie Owen, 'Government household surveys', in Daniel Dorling and Stephen Simpson (eds), *Statistics in Society: The Arithmetic of Politics* (London: Arnold, 1999), pp. 19–28.

119 *Annual Report of the Office for National Statistics, 1999–2000*, p. 30, National Statistics website: http://www.statistics.gov.uk/about_ns/ONS/downloads/AnnRep200.pdf.

120 PRO: RG 20/81 Complement of Staff up to Higher Executive Level; Martin Bulmer, 'Social science research and policy-making in Britain', in Martin Bulmer (ed.), *Social Policy Research* (London: Macmillan, 1978), p. 32.

121 Catherine Marsh, 'Informants, respondents and citizens', in Martin Bulmer (ed.), *Essays on the History of British Sociological Research* (Cambridge: Cambridge University Press, 1985), pp. 206–27.

122 Sir Claus Moser, 'Social indicators: systems, methods and problems', in Martin Bulmer (ed.), *Social Policy Research* (London: Macmillan, 1978), pp. 203–14.

123 Ian Miles and John Irvine, 'The critique of official statistics', in John Irvine, Ian Miles and Jeff Evans (eds), *Demystifying Social Statistics* (London: Pluto Press, 1979), pp. 113–29. See also: L. J. Sharpe, 'Government as client for social policy research', in Martin Bulmer (ed.), *Social Policy Research* (London: Macmillan, 1978), p. 72; John Edwards, 'Social indicators, urban deprivation and positive discrimination', in Martin Bulmer (ed.), *Social Policy Research* (London: Macmillan, 1978), pp. 222–4.

124 Philip Abrams, 'The uses of British sociology, 1831–1981', in Martin Bulmer (ed.), *Essays on the History of British Sociological Research*

(Cambridge: Cambridge University Press, 1985), pp. 181–205; Peter Townsend, 'Surveys of poverty to promote democracy', in Martin Bulmer (ed.), *Essays on the History of British Sociological Research* (Cambridge: Cambridge University Press, 1985), pp. 228–35.

125 Miles and Irvine, 'The critique of official statistics', p. 126.

126 Lesley Doyal, 'A matter of life and death: medicine, health and statistics', in John Irvine, Ian Miles and Jeff Evans (eds), *Demystifying Social Statistics* (London: Pluto Press, 1979), pp. 241–6.

127 Catherine Hakim, 'Social monitors: population censuses as social surveys', in Martin Bulmer (ed.), *Essays on the History of British Sociological Research* (Cambridge: Cambridge University Press, 1985), p. 41.

128 L. J. Sharpe, 'The social scientist and policy-making in Britain and America: a comparison', in Martin Bulmer (ed.), *Social Policy Research* (London: Macmillan, 1978), pp. 308–9.

129 Ian Miles and John Irvine, 'The critique of official statistics', p. 126.

130 Bulmer, 'Social science research', p. 24.

131 Peter Townsend, Nick Davidson and Margaret Whitehead (eds), *Inequalities in Health: the Black Report* (London: Penguin, 1988), pp. 1–4.

132 Ray Thomas, 'The politics and reform of unemployment and employment statistics', in Daniel Dorling and Stephen Simpson (eds), *Statistics in Society: The Arithmetic of Politics* (London: Arnold, 1999), pp. 327–8.

133 Edward Higgs, *A Clearer Sense of the Census: The Victorian Censuses and Historical Research* (London: HMSO, 1996), *passim*.

134 Edward Higgs, 'Women, occupations and work in the nineteenth-century censuses', *History Workshop Journal* 23 (1987), pp. 59–80.

135 Christopher Hamlin, *Public Health and Social Justice in the Age of Chadwick: Britain, 1800–1854* (Cambridge: Cambridge University Press, 1998), *passim*.

136 Sir Bernard Mallet, *British Budgets 1887–1913* (London: Macmillan, 1913) *passim*; Josiah Stamp, *British Incomes and Property: The Application of Official Statistics to Economic Problems* (London: P. S. King & Son, 1916) *passim*; Arthur Bowley and Margaret H. Hogg, *Has Poverty Diminished?: A Sequel to 'Livelihood and poverty'* (London: P. S. King, 1925).

137 For examples of their use to calculate wealth see, for example A. B. Atkinson and A. J. Harrison, *Distribution of Personal Wealth in Britain* (Cambridge: Cambridge University Press, 1978); W. D. Rubinstein, *Men of Property: The Very Wealthy in Britain since the Industrial Revolution* (London: Croom Helm, 1981), *passim*.

138 W. R. Garside, *The Measurement of Unemployment: Methods and Sources in Great Britain, 1850–1979* (Oxford: Blackwell, 1980), *passim*.

139 For an exploration of some of these themes in medicine, see Robert A. Aronowitz, *Making Sense of Illness: Science, Society and Disease* (Cambridge: Cambridge University Press, 1998).

140 See, for example, Campbell and Connor, *On the Record*, p. 73.

7   The Information State in the age of information technology

1 Bryan S. Turner, 'Outline of a theory of citizenship', in Bryan S. Turner and Peter Hamilton (eds), *Citizenship: Critical Concepts*, vol. 1 (London: Routledge, 1994), pp. 199–226.

2 David Vincent, *The Culture of Secrecy: Britain, 1832–1998* (Oxford: Oxford University Press, 1998), pp. 244–56.

3 José Harris, 'Society and the state in twentieth-century Britain', in F. M. L. Thompson (ed.), *The Cambridge Social History of Britain, 1750–1950*, vol. 3: *Social Agencies and Institutions* (Cambridge: Cambridge University Press, 1990), p. 64.

4 Martin Campbell-Kelly, *ICL: A Business and Technical History* (Oxford: Oxford University Press, 1989), pp. 204–5.

5 Michael Wettengel, 'German unification and electronic records', in Edward Higgs (ed.), *History and Electronic Artefacts* (Oxford: Clarendon Press, 1998), pp. 269–70.

6 *Report of the [Younger] Committee on Privacy*, PP 1971–72 XXII, pp. 179–80.

7 Christine Bellamy and John A. Taylor, *Governing in the Information Age* (Buckingham: Open University Press, 1998), pp. 8–9, 39.

8 Duncan Campbell and Steve Connor, *On the Record: Surveillance, Computers and Privacy – the Inside Story* (London: Michael Joseph, 1986), 61.

9 *Report of the (Lindop) Committee on Data Protection*, Appendix 6; Campbell and Connor, *On the Record*, pp. 62–5.

10 Bellamy and Taylor, *Governing in the Information Age*, pp. 64–89; Campbell and Connor, *On the Record*, p. 87.

11 *Computers and Privacy*, PP 1975–76 XX, p. 4.

12 Campbell and Connor, *On the Record*, p. 90.

13 Bellamy and Taylor, *Governing in the Information Age*, p. 85.

14 *3rd Annual Report of the Data Protection Registrar* [hereafter ARDPR] *June 1987*, PP 1987–88 33, p. 5; *4th ARDPR June 1988*, PP 1987–88 570, pp. 13–14.

15 *Independent*, 30 November 1999.

16 Information Commissioner's website: DSS registration, http://www.dpr.gov.uk/cgi-bin/dpr98-fetch.pl?source= DPR&dcid=155219 (12 September 2001).

17 Performance and Innovation Unit website: Privacy and data-sharing: The way forward for public services, http://www. cabinet-office.gov.uk/innovation/2002/privacy/report/index.htm (12 April 2002).

18 *13th ARDPR June 1997*, PP 1997–98 122, p. 36.

19 *14th ARDPR June 1998*, PP 1997–98 910, p. 37.

20 *12th ARDPR June 1996*, PP 1995–96 574, p. 38.

21 *5th ARDPR June 1989*, PP 1988–89 472, p. 35.

22 *Report of the (Lindop) Committee on Data Protection*, p. 54.

23 *8th ARDPR June 1992*, PP 1992–93 64, p. 15.

24 For the theory of relational databases in the context of historical research, see Charles Harvey and Jon Press, *Databases in Historical Research* (Basingstoke: Palgrave Macmillan, 1996).

25 *6th ARDPR June 1990*, PP 1989–90 472, pp. 3–4; *10th ARDPR June 1994*, PP 1993–94 453, p. 8.

26 *7th ARDPR June 1991*, PP 1990–91 553, p. 7.

27 *14th ARDPR June 1998*, p. 38.

28 PRO: PIN 23/49 Divulgence of Information about Insured Persons and Pensions: Policy.

29 Wettengel, 'German unification', p. 272.

30 Robert Baldwin and Richard Kinsey, *Police Powers and Politics* (London: Quartet Books, 1982), pp. 30–2; Clive Emsley, *The English Police: A Political and Social History* (Hemel Hempstead: Harvester Wheatsheaf, 1991), p. 166; Sarah Manwaring-White, *The Policing Revolution* (Brighton: Harvester, 1983), pp. 24–5.

31 Baldwin and Kinsey, *Police Powers and Politics*, pp. 41, 77.

32 T. A. Critchley, *A History of Police in England and Wales* (London: Constable, 1978), p. 308.

33 Baldwin and Kinsey, *Police Powers and Politics*, pp. 27–8.

34 See C. Norris, J. Moran, and G. Armstrong (eds), *Surveillance, Closed Circuit Television and Social Control* (Aldershot: Ashgate, 1998).

35 Manwaring-White, *The Policing Revolution*, p. 55.

36 *Report of the (Lindop) Committee on Data Protection*, p. 81.

37 *Hansard, 5th Series, Commons*, vol. 773, 11–22 November 1968, col. 1698.

38 Manwaring-White, *The Policing Revolution*, p. 59.

39 *Report of the (Lindop) Committee on Data Protection*, pp. 80–1.

40 Campbell and Connor, *On the Record*, pp. 227–8.

41 *Independent*, 19 February 2000.

42 Baldwin and Kinsey, *Police Powers and Politics*, pp. 82–3; Manwaring-White, *The Policing Revolution*, pp. 65–6.

43 Baldwin and Kinsey, *Police Powers and Politics*, pp. 82–3.

44 Campbell and Connor, *On the Record*, p. 204.

45 Peter Gill, *Policing Politics: Security Intelligence and the Liberal Democratic State* (London: Frank Cass, 1994), p. 144.

46 Ibid., p. 145.

47 Campbell and Connor, *On the Record*, p. 199.

48 Ibid., pp. 193–6.

49 *Computers: Safeguards for Privacy*, PP 1975–76 XX, p. 30.

50 *8th ARDPR*, p. 6.

51 *10th ARDPR*, p. 14.

52 *Guardian*, 15 December 1998.

53 *Independent*, 11 July 2001.

54 Campbell and Connor, *On the Record*, p. 111.

55 Pamela Sankar, 'DNA-typing: Galton's eugenic dream realized?', in Jane Caplan and John Torpey (eds), *Documenting Individual Identity* (Princeton, NJ: Princeton University Press, 2001), pp. 279–90.

56 *7th ARDPR*, pp. 5–6; *11th ARDPR June 1995*, PP 1994–95 629, p. 29.

57 David Lyon, 'Under my skin: from identification to body surveillance', in Jane Caplan and John Torpey (eds), *Documenting Individual Identity: The Development of State Practices in the Modern World* (Princeton, NJ: Princeton University Press, 2001), pp. 291–310.

58 Home Office website: http://www.homeoffice.gov.uk/ripa/ripact.htm (12 June 2002); Liberty website: http://www.liberty-human-rights.org.uk/impress112.html (12 June 2002); Guardian Unlimited Observer website: http://www.observer.co.uk/politics/story/0,6903,730091,00.html (12 June 2002).

59 *10th ARDPR*, p. 16.

60 Manwaring-White, *The Policing Revolution*, p. 32.

61 David Charters, 'Intelligence and psychological warfare operations in Northern Ireland', *Journal of the Royal United Services Institute* 122 (1977), pp. 22–7.

62 Manwaring-White, *The Policing Revolution*, p. 32.

63 Richard Thurlow, *The Secret State: British Internal Security in the Twentieth Century* (Oxford: Blackwell, 1994), p. 372.

64 *5th ARDPR*, p. 5.

65 *7th ARDPR*, p. 7.

66 *10th ARDPR*, p. 8; *Guardian*, 25 May 1999.

67 *10th ARDPR*, p. 7.

68 *Identity Cards. A Consultation Document*, PP 1994–95, 2879, p. 25.

69 *10th ARDPR*, p. 7; *12th ARDPR*, p. 37.

70 James B. Rule, *Private Lives and Public Surveillance* (London: Allen Lane, 1973), p. 120.

71 *Independent*, 24 November 2001.
72 *Independent*, 9 January 2001.
73 Home Office website: Entitlement cards and identity fraud; http://www.homeoffice.gov.uk/cpd/entitlement_cards.pdf (5 August 2002); Japan Local Government Centre website: Basic Resident Register Network: Standardization, simplification and savings: http://www.jlgc.org/jlgcnews/032?BasciResidentRegisterNetwork.html (5 August 2002).
74 Information Commissioner's website: Press release: http://www.dataprotection.gov.uk/dpr/dpdoc1.nsf (13 February 2003).
75 Michel Foucault, *Discipline and Punish* (Harmondsworth: Penguin Books, 1991), pp. 265–77, 282–6, 300–2.
76 Baldwin and Kinsey, *Police Powers and Politics*, pp. 99–100.
77 For the problems with the data on the PNC, see Campbell and Connor, *On the Record*, pp. 75–7; Information Commissioner's website: *UK Information Commissioner's Report for 2001*, Chapter 2, Data Protection Registrar's website, http://www.dpr.gov.uk/ar2001/annrep/htmlrep/000index.html (21 September 2001).
78 This was certainly the argument of the Lindop Committee: *Report of the (Lindop) Committee on Data Protection*, pp. 260–4.
79 Claes Gränström, 'Swedish society and electronic data', in Edward Higgs (ed.), *History and Electronic Artefacts* (Oxford: Oxford University Press, 1998), pp. 317–18.
80 Vincent, *The Culture of Secrecy*, p. 91.
81 PRO website: Access to public records: http://www.pro.gov.uk/recordsmanagement/access/Access2.html (2 October 2001).
82 Campbell and Connor, *On the Record*, pp. 23–4.
83 *Report of the (Lindop) Committee on Data Protection*, pp. 83–4, 222.
84 Council of Europe: European Treaty Series, no. 108. *Convention for the Protection of Individuals with Regard to Automatic Processing of Personal Data.*
85 Campbell and Connor, *On the Record*, pp. 27–8; Richard Sizer and Philip Newman, *The Data Protection Act: A Practical Guide* (Aldershot: Gower, 1984), p. 31.
86 *Report of the (Lindop) Committee on Data Protection*, p. 201.
87 *3rd ARDPR*, p. 2.
88 Directive 95/46/EC of the European Parliament and the Council of Ministers of 24 October 1995 on the protection of individuals with regard to the processing of personal data... , *Official Journal of the European Community* L, 281 (23 November 1995), p. 31.
89 *Report of the (Lindop) Committee on Data Protection*, p. 11.
90 Martin Bulmer, 'The impact of privacy upon social research', in Martin Bulmer (ed.), *Censuses, Surveys and Privacy* (London: Macmillan, 1979), pp. 4–5.

91 James Michael, *The Politics of Secrecy* (Harmondsworth: Penguin Books, 1982), pp. 126–46.

92 Data Protection Registrar's website: *UK Information Commissioner's Report for 2001: Commissioner's foreword*: http:// www.dpr.gov.uk/ar2001/annrep/htmlrep/000index.html (21 September 2001).

93 A. P. Tant, *British Government: The Triumph of Elitism: A Study of the British Political Tradition and Its Major Challenges* (Aldershot: Dartmouth, 1993), pp. 23, 57–91.

94 Quoted in Tant, *British Government: The Triumph of Elitism*, p. 201.

95 Campbell and Connor, *On the Record*, pp. 27–8.

96 *7th ARDPR*, p. 15.

97 *11th ARDPR*, pp. 83–8.

98 *12th ARDPR*, p. 57.

99 *14th ARDPR*, pp. 61–2.

100 *9th ARDPR June 1993*, PP 1992–93 736, pp. 4–9.

101 Elizabeth M. Hallam, *Domesday Book through Nine Centuries* (London: Thames and Hudson, 1986), pp. 32–51.

102 Donald W. Sutherland, *Quo warranto Proceedings in the Reign of Edward I, 1278–1294* (Oxford: Oxford University Press, 1963), p. 82.

8 Towards a conclusion: social control or a hegemony of citizenship?

1 For example, John Rawls, *A Theory of Justice* (Oxford: Oxford University Press, 1999).

Bibliography

British Parliamentary Papers

3rd Annual Report of the Data Protection Registrar [hereafter ARDPR] *June 1987*, PP 1987–88 33.
4th ARDPR June 1988, PP 1987–88 570.
5th ARDPR June 1989, PP 1988–89 472.
6th ARDPR June 1990, PP 1989–90 472.
7th ARDPR June 1991, PP 1990–91 553.
8th ARDPR June 1992, PP 1992–93 64.
9th ARDPR June 1993, PP 1992–93 736.
10th ARDPR June 1994, PP 1993–94 453.
11th ARDPR June 1995, PP 1994–95 629.
12th ARDPR June 1996, PP 1995–96 574.
13th ARDPR June 1997, PP 1997–98 122.
14th ARDPR June 1998, PP 1997–98 910.
Census of 1911, vol. XIII: *Fertility of Marriage Report, Part I*, PP 1917–18 XXXV, Cd 8678.
Census of 1911, vol. XIII: *Fertility of Marriage Report, Part II*, PP 1923, Cd 2175.
Computers and Privacy, PP 1975–76 XX, Cmnd 6353.
Computers: Safeguards for Privacy, PP 1975–76 XX, Cmnd 6354.
Estimates for Civil Services for the Year Ending 31 March 1926, PP 1924–25 XIX, 35.
General Report of the Commissioners on the Public Records, PP 1837 XXXIV, Pt 1.
Hansard, 3rd, 4th and 5th series.
Identity Cards: A Consultation Document, PP 1994–95, Cm 2879.
Memorandum Explanatory of the Wireless Telegraphy Bill, PP 1904 LXXIX, 271.
Report of a committee appointed by the secretary of state to inquire into the best means available for identifying habitual criminals..., PP 1893–94 LXXII, c. 7263.
Report of the (Desborough) Committee on the Police Service of England, Wales and Scotland. Minutes of Evidence, PP 1920 XXII, Cmd 874.
Report of the (Lindop) Committee on Data Protection, PP 1978–79, V, Cmnd 7341.

Report of the Royal Commission on Income Tax, PP 1920, XVIII, Cmd 615.

Report of the Treasury Committee on the Census, PP 1890 LVIII, *c.* 6071.

Report of the [Younger] Committee on Privacy, PP 1971–72 XXII, Cmnd 5012.

Second report of the Royal Sanitary Commission, vol. 1, 1871 XXXV, *c.* 281.

European Union papers

Council of Europe: European Treaty Series, no. 108, *Convention for the Protection of Individuals with Regard to Automatic Processing of Personal Data.*

Directive 95/46/EC of the European Parliament and the Council of Ministers of 24 October 1995 on the protection of individuals with regard to the processing of personal data…, *Official Journal of the European Community*, no. L, 281 (23 November 1995).

Public Record Office sources

Board of Inland Revenue: Commissioners of Inland Revenue: Reports (IR 15).

Board of Inland Revenue: Private Office Papers: Memoranda (IR 74).

Board of Inland Revenue: Statistics and Intelligence Division: Correspondence and Papers (IR 64).

Cabinet Office: Miscellaneous Committees: Minutes and Papers (General Series) (CAB 134).

Committee of Imperial Defence: Ad-Hoc Sub-Committees: Minutes, Memoranda and Reports (CAB 16).

Department of Employment (and predecessors): Establishment Division (and predecessors), Registered Files (LAB 12).

Government Social Survey Department: Social Surveys, Reports and Papers (RG 23).

General Register Office (hereafter GRO): Census Returns, Correspondence and Papers (RG 19).

GRO: Census Returns, Specimens of Forms and Documents (RG 27).

GRO: Establishment and Accounts Division, Correspondence and Papers (RG 20).

GRO: Letter Books (RG 29).

GRO: National Registration: Correspondence and Papers (RG 28).

GRO: Population and Medical Statistics: Correspondence and Papers (RG 26).

GRO: Registration of Births, Deaths and Marriages: Correspondence and Papers (RG 48).

GRO: Royal Commission on Population, 1944–9 (RG 24).

Home Office: Domestic Correspondence from1773 to 1861 (HO 44).

Home Office: Registered Papers (HO 45).

Home Office Registered Papers, Supplementary (HO 144).

Home Office and Prison Commission: Prisons Records, Series I (PCOM 2).

Local Government Board: Correspondence and Papers (MH 19).

Metropolitan Police; Criminal Record Office: Habitual Criminals Registers and Miscellaneous Papers (MEPO 6).

Ministry of National Insurance and successors: Staff and Establishment, Registered Files (PIN 23).

Transport Departments: Road Traffic and Safety Correspondence and Papers (MT 34): MT 34/39 Motor Car Act, 1903, Amending Motor Car (Registration and Licencing) Orders 1903.

Security Services: First World War Historical Reports and Other Papers (KV 1).

Security Services: Policy (POL F Series) Files (KV 4).

Treasury: Treasury Blue Notes (T 165).

Treasury: Treasury Board Papers (T 1).

Other manuscript sources

Greater London Record Office: London School Board Statistical Committee (SBL 908).

Newspapers

The Guardian
The Independent

Websites

Confederation of British Industry website: http://www.cbi.org.uk

Data Protection Registrar's website (see Information Commissioner's website).

Department of Social Security website: http://www.dss.gov.uk

Guardian Unlimited Observer website: http://www.observer.co.uk

Health of the Body Politic website: http://www.cimm.jcu.edu.au/hist/stat

Home Office website: http://www.homeoffice.gov.uk

Information Commissioner's website: http://www.dpr.gov.uk

Inland Revenue website: http://www.inlandrevenue.gov.uk

International Development Research Centre website: http://www.idrc.ca

Japan Local Government Centre website: http://www.jlgc.org

Liberty website: http://www.liberty-human-rights.org.uk

Metropolitan Police website: http://www.met.police.uk

MI5 website: http://www.mi5.gov.uk

National Statistics website: http://www.statistics.gov.uk

Performance and Innovation Unit website: http://www.cabinet-office.gov.uk/innovation

Public Record Office website: http://www.pro.gov.uk

Records of Earls Colne website: http://linux02.lib.cam.ac.uk/earlsecolne/

UK Passport Service website: http://www.ukpa.gov.uk

Books and articles

Abrams, Philip, *The Origins of British Sociology: 1834–1914* (Chicago, IL: University of Chicago, 1968).

Abrams, Philip, 'The uses of British sociology, 1831–1981', in Martin Bulmer (ed.), *Essays on the History of British Sociological Research* (Cambridge: Cambridge University Press, 1985), pp. 181–205.

Agar, Jon, 'Modern horrors: British identity and identity cards', in Jane Caplan and John Torpey (eds), *Documenting Individual Identity: The Development of State Practices in the Modern World* (Princeton, NJ: Princeton University Press, 2001), pp. 101–20.

Anderson, Benedict, *Imagined Communities: Reflections on the Origin and Spread of Nationalism* (London: Verso, 1983).

Anderson, Margo, *The American Census: A Social History* (New Haven, CT: Yale University Press, 1988).

Anderson, Michael, *Family Structure in Nineteenth-Century Lancashire* (Cambridge: Cambridge University Press, 1971).

Andrew, Christopher, 'Introduction', in Christopher Andrew (ed.), *The Security Service: The Official History* (London: Public Record Office, 1999).

Armstrong, David, 'The invention of infant mortality', *Sociology of Health and Illness* 8(3), (1986), pp. 211–32.

Aronowitz, Robert A., *Making Sense of Illness: Science, Society and Disease* (Cambridge: Cambridge University Press, 1998).

Atkinson, A. B. and Harrison, A. J., *Distribution of Personal Wealth in Britain* (Cambridge: Cambridge University Press, 1978).

Bailey, Victor, 'Introduction', in Victor Bailey (ed.), *Policing and Punishment in Nineteenth-Century Britain* (London: Croom Helm, 1981), pp. 11–24.

Bailey, Victor, 'The Metropolitan Police, the Home Office and the threat of outcast London', in Victor Bailey (ed.), *Policing and Punishment in Nineteenth-Century Britain* (London: Croom Helm, 1981), pp. 94–125.

Baldwin, Robert and Kinsey, Richard, *Police Powers and Politics* (London: Quartet Books, 1982).

Banks, J. A., *Prosperity and Parenthood: A Study of Family Planning among the Victorian Middle Classes* (London: Routledge Kegan Paul, 1954).

Bartrip, Peter W. J., 'Public opinion and law enforcement: the ticket-of-leave scares in mid-Victorian Britain', in Victor Bailey (ed.), *Policing and Punishment in Nineteenth-Century Britain* (London: Croom Helm, 1981), pp. 150–81.

Becker, Peter, 'The standardized gaze: the standardization of the search warrant in nineteenth-century Germany', in Jane Caplan and John Torpey (eds), *Documenting Individual Identity: The Development of State Practices in the Modern World* (Princeton, NJ: Princeton University Press, 2001), pp. 139–63.

Bellamy, Christine, *Administering Central–Local Relations, 1871–1919: The Local Government Board in Its Fiscal and Cultural Context* (Manchester: Manchester University Press, 1988).

Bellamy, Christine and Taylor, John A., *Governing in the Information Age* (Buckingham: Open University Press, 1998).

Beniger, James R., *The Control Revolution: Technology and the Economic Origins of the Information Society* (Cambridge, MA: Harvard University Press, 1986).

Beresford, M. W., 'The poll taxes of 1377, 1379 and 1381', *The Amateur Historian* 3 (1958), pp. 271–8.

Berger, John, *Ways of Seeing* (London: Penguin, 1972).

Bevan, Colin, *Fingerprints: Murder and the Race to Uncover the Science of Identity* (London: Fourth Estate, 2002).

Biagini, Eugenio F., 'Liberalism and direct democracy: John Stuart Mill and the model of ancient Athens', in Eugenio F. Biagini (ed.), *Citizenship and Community: Liberals, Radicals and Collective Identities in the British Isles, 1865–1931* (Cambridge: Cambridge University Press, 1996), pp. 21–44.

Black, Alistair and Brunt, Rodney, 'Information management in MI5 before the age of the computer', *Intelligence and National Security* 16(2) (Summer 2001), pp. 158–65.

Black, Edwin, *IBM and the Holocaust* (London: Little, Brown, 2001).

Bowley, Arthur and Hogg, Margaret H., *Has Poverty Diminished? A Sequel to 'Livelihood and Poverty'* (London: P. S. King, 1925).

Braddick, Michael J., 'State formation and social change in early modern England: a problem stated and approaches suggested', *Social History* 16 (1991), pp. 1–17.

Braddick, Michael J., *Parliamentary Taxation in Seventeenth-century England: Local Administration and Response* (Woodbridge: Boydell Press, 1994).

Braddick, Michael J., *The Nerves of State: Taxation and the Finance of the English State, 1558–1714* (Manchester: Manchester University Press, 1996).

Braddick, Michael J., *State Formation in Early Modern England c.1550–1700* (Cambridge: Cambridge University Press, 2000).

Brand, Jeanne L., *Doctors and the State: The British Medical Profession and Government Action in Public Health, 1870–1912* (Baltimore, MD: Johns Hopkins University Press, 1965).

Breight, Curtis C., *Surveillance, Militarism and Drama in the Elizabethan Era* (Basingstoke: Palgrave Macmillan, 1996).

Brewer, John, *The Sinews of Power: War, Money and the English State, 1688–1783* (London: Unwin Hyman, 1989).

Briggs, Asa, *Social Thought and Social Action: A Study of the Work of Seebohm Rowntree, 1871–1954* (London: Longman, 1961).

Briggs, Asa, *The History of Broadcasting in the United Kingdom*, vol. II: *The Golden Age of Wireless* (London: Oxford University Press, 1965).

British Imperial Calendar for 1863 (London: HMSO, 1863).

British Imperial Calendar for 1875 (London: HMSO, 1875).

British Imperial Calendar for 1876 (London: HMSO, 1876).

British Imperial Calendar for 1877 (London: HMSO, 1877).

Brown, John, 'Social control and the modernisation of social policy, 1890–1929', in Pat Thane (ed.), *The Origins of British Social Policy* (London: Croom Helm, 1978), pp. 126–46.

Brundage, Anthony, *England's 'Prussian Minister': Edwin Chadwick and the Politics of Government Growth, 1832–1854* (University Park: Pennsylvania State University Press, 1988).

Bulmer, Martin, 'Social science research and policy-making in Britain', in Martin Bulmer (ed.), *Social Policy Research* (London: Macmillan, 1978), pp. 3–43.

Bulmer, Martin, 'The impact of privacy upon social research', in Martin Bulmer (ed.), *Censuses, Surveys and Privacy* (London: Macmillan, 1979), pp. 3–21.

Burns, John, 'Presidential address delivered to the First National Conference on Infantile Mortality on June 13, 1906', in G. F. McCleary, *The Early History of the Infant Welfare Movement* (London: H. K. Lewis, 1933), pp. 151–68.

Bush, M. L., *The Government Policy of Protector Somerset* (London: Edward Arnold, 1975).

Campbell, Duncan and Connor, Steve, *On the Record: Surveillance, Computers and Privacy – The Inside Story* (London: Michael Joseph, 1986).

Campbell-Kelly, Martin, *ICL: A Business and Technical History* (Oxford: Oxford University Press, 1989), pp. 8–13.

Caplan, Jane, ' "This or that person": protocols of identification in nineteenth-century Europe', in Jane Caplan and John Torpey (eds), *Documenting Individual Identity: The Development of State Practices in the Modern World* (Princeton, NJ: Princeton University Press, 2001), pp. 49–66.

Caplan, Jane and Torpey, John, 'Introduction', in Jane Caplan and John Torpey (eds), *Documenting Individual Identity: The Development of State Practices in the Modern World* (Princeton, NJ: Princeton University Press, 2001), pp. 1–11.

Chadwick, Edwin, *Report on the Sanitary Condition of the Labouring Population of Great Britain* (Edinburgh: Edinburgh University Press, 1965).

Charters, David, 'Intelligence and psychological warfare operations in Northern Ireland', *Journal of the Royal United Services Institute* 122(3), (1977), pp. 22–7.

Clanchy, M. T., *From Memory to Written Record. England, 1066–1307* (London: Edward Arnold, 1979).

Clarke, Peter, 'The end of laissez faire and the politics of cotton', *Historical Journal* 15 (1972), pp. 493–512.

Cobbett, William, *Rural Rides* (Harmondsworth: Penguin, 1983).

Cohen, Stanley, *Visions of Social Control: Crime, Punishment and Classification* (Cambridge: Polity Press, 1985).

Cook, Chris and Keith, Brendan, *British Historical Facts, 1830–1900* (New York: St Martin's Press, 1975).

Cope, David R., 'Census-taking and the debate on privacy: a sociological view', in Martin Bulmer (ed.), *Censuses, Surveys and Privacy* (London: Macmillan, 1979), pp. 184–98.

Copley, Frank Barkley, *Frederick W. Taylor: Father of Scientific Management* (London: Routledge, 1993).

Corfield, Penelope J., *Power and the Professions in Britain, 1700–1850* (London: Routledge, 1995).

Corrigan, Philip and Sayer, Derek, *The Great Arch: English State Formation as Cultural Revolution* (Oxford: Blackwell, 1985).

Critchley, T. A., *A History of Police in England and Wales* (London: Constable, 1978).

Crook, David, *Records of the General Eyre* (London: HMSO, 1982).

Cullen, Michael J., 'The making of the Civil Registration Act of 1836', *Journal of Ecclesiastical History* 25 (1974), pp. 39–59.

Cullen, Michael J., *The Statistical Movement in Early Victorian Britain* (Hassocks: Harvester Press, 1975).

Curry, John, 'The Security service: its problems and organisational adjustments, 1908–1945', in Christopher Andrew (ed.), *The Security Service: The Official History* (London: Public Record Office, 1999).

Curtis, Bruce, *The Politics of Population: State Formation, Statistics and the Census of Canada, 1840–1875* (Toronto: University of Toronto Press, 2001).

Dandeker, Christopher, *Surveillance, Power and Modernity: Bureaucracy and Discipline from 1700 to the Present Day* (Cambridge: Polity Press, 1990).

Darby, H. C., *Domesday England* (Cambridge: Cambridge University Press, 1977).

Daunton, Martin, 'Introduction', in Martin Daunton (ed.), *Charity, Self-interest and Welfare in the English Past* (London: UCL Press, 1996), pp. 1–22.

Davidson, Roger, *Whitehall and the Labour Problem in Late-Victorian and Edwardian Britain* (London: Croom Helm, 1985).

Davin, Anna, 'Working or helping? London working-class children in the domestic economy', in J. Smith, I. Wallerstein and H. Evers (eds), *Households and the World Economy* (London: Sage, 1984), pp. 215–32.

Davin, Anna, *Growing Up Poor: Home, School and Street in London, 1870–1914* (London: Rivers Oram Press, 1996).

Deacon, Richard, *British Secret Service* (London: Grafton, 1991).

Desrosières, Alain, *La politique des grands nombres: histoire de la raison statistique* (Paris: Éditions la Découverte, 1993).

Dicey, A. V., *Lectures on the Relation between Law and Public Opinion in England during the Nineteenth Century* (London: Macmillan, 1905).

Digby, Ann, *Making a Medical Living: Doctors and Patients in the English Market for Medicine, 1720–1911* (Cambridge: Cambridge University Press, 1994).

Discussion Group on the State, 'When and what was the State? St Peter's, Oxford, 29–31 March, 2001', *Journal of Historical Sociology* 15 (2002), pp. 59–165.

Donajgrodzki, A. P., 'Introduction', in A. P. Donajgrodzki (ed.), *Social Control in Nineteenth-Century Britain* (London: Croom Helm, 1977), pp. 9–26.

Donajgrodzki, A. P., ' "Social police" and the bureaucratic elite: a vision of order in the age of reform', in A. P. Donajgrodzki (ed.), *Social Control in Nineteenth-Century Britain* (London: Croom Helm, 1977), pp. 51–76.

Douglas, Roy, *Taxation in Britain since 1660* (London: Macmillan, 1999).

Doyal, Lesley, 'A matter of life and death: medicine, health and statistics', in John Irvine, Ian Miles and Jeff Evans (eds), *Demystifying Social Statistics* (London: Pluto Press, 1979), pp. 237–54.

Drake, Michael, *Population and Society in Norway, 1735–1865* (Cambridge: Cambridge University Press, 1969).

Dunn, C. L. (ed.), *The Emergency Medical Services* (London: HMSO, 1952–3).

Dupâquier, Jacques and Michel, *Histoire de la démographie: La statistique de la population des origines à 1914* (Paris: Libr. Academique Perrin, 1985).

Durbach, Nadja, ' "They might as well brand us": working-class resistance to compulsory vaccination in Victorian England', *Social History of Medicine* 13 (2000), pp. 45–62.

Dwork, Deborah, *War is Good for Babies and Other Young Children* (London: Tavistock, 1987).

Eastwood, David, ' "Amplifying the province of the Legislature": the flow of information and the English State in the early nineteenth century', *Historical Research* LXII (1989), pp. 276–94.

Eastwood, David, *Governing Rural England: Tradition and Transformation in Local Government, 1780–1840* (Oxford: Oxford University Press, 1994).

Eastwood, David, *Government and Community in the English Provinces, 1700–1870* (Basingstoke: Palgrave Macmillan, 1997).

Edwards, John, 'Social indicators, urban deprivation and positive discrimination', in Martin Bulmer (ed.), *Social Policy Research* (London: Macmillan, 1978), pp. 215–27.

Elias, Norbert, *The Civilizing Process* (Oxford: Blackwell, 2000).

Elton, G. R., *Policy and Police: The Enforcement of the Reformation in the Age of Thomas Cromwell* (Cambridge: Cambridge University Press, 1972).

Emsley, Clive, *Crime and Society in England, 1750–1900* (London: Longman, 1987).

Emsley, Clive, ' "Mother, what *did* policemen do when there weren't any motors?" The law, the police and the regulation of motor traffic in England, 1900–1939', *Historical Journal* 36 (1993), pp. 357–81.

Emsley, Clive, *The English Police: A Political and Social History* (Hemel Hempstead: Harvester Wheatsheaf, 1991).

Emy, H. V., *Liberals, Radicals and Social Politics, 1892–1914* (Cambridge: Cambridge University Press, 1973).

Eyler, John M., *Victorian Social Medicine: The Ideas and Methods of William Farr* (London: Johns Hopkins University Press, 1979).

Fairbank, John King, *China: A New History* (London: Harvard University Press, 1992).

Finer, S. E., *The Life and Times of Sir Edwin Chadwick* (London: Methuen, 1952).

Finlayson, George, *Citizen, State and Social Welfare in Britain, 1830–1990* (Oxford: Oxford University Press, 1994).

Fletcher, Anthony, *Reform in the Provinces: The Government of Stuart England* (London: Yale University Press, 1986).

Foster, John, *Class Struggle and the Industrial Revolution: Early Industrial Capitalism in Three English Towns* (London: Methuen, 1974).

Foucault, Michael, *Discipline and Punish: The Birth of the Prison* (London: Allen Lane, 1977).

Foucault, Michel, *Discipline and Punish* (Harmondsworth: Penguin Books, 1991).

Foucault, Michel, 'Governmentality', in Graham Burchell, Colin Gordon and Peter Miller (eds), *The Foucault Effect: Studies in Governmentality* (London: Harvester Wheatsheaf, 1991), pp. 87–104.

Foucault, Michel, 'The subject and power', in Hubert L. Dreyfus and Paul Rabinow (eds), *Michel Foucault: Beyond Structuralism and Hermeneutics, with an Afterword by Michel Foucault* (Brighton: Harvester, 1982), pp. 208–26.

Fowler, Simon and Spencer, William, *Army Records for Family Historians* (London: PRO Publications, 1998).

Fox, Barry, 'More money than sense', *Personal Computer World* (November 2002), p. 35.

French, David, *British Strategy and War Aims, 1914–1916* (London: Allen & Unwin, 1986).

French, H. R., 'Social status, localism and the "middle sort of people" in England, 1620–1750', *Past and Present* 166 (2000), pp. 66–99.

Fried, Albert and Elman, Richard M., *Charles Booth's London: A Portrait of the Poor at the Turn of the Century Drawn from His 'Life and Labour of the People in London'* (London: Hutchinson, 1969).

Galton, Francis, *Finger Prints* (London: Macmillan, 1892).

Garcelon, Marc, 'Colonizing the subject: the genealogy and legacy of the Soviet internal passport', in Jane Caplan and John Torpey (eds), *Documenting Individual Identity: The Development of State Practices in the Modern World* (Princeton, NJ: Princeton University Press, 2001), pp. 83–100.

Garside, W. R., *The Measurement of Unemployment: Methods and Sources in Great Britain, 1850–1979* (Oxford: Blackwell, 1980).

Gatrell, V. A. C. and Hadden, T. B., 'Criminal statistics and their interpretation', in E. A. Wrigley (ed.), *Nineteenth-century Society: Essays in the Use of Quantitative Methods for the Study of Social Data* (Cambridge: Cambridge University Press, 1972), pp. 336–96.

Gatrell, V. A. C., 'Crime, authority and the police-man state', in F. M. L. Thompson (ed.), *The Cambridge Social History of Britain, 1750–1950*, vol. 3: *Social Agencies and Institutions* (Cambridge: Cambridge University Press, 1990), pp. 243–310.

Geary, Roger, *Policing Industrial Disputes: 1893 to 1985* (Cambridge: Cambridge University Press, 1985).

General Register Office, *16th Annual Report of the Registrar General of Births, Marriages and Deaths for England and Wales* [hereafter ARRG] *for 1853* (London: HMSO, 1856).

General Register Office, *22nd ARRG for 1859* (London: HMSO, 1861).

General Register Office, *25th ARRG for 1862* (London: HMSO, 1864).

General Register Office, *34th ARRG for 1871* (London: HMSO, 1873).

General Register Office, *51st ARRG for 1888* (London: HMSO, 1889).

General Register Office, *59th ARRG for 1896* (London: HMSO, 1897).

General Register Office, *67th ARRG for 1904* (London: HMSO, 1906).

General Register Office, *68th ARRG for 1905* (London: HMSO, 1907).

General Register Office, *77th ARRG for 1914* (London: HMSO, 1916).

General Register Office, *National Registration: Statistics of Population on 29 September 1939 by Age, Sex and Marital Condition: Report and Tables* (London: HMSO, 1944).

General Register Office, *Registrar General's Statistical Review for 1921* (London: HMSO, 1923).

General Register Office, *Registrar General's Statistical Review for 1938: Civil Tables* (London: HMSO, 1944).

General Register Office, *Registrar General's Statistical Review for 1938 and 1939* (London: HMSO, 1947).

General Register Office, *Registrar General's Statistical Review for 1946–1947 Medical* (London: HMSO, 1949).

General Register Office, *Registrar General's Statistical Review for 1951: Text* (London: HMSO, 1954).

General Register Office, *Supplement to the 35th ARRG. Letter to the Registrar General on the Mortality in the Registration Districts of England during the 10 years 1861–70, by Wm Farr* (London: HMSO, 1875).

General Register Office, *Supplement to the 65th ARRG. Letter to the Registrar General on the Mortality in the Registration Districts of England and Wales during the 10 years 1891–1900, by John Tatham* (London: HMSO, 1907).

General Register Office, *Supplement to the 75th ARRG: Part III. Registration Summary Tables: Review of the Vital Statistics of England and Wales during the 10 years 1901–1911, by T. H. C. Stevenson* (London: HMSO, 1919).

Geselle, Andrea, 'Domenica Saba takes to the road: origins and development of a modern passport system in Lombardy–Veneto', in Jane Caplan and John Torpey (eds), *Documenting Individual Identity: The Development of State Practices in the Modern World* (Princeton, NJ: Princeton University Press, 2001), pp. 199–217.

Giddens, Anthony, *The Constitution of Society* (Cambridge: Polity Press, 1986).

Giddens, Anthony, *The Nation-state and Violence: Volume Two of a Contemporary Critique of Historical Materialism* (Cambridge: Polity Press, 1987).

Giddens, Anthony, *The Consequences of Modernity* (Cambridge: Polity Press, 1991).

Giddens, Anthony, *A Contemporary Critique of Historical Materialism* (Basingstoke: Palgrave Macmillan, 1995).

Giddens, Anthony, *The Third Way: The Renewal of Social Democracy* (Cambridge: Polity Press, 1998).

Gilbert, Bentley B., *British Social Policy, 1914–1939* (London: B. T. Batsford, 1970).

Gill, Peter, *Policing Politics: Security Intelligence and the Liberal Democratic State* (London: Frank Cass, 1994).

Gladstone, David, *The Twentieth-century Welfare State* (Basingstoke: Palgrave, 1999).

Glass, D. V., *Numbering the People* (London: Gordon and Cremonesi, 1978).

Glass, D. V., 'Two papers on Gregory King', in D. V. Glass and D. E. C. Eversley (eds), *Population in History: Essays in Historical Demography* (London: Edward Arnold, 1965), pp. 159–220.

Goldie, Mark, 'The unacknowledged republic: officeholding in early modern England', in Tim Harris (ed.), *The Politics of the Excluded, c.1500–1850* (Basingstoke: Palgrave Macmillan, 2001), pp. 153–94.

Gränström, Claes, 'Swedish society and electronic data', in Edward Higgs (ed.), *History and Electronic Artefacts* (Oxford: Oxford University Press, 1998), pp. 317–38.

Grieves, Keith, *The Politics of Manpower, 1914–19* (Manchester: Manchester University Press, 1988).

Griffiths, Paul, Fox, Adam and Hindle, Steve, 'Introduction', in Paul Griffiths, Adam Fox and Steve Hindle (eds), *The Experience of Authority in Early Modern England* (Basingstoke: Palgrave Macmillan, 1996), pp. 1–9.

Guinn, Paul, *British Strategy and Politics, 1914 to 1918* (Oxford: Oxford University Press, 1965).

Habermas, Jürgen, *The Theory of Communicative Action: The Critique of Functionalist Reason*, vol. 2 (Cambridge: Polity, 1989).

Habermas, Jürgen, *The Structural Transformation of the Public Sphere: An Inquiry into a Category of Bourgeois Society* (Cambridge: Polity Press, 1992).

Hacking, Ian, *The Emergence of Probability* (Cambridge: Cambridge University Press, 1975).

Hacking, Ian, *The Taming of Chance* (Cambridge: Cambridge University Press, 1990).

Hakim, Catherine, 'Social monitors: population censuses as social surveys', in Martin Bulmer (ed.), *Essays on the History of British Sociological Research* (Cambridge: Cambridge University Press, 1985), pp. 39–51.

Hall, Catherine, McClelland, Keith and Rendall, Jane, *Defining the Victorian Nation: Class, Race, Gender and the British Reform Act of 1867* (Cambridge: Cambridge University Press, 2000).

Hall, J. A., 'Capstones and organisms: political forms and the triumph of capitalism', *Sociology* 19 (1985), pp. 173–92.

Hall, John A., *Powers and Liberties: The Causes and Consequences of the Rise of the West* (Oxford: Basil Blackwell, 1985).

Hall, Stuart and Schwarz, Bill, 'State and society, 1880–1930', in Mary Langan and Bill Schwarz (eds), *Crises in the British State, 1880–1930* (London: Hutchinson, 1985), pp. 7–32.

Hallam, Elizabeth M., *Domesday Book though Nine Centuries* (London: Thames & Hudson, 1986).

Hamlin, Christopher, 'Could you starve to death in England in 1839? The Chadwick–Farr controversy and the loss of the "social" in public health', *American Journal of Public Health* 85 (1995), pp. 856–66.

Hamlin, Christopher, *Public Health and Social Justice in the Age of Chadwick: Britain, 1800–1854* (Cambridge: Cambridge University Press, 1998).

Hannah, Leslie, *The Rise of the Corporate Economy* (London: Methuen, 1976).

Hardy, Anne, ' "Death is the cure of all diseases": using the General Register Office cause of death statistics for 1837–1920', *Social History of Medicine* 7 (1994), pp. 472–92.

Harling, Philip, 'The power of persuasion: central authority, local bureaucracy and the New Poor Law', *English Historical Review* 107 (1992), pp. 30–53.

Harling, Philip, 'The politics of administrative change in Britain, 1780–1850', *Yearbook of European Administrative History* 8 (Baden-Baden: Nomos Verlagsgesellschaft, 1996), pp. 191–212.

Harling, Philip, *The Modern British State: An Historical Introduction* (Cambridge: Polity Press, 2001).

Harris, José, *William Beveridge: A Biography* (Oxford: Oxford University Press, 1977).

Harris, José, *Unemployment and Politics: A Study in English Social Policy, 1886–1914* (Oxford: Oxford University Press, 1984).

Harris, José, 'Society and the state in twentieth-century Britain', in F. M. L. Thompson (ed.), *The Cambridge Social History of Britain, 1750–1950*, vol. 3: *Social Agencies and Institutions* (Cambridge: Cambridge University Press, 1990), pp. 63–118.

Harris, José, *Private Lives, Public Spirit: A Social History of Britain, 1870–1914* (London: Penguin, 1994).

Harris, José, 'Political thought and the Welfare State, 1870–1940: an intellectual framework for British social policy', in David Gladstone (ed.), *Before Beveridge: Welfare before the Welfare State* (London: IEA Health and Welfare Unit, 1999), pp. 43–63.

Harris, José, 'General introduction', in Ferdinand Tönnies, *Community and Civil Society (Gemeinschaft und Gesellschaft)* (Cambridge: Cambridge University Press, 2001), pp. ix–xxx.

Harrison, Brian, *The Transformation of British Politics, 1860–1995* (Oxford: Oxford University Press, 1996).

Harriss, Gerald, 'Political society and the growth of government in late medieval England', *Past and Present* 138 (1993), pp. 28–57.

Harvey, Charles and Press, Jon, *Databases in Historical Research* (Basingstoke: Palgrave Macmillan, 1996).

Hay, J. R., 'Employers' attitudes to social policy and the concept of "social control", 1900–1920', in Pat Thane (ed.), *The Origins of British Social Policy* (London: Croom Helm, 1978), pp. 107–25.

Headrick, Daniel, *The Invisible Weapon: Telecommunications and International Politics, 1851–1945* (Oxford: Oxford University Press, 1991).

Headrick, Daniel, *When Information Came of Age: Technologies of Knowledge in the Age of Reason and Revolution, 1700–1850* (New York: Oxford University Press, 2000).

Hennessy, Peter, *The Secret State: Whitehall and the Cold War* (London: Penguin, 2002).

Hennock, E. P., *Fit and Proper Persons: Ideal and Reality in Nineteenth-century Urban Government* (London: Edward Arnold, 1973).

Hennock, E. P., 'Poverty and social theory in England: the experience of the eighteen-eighties', *Social History* 1 (1976), pp. 67–91.

Hennock, E. P., 'Poverty and social reforms', in Paul Johnson (ed.), *Twentieth-century Britain: Economic, Social and Cultural Change* (London: Longman, 1994), pp. 79–93.

Hennock, E. P., 'Vaccination policy against smallpox, 1835–1914: a comparison of England with Prussia and Imperial Germany', *Social History of Medicine* 11 (1998), pp. 49–72.

Henriques, Ursula R. Q., *The Early Factory Acts and their Enforcement* (London: Historical Association, 1971).

Hey, David, *The Oxford Companion to Local and Family History* (Oxford: Oxford University Press, 1998).

Higgs, Edward, 'Women, occupations and work in the nineteenth-century censuses', *History Workshop Journal* 23 (1987), pp. 59–80.

Higgs, Edward, *Making Sense of the Census: The Manuscript Returns for England and Wales, 1801–1901* (London: HMSO, 1989).

Higgs, Edward, 'Diseases, febrile poisons, and statistics: the census as a medical survey', *Social History of Medicine* 4 (1991), pp. 465–78.

Higgs, Edward, *A Clearer Sense of the Census: The Victorian Censuses and Historical Research* (London: HMSO, 1996), pp. 155–6.

Higgs, Edward, 'A cuckoo in the nest? The origins of civil registration and state medical statistics in England and Wales', *Continuity and Change* 11 (1996), pp. 115–34.

Higgs, Edward, 'The statistical Big Bang of 1911: ideology, technological innovation and the production of medical statistics', *Social History of Medicine* 9 (1996), pp. 409–26.

Higgs, Edward, 'From medieval erudition to information management: the evolution of the archival profession', *Archivum (Proceedings of the XIII International Congress on Archives, Beijing, 2–7 September 1996)* XLIII (1997), pp. 136–44.

Higgs, Edward, '*The Annual Report of the Registrar General*, 1839–1920: a textual history', in Eileen Magnello and Anne Hardy (eds), *The Road to Medical Statistics* (Amsterdam: Rodopi, 2002), pp. 55–76.

Hill, Christopher, *Liberty against the Law: Some Seventeenth-century Controversies* (London: Allen Lane, 1996).

Hindle, Steve, 'The keeping of the public peace', in Paul Griffiths, Adam Fox and Steve Hindle (eds), *The Experience of Authority in Early Modern England* (Basingstoke: Palgrave Macmillan, 1996), pp. 213–48.

Hindle, Steve, *The State and Social Change in Early Modern England, c. 1550–1640* (Basingstoke: Palgrave Macmillan, 2000).

Holdsworth, Sir William, *A History of English Law*, vol. 13 (London: Sweet and Maxwell, 1952).

Holmes, G. S., 'Gregory King and the social structure of pre-industrial England', *Transactions of the Royal Historical Society*, Fifth Series, 27 (1977), pp. 41–68.

Hopkins, E., *Working-class Self Help in Nineteenth-century England: Responses to Industrialisation* (London: UCL Press, 1995).

Hoppen, K. Theodore, *The Mid-Victorian Generation, 1846–1886* (Oxford: Oxford University Press, 1998).

Horn, Pamela, 'Child workers in the Victorian countryside: the case of Northamptonshire', *Northamptonshire Past and Present* VII (1985–6), pp. 173–85.

Houlbrooke, Ralph A., *Church Courts and the People during the English Reformation, 1520–1570* (Oxford: Oxford University Press, 1979).

Hurt, J. S., *Elementary Schooling and the Working Classes, 1860–1918* (London: Routledge and Kegan Paul, 1979).

Ignatieff, Michael, *A Just Measure of Pain: The Penitentiary in the Industrial Revolution, 1750–1850* (London: Macmillan, 1978).

Ignatieff, Michael, 'State, civil society and total institutions: a critique of recent social histories of punishment', in Stanley Cohen and Andrew Scull (eds), *Social Control and the State: Historical and Comparative Essays* (Oxford: M. Robertson, 1983), pp. 75–105.

Ingram, Martin, *Church Courts, Sex and Marriages in England, 1570–1640* (Cambridge: Cambridge University Press, 1990).

Janowitz, M., 'Sociological theory and social control', *American Journal of Sociology* 81 (1975), pp. 82–95.

Jarvis, Rupert C., 'Official trade and revenue statistics', *Economic History Review* XVII (1964–65), pp. 43–62.

Joas, Hans, *G. H. Mead: A Contemporary Re-examination of His Thought* (Cambridge: Polity Press, 1985).

Johnson, Paul, 'The role of the State in twentieth-century Britain', in Paul Johnson (ed.), *Twentieth-century Britain: Economic, Social and Cultural Change* (Harlow: Longman, 1994), pp. 476–91.

Johnson, Paul, 'Risk, redistribution and social welfare in Britain from the poor law to Beveridge', in Martin Daunton (ed.), *Charity, Self-interest and Welfare in the English Past* (London: UCL Press, 1996), pp. 225–48.

Jones, David Martin, *Conscience and Allegiance in Seventeenth-century England: The Political Significance of Oaths and Engagements* (New York: University of Rochester Press, 1999).

Jones, Gareth Stedman, 'Class expression versus social control? A critique of recent trends in the social history of "leisure"', *History Workshop Journal* 4 (1977), pp. 162–70.

Jones, Gareth Stedman, *Outcast London: A Study in the Relationship Between Classes in Victorian Society* (Harmondsworth: Penguin, 1984).

Jones, Greta, *Social Hygiene in Twentieth-century Britain* (London: Croom Helm, 1986).

Joseph, Anne M., 'Anthropometry, the police expert, and the Deptford Murders: the contested introduction of fingerprinting for the identification of criminals in late Victorian and Edwardian Britain', in Jane Caplan and John Torpey (eds), *Documenting Individual Identity: The Development of State Practices in the Modern World* (Princeton, NJ: Princeton University Press, 2001), pp. 164–83.

Joyce, Patrick, *Visions of the People: Industrial England and the Question of Class, 1848–1914* (Cambridge: Cambridge University Press, 1991).

Jurkowski, M., Smith, C. and Crook, D., *Lay Taxes in England and Wales, 1188–1688* (London: Public Record Office, 1998).

Kaluszynski, Martine, 'Republican identity: Bertillonage as government technique', in Jane Caplan and John Torpey (eds), *Documenting Individual Identity: The Development of State Practices in the Modern World* (Princeton, NJ: Princeton University Press, 2001), pp. 123–38.

Kearns, Gerry, 'Private property and public health reform, 1830–70', *Social Science & Medicine* 26 (1988), pp. 187–99.

Kent, Joan R., 'The centre and the localities: state formation and parish government in England, circa 1640–1740', *Historical Journal* 38 (1995), pp. 363–404.

Kidd, Alan, *State, Society and the Poor in Nineteenth-century England* (Basingstoke: Palgrave Macmillan, 1999).

Kidd, Alan, 'The "Liberal State" civil society and social welfare in nineteenth-century England', *Journal of Historical Sociology* 15 (2002), pp. 114–20.

Killingback, W. J., *The Work of the Registry of Shipping and Seamen and of the Mercantile Marine Office* (n/a: W. J. Killingback, 1945).

King, Sir Geoffrey S., *The Ministry of Pensions and National Insurance* (London: Allen & Unwin, 1958).

Kreager, Philip, 'Quand une population est-elle un nation? Quand une nation est-elle un état? La démographie et l'emergence d'un dilemme moderne, 1770–1870', *Population* 6 (1992), pp. 1639–56.

Kuznets, Lois R., *Kenneth Grahame* (Boston, MA: Twayne Publishers, 1987).

La Berge, Anna, 'Edwin Chadwick and the French connection', *Bulletin of the History of Medicine* 62 (1988), pp. 23–41.

Lambert, R. J., 'A Victorian National Health Service: State vaccination 1855–1871', *Historical Journal* V (1962), pp. 1–18.

Landau, N., 'Laws of settlement and surveillance of immigration in eighteenth-century Kent', *Continuity and Change* 3 (1988), pp. 391–420.

Laslett, Peter, 'Gregory King, Thomas Malthus and the origins of English social realism', *Population Studies* 39 (1985), pp. 351–62.

Laslett, Peter, 'Natural and political observations on the population of the late seventeenth-century England: reflection on the work of Gregory King and John Graunt', in Kevin Schürer and Tom Arkell (eds), *Surveying the People: The Interpretation and Use of Document Sources for the Study of Population in the Later Seventeenth Century* (Oxford: Leopard's Head Press, 1992), pp. 6–30.

Lawes, Aidan, *Chancery Lane, 1377–1977: The Strong Box of the Empire* (Kew: PRO Publications, 1996).

Lewis, Jane, *The Politics of Motherhood: Child and Maternal Welfare in England, 1900–1939* (London: Croom Helm, 1980).

Logan, W. P. D. and Brooke, Eileen M., *The Survey of Sickness, 1943 to 1952: General Register Office Studies on Medical and Population Subjects*, no. 12 (London: HMSO, 1952).

Longman, Timothy, 'Identity cards, ethnic self-perception, and genocide in Rwanda', in Jane Caplan and John Torpey (eds), *Documenting Individual Identity: The Development of State Practices in the Modern World* (Princeton, NJ: Princeton University Press, 2001), pp. 345–57.

Lonsdale, Roger (ed.), *Eighteenth-Century Verse* (Oxford: Oxford University Press, 1987).

Loudon, Irvine. *Medical Care and the General Practitioner, 1750–1850* (Oxford: Oxford University Press, 1986).

Lowe, Rodney, *Adjusting to Democracy: The Role of the Ministry of Labour in British Politics, 1916–1939* (Oxford: Oxford University Press, 1986).

Lucassen, Leo, 'A many-headed monster: the evolution of the passport system in the Netherlands and Germany in the long nineteenth century', in Jane Caplan and John Torpey (eds), *Documenting Individual Identity: The Development of State Practices in the Modern World* (Princeton, NJ: Princeton University Press, 2001), pp. 235–54.

Luebke, David Martin and Milton, Sybil, 'Locating the victim: an overview of census-taking, tabulation technology, and persecution in Nazi Germany', *IEEE Annals of the History of Computing* 16 (1994), pp. 25–39.

Luhmann, Niklas, *The Differentiation of Society* (New York: Columbia University Press, 1982).

Luhmann, Niklas, *Social Systems* (Stanford, CA: Stanford University Press, 1995).

Lyon, David, *The Electronic Eye: The Rise of the Surveillance Society* (Cambridge: Polity, 1994).

Lyon, David, 'Under my skin: from identification to body surveillance', in Jane Caplan and John Torpey (eds), *Documenting Individual Identity: The Development of State Practices in the Modern World* (Princeton, NJ: Princeton University Press, 2001), pp. 291–310.

MacCaffrey, Wallace, *Elizabeth I* (London: Edward Arnold, 1993).

MacDonagh, Oliver, 'The nineteenth-century revolution in government: a reappraisal', *The Historical Journal* I (1958), pp. 52–67.

MacDonagh, Oliver, *A Pattern of Government Growth: The Passenger Acts and Their Enforcement, 1800–1860* (London: MacGibbon and Kee, 1961).

MacDonagh, Oliver, *Early Victorian Government, 1830–1870* (London: Weidenfeld and Nicolson, 1977).

McDonald, John and Snooks, G. D., *Domesday Economy: A New Approach to Anglo-Norman History* (Oxford: Oxford University Press, 1986).

Macfarlane, Alan, *Reconstructing Historical Communities* (Cambridge, Cambridge University Press, 1977).

Macfarlane, Alan, *The Origins of English Individualism* (Oxford: Blackwell, 1978).

McHugh, Paul, *Prostitution and Victorian Social Reform* (London: Croom Helm, 1980).

McIntosh, Marjorie Keniston, *Controlling Misbehaviour in England, 1370–1600* (Cambridge: Cambridge University Press, 1998).

MacLeod, R. M., 'Law, medicine and public opinion: the resistance to compulsory health legislation, 1870–1907: Part I and II', *Public Law* (1967), pp. 107–28, 189–211.

Mallet, Sir Bernard, *British Budgets, 1887–1913* (London: Macmillan, 1913).

Mallet, Sir Bernard, 'The organisation of registration in its bearings on vital statistics', *Journal of the Royal Statistical Society* LXXX (1917), pp. 1–24.

Manchester, A. H., *A Modern Legal History of England and Wales, 1750–1950* (London: Butterworths, 1980).

Mann, Michael, *The Sources of Social Power*, vol. I: *A History of Power from the Beginning to AD1760* (Cambridge: Cambridge University Press, 1986).

Mann, Michael, *States, War and Capitalism: Studies in Political Sociology* (Oxford: Blackwell, 1988).

Mann, Michael, *The Sources of Social Power*, vol. II: *The Rise of Classes and Nation-States* (Cambridge: Cambridge University Press, 1993).

Manwaring-White, Sarah, *The Policing Revolution* (Brighton: Harvester, 1983).

Mappen, Ellen F., 'Strategists for change: social feminist approaches to the problems of women's work', in Angela V. John (ed.), *Unequal Opportunities: Women's Employment in England, 1800–1918* (Oxford: Blackwell, 1986), pp. 235–60.

Marsh, Catherine, 'Informants, respondents and citizens', in Martin Bulmer (ed.), *Essays on the History of British Sociological Research* (Cambridge: Cambridge University Press, 1985), pp. 206–25.

Marshall, T. H., 'Citizenship and social class', in Bryan S. Turner and Peter Hamilton (eds), *Citizenship: Critical Concepts*, vol. II (London: Routledge, 1994), pp. 5–44.

Mattelart, Armand, *The Invention of Communication* (London: University of Minnesota Press, 1996).

Mayer, John A., 'Notes towards a working definition of social control in historical analysis', in Stanley Cohen and Andrew Scull (eds), *Social Control and the State: Historical and Comparative Essays* (Oxford: M. Robertson, 1983), pp. 17–38.

Mazumdar, Pauline M. H., *Eugenics, Human Genetics and Human Failings: The Eugenics Society, Its Sources and Its Critics in Britain* (London: Routledge, 1992).

Michael, James, *The Politics of Secrecy* (Harmondsworth: Penguin, 1982).

Miles, Ian and Irvine, John, 'The critique of official statistics', in John Irvine, Ian Miles and Jeff Evans (eds), *Demystifying Social Statistics* (London: Pluto Press, 1979), pp. 113–29.

Mill, John Stuart, 'Bentham', in John Stuart Mill and Jeremy Bentham, *Utilitarianism and Other Essays* (London: Penguin, 1987).

Mill, John Stuart, 'Considerations on representative government', in *Utilitarianism, On Liberty, Considerations on Representative Government* (London: J. M. Dent, 1993).

Ministry of Labour, *Report on National Unemployment Insurance to July 1923* (London: HMSO, 1923).

Mitchison, Rosalind, *British Population Change since 1860* (London: Macmillan, 1977).

Morris, R. J., *Class, Sect and Party: The Making of the British Middle Class: Leeds 1820–1850* (Manchester: Manchester University Press, 1990).

Mort, Frank, *Dangerous Sexualities: Medico-moral Politics in England since 1830* (London: Routledge & Kegan Paul, 1987).

Moser, Sir Claus, 'Social indicators: systems, methods and problems', in Martin Bulmer (ed.), *Social Policy Research* (London: Macmillan, 1978), pp. 203–14.

Moss, Louis, *The Government Social Survey: A History* (London: HMSO, 1991).

Musson, A. J., 'Sub-keepers and constables: the role of local officers in keeping the peace in fourteenth-century England', *English Historical Review* CXVII, 470 (2002), pp. 1–24.

National Conference on Infantile Mortality, *Report of the Proceedings of the National Conference on Infantile Mortality… 23rd, 24th, and 25th March 1908* (London: P. S. King & Son, 1908).

Nelson, Daniel, *Frederick W. Taylor and the Rise of Scientific Management* (Madison: University of Wisconsin Press, 1980).

Nissel, Muriel, *People Count: A History of the General Register Office* (London: HMSO, 1996).

Noiriel, Gerard, 'The identification of the citizen: the birth of republican civil status in France', in Jane Caplan and John Torpey (eds), *Documenting Individual Identity: The Development of State Practices in the Modern World* (Princeton, NJ: Princeton University Press, 2001), pp. 28–48.

Norris, C., Moran, J. and Armstrong, G. (eds), *Surveillance, Closed Circuit Television and Social Control* (Aldershot: Ashgate, 1998).

O'Brien, Patrick K., 'The political economy of British taxation, 1660–1815', *Economic History Review*, 2nd ser., XLI (1988), pp. 1–32.

O'Farrell, Patrick, *Ireland's English Question* (London: B. T. Batsford, 1971).

Office of Population Censuses and Surveys and the General Register Office, Edinburgh, *Guide to Census Reports, Great Britain, 1801–1966* (London: HMSO, 1977).

Ogg, David, *England in the Reign of Charles II* (Oxford: Oxford University Press, 1934).

Oman, Carola, *Nelson* (London: Hodder and Stoughton, 1967).

Owen, Charlie, 'Government household surveys', in Daniel Dorling and Stephen Simpson (eds), *Statistics in Society: The Arithmetic of Politics* (London: Arnold, 1999), pp. 19–28.

Palmowski, Jan, 'Liberalism and local government in late nineteenth-century Germany and England', *Historical Journal* 45 (2002), pp. 381–410.

Parker, H. M. D., *Manpower: A Study of War-time Policy and Administration* (London: HMSO, 1957).

Parkhurst, P. G., *Ships of Peace* (New Malden: P. G. Parkhurst, 1962).

Parsons, Talcott, *The Social System* (London: Routledge & Kegan Paul, 1951).

Patriarca, Silvana, *Numbers and Nationhood: Writing Statistics in Nineteenth-century Italy* (Cambridge: Cambridge University Press, 1996).

Peacock, A. T. and Jack Wiseman, *The Growth of Public Expenditure in the United Kingdom* (London: Allen and Unwin, 1967).

Pedersen, Susan, *Family, Dependence, and the Origins of the Welfare State* (Cambridge: Cambridge University Press, 1993).

Perkin, Harold, *The Rise of Professional Society: England since 1880* (London: Routledge, 1989).

Perrot, Jean-Claude and Woolf, Stuart J., *State and Statistics in France, 1789–1815* (New York: Harwood Academic Publishers, 1984).

Philips, David, *Crime and Authority in Victorian England: The Black Country, 1835–1860* (London: Croom Helm, 1977).

Philips, David, ' "A new engine of power and authority": the institution-alization of law-enforcing in England, 1780–1830', in V. Gatrell, B. Lenman and G. Parker (eds), *Crime and the Law: The Social History of Crime in Western Europe since 1500* (London: Europa Publications, 1980), pp. 155–89.

Porter, Bernard, *The Origins of the Vigilant State: The London Metropolitan Police Special Branch before the First World War* (London: Weidenfeld and Nicolson, 1987).

Porter, Theodore M., *The Rise of Statistical Thinking, 1820–1900* (Princeton, NJ: Princeton University Press, 1986).

Postema, Gerald J., *Bentham and the Common Law Tradition* (Oxford: Oxford University Press, 1986).

Public Record Office, *Current Guide* (London: Public Record Office, n.d.).

Public Record Office, *Guide to the Contents of the Public Record Office*, vol. I: *Legal Records, etc.* (London: HMSO, 1963).

Public Record Office, *Guide to the Contents of the Public Record Office*, vol. II: *State Papers and Departmental Records* (London: HMSO, 1963).

Pugh, Martin, 'Working-class experience and state social welfare, 1908–1914: old age pensions reconsidered', *The Historical Journal* 45 (2002), pp. 775–97.

Randeraad, Nico, 'Nineteenth-century population registers as statistical source and instrument of social control (Belgium, Italy and the Netherlands)', *Tijdschrift voor sociale geschiedenis* 21 (1995), pp. 319–42.

Rawls, John, *A Theory of Justice* (Oxford: Oxford University Press, 1999).

Reiner, Robert, *The Politics of the Police* (Oxford: Oxford University Press, 2000).

Rodger, N. A. M., *The Admiralty* (Lavenham: Terence Dalton, 1979).

Rodger, N. A. M., *The Wooden World: An Anatomy of the Georgian Navy* (London: Collins, 1986).

Rodger, N. A. M., *Naval Records for Genealogists* (London: PRO Publications, 1988).

Rodger, N. A. M., *The Wooden World: An Anatomy of the Georgian Navy* (London: Fontana, 1988).

Rothman, David J., 'Social control: the uses and abuses of the concept in the history of incarceration', in Stanley Cohen and Andrew Scull (eds), *Social Control and the State: Historical and Comparative Essays* (Oxford: Martin Robertson, 1983), pp. 106–17.

Rouche, Michel, 'Autopsy of the West: the early fifth century', in Robert Fossier (ed.), *The Cambridge Illustrated History of the Middle Ages, 350–950* (Cambridge: Cambridge University Press, 1997), pp. 17–51.

Rowntree, Seebohm, *Poverty: A Study of Town Life* (London: Macmillan, 1902).

Rubinstein, W. D., *Men of Property: The Very Wealthy in Britain since the Industrial Revolution* (London: Croom Helm, 1981).

Ruggiero, Kristin, 'Fingerprinting and the Argentine plan for universal identification in the late nineteenth and early twentieth centuries', in Jane Caplan and John Torpey (eds), *Documenting Individual Identity: The Development of State Practices in the Modern World* (Princeton, NJ: Princeton University Press, 2001), pp. 184–96.

Rule, James B., *Private Lives and Public Surveillance* (London: Allen Lane, 1973).

Sabine, B. E. V., *A History of the Income Tax* (London: Allen & Unwin, 1966).

Sankar, Pamela, 'DNA-typing: Galton's eugenic dream realized?', in Jane Caplan and John Torpey (eds), *Documenting Individual*

Identity: The Development of State Practices in the Modern World (Princeton, NJ: Princeton University Press, 2001), pp. 273–90.

Scannell, Paddy and Cardiff, David, *A Social History of British Broadcasting*, vol. 1: *1922–1939: Serving the Nation* (Oxford: Blackwell, 1991).

Schürer, Kevin, 'The 1891 census and local population studies', *Local Population Studies* 47 (1991), pp. 16–29.

Searle, G. R., *The Quest for National Efficiency: A Study in British Politics and Political Thought, 1899–1914* (Oxford: Basil Blackwell, 1971).

Sharpe, J. A., *Crime in Early Modern England, 1550–1750* (London: Longman, 1984).

Sharpe, L. J., 'Government as client for social policy research', in Martin Bulmer (ed.), *Social Policy Research* (London: Macmillan, 1978), pp. 67–84.

Sharpe, L. J., 'The social scientist and policy-making in Britain and America: a comparison', in Martin Bulmer (ed.), *Social Policy Research* (London: Macmillan, 1978), pp. 302–12.

Simpson, A. W., *In the Highest Degree Odious: Detention without Trial in Wartime Britain* (Oxford: Oxford University Press, 1992).

Sizer, Richard and Newman, Philip, *The Data Protection Act: A Practical Guide* (Aldershot: Gower, 1984).

Skocpol, Theda, *States and Social Revolutions: A Comparative Analysis of France, Russia and China* (Cambridge: Cambridge University Press, 1979).

Skocpol, Theda and Rueschemeyer, Dietrich, 'Introduction', in Dietrich Rueschemeyer and Theda Skocpol (eds), *States, Social Knowledge, and the Origins of Modern Social Policy* (Princeton, NJ: Princeton University Press, 1996), pp. 3–14.

Slack, Paul, *Poverty and Policy in Tudor and Stuart England* (London: Longman, 1988).

Smith, F. B., 'The Contagious Diseases Act reconsidered', *Social History of Medicine* 3 (1990), pp. 197–217.

Smith, Michael, *New Cloak, Old Dagger: How Britain's Spies Came in from the Cold* (London: Victor Gollancz, 1996).

Smith, R. M., ' "Modernisation" and the corporate medieval community in England: some sceptical reflections', in A. H. R. Baker and D. Gregory (eds), *Explorations in Historical Geography* (Cambridge: Cambridge University Press, 1984), pp. 140–79.

Snell, K. D. M., *Annals of the Labouring Poor: Social Change and Agrarian England, 1660–1900* (Cambridge: Cambridge University Press, 1987).

Snell, K. D. M., 'Pauper settlement and the right to relief in England and Wales', *Continuity and Change* 6 (1991), pp. 375–415.

Snellen, Ignace Th.M., 'From societal scanning to policy feedback: two hundred years of government information processing in the

Netherlands', *Yearbook of European Administrative History* 9 (Baden-Baden: Nomos Verlagsgesellschaft, 1997), pp. 195–212.

Soloway, Richard A., *Demography and Degeneration: Eugenics and the Declining Birthrate in Twentieth-century Britain* (London: University of North Carolina Press, 1990).

Somerville, Johann P., *Thomas Hobbes: Political Ideas in Historical Context* (Basingstoke: Palgrave Macmillan, 1992).

Spitzer, Steven, 'The rationalization of crime control in capitalist society', in Stanley Cohen and Andrew Scull (eds), *Social Control and the State: Historical and Comparative Essays* (Oxford: Martin Robertson, 1983), pp. 312–33.

Stammers, Neil, *Civil Liberties in Britain during the Second World War* (London: Croom Helm, 1983).

Stamp, Josiah, *British Incomes and Property: the Application of Official Statistics to Economic Problems* (London: P. S. King & Son, 1916).

Stanziani, Alessandro, 'Les sources démographiques entre contrôle policier et utopies technocratiques: le cas russe, 1870–1926', *Cahiers du monde russe* 38 (1997), pp. 457–88.

Steinwedel, Charles, 'Making social groups, one person at a time: the identification of individuals by estate, religious confession, and ethnicity in late Imperial Russia', in Jane Caplan and John Torpey (eds), *Documenting Individual Identity: The Development of State Practices in the Modern World* (Princeton, NJ: Princeton University Press, 2001), pp. 67–82.

Stenton, F. M., *Anglo-Saxon England* (Oxford: Oxford University Press, 1971).

Stewart, Robert Mackenzie, *Henry Brougham, 1778–1868: His Public Career* (London: Bodley Head, 1986).

Strachan, Hew, *European Armies and the Conduct of War* (London: George Allen & Unwin, 1983).

Sumner, Colin, 'Social control: the history and politics of a central concept in Anglo-American sociology', in Roberto Bergalli and Colin Sumner (eds), *Social Control and Political Orders: European Perspectives at the End of the Century* (London: Sage, 1997), pp. 1–33.

Sutherland, Donald W., *Quo Warranto Proceedings in the Reign of Edward I, 1278–1294* (Oxford: Oxford University Press, 1963).

Szreter, Simon, 'The GRO and the public health movement in Britain, 1837–1914', *Social History of Medicine* 4 (1991), pp. 435–64.

Szreter, Simon, *Fertility, Class and Gender in Britain, 1860–1940* (Cambridge: Cambridge University Press, 1996).

Tant, A. P., *British Government: The Triumph of Elitism: A Study of the British Political Tradition and Its Major Challenges* (Aldershot: Dartmouth, 1993).

Tate, W. E., *The Parish Chest: A Study of the Records of Parochial Administration in England* (Cambridge: Cambridge University Press, 1951).

Taylor, Charles, *Sources of the Self: The Making of Modern Identity* (Cambridge: Cambridge University Press, 1989).

Taylor, Howard, 'Rationing crime: the political economy of criminal statistics since the 1850s', *Economic History Review* LI (1998), pp. 569–90.

Thane, Pat, 'Non-contributory versus insurance pensions, 1878–1908', in Pat Thane (ed.), *The Origins of British Social Policy* (London: Croom Helm, 1978), pp. 84–106.

Thane, Pat, *The Foundations of the Welfare State* (London: Longman, 1982).

Thane, Pat, 'Government and society in England and Wales, 1750–1914', in F. M. L. Thompson (ed.), *The Cambridge Social History of Britain, 1750–1950*, vol. 3: *Social Agencies and Institutions* (Cambridge: Cambridge University Press, 1990), pp. 1–62.

Thane, Pat, 'Old people and their families in the English past', in Martin Daunton (ed.), *Charity, Self-interest and Welfare in the English Past* (London: UCL Press, 1996), pp. 113–38.

Thane, Pat, 'The working class and state "welfare" in Britain, 1880–1914', in David Gladstone, *Before Beveridge: Welfare before the Welfare State* (London: IEA Health and Welfare Unit, 1999), pp. 86–112.

Thirsk, Joan and Cooper, J. P., *Seventeenth-century Economic Documents* (Oxford: Oxford University Press, 1972).

Thomas, Ray, 'The politics and reform of unemployment and employment statistics', in Daniel Dorling and Stephen Simpson (eds), *Statistics in Society: The Arithmetic of Politics* (London: Arnold, 1999), pp. 324–34.

Thompson, E. P., *The Making of the English Working Class* (Harmondsworth: Penguin Books, 1968).

Thompson, E. P., *Whigs and Hunters: The Origin of the Black Act* (Harmondsworth: Penguin, 1977).

Thompson, F. M. L., 'Social control in Victorian Britain', *Economic History Review*, 2nd ser., XXXIV (1981), pp. 189–208.

Thurlow, Richard, *The Secret State: British Internal Security in the Twentieth Century* (Oxford: Blackwell, 1994).

de Tocqueville, Alexis, *The Old Regime and the French Revolution* (New York: Doubleday, 1955).

de Tocqueville, Alexis, *Journeys to England and Ireland* (London: Faber and Faber, 1958).

Tönnies, Ferdinand, *Community and Civil Society (Gemeinschaft und Gesellschaft)* (Cambridge: Cambridge University Press, 2001).

Torpey, John, 'The Great War and the birth of the modern passport system', in Jane Caplan and John Torpey (eds), *Documenting Individual*

Identity: The Development of State Practices in the Modern World (Princeton, NJ: Princeton University Press, 2001), pp. 256–70.

Townsend, Peter, 'Surveys of poverty to promote democracy', in Martin Bulmer (ed.), *Essays on the History of British Sociological Research* (Cambridge: Cambridge University Press, 1985), pp. 228–35.

Townsend, Peter, Davidson, Nick and Whitehead, Margaret (eds), *Inequalities in Health: The Black Report* (London: Penguin, 1988).

Turner, Bryan S., 'Outline of a theory of citizenship', in Bryan S. Turner and Peter Hamilton (eds), *Citizenship: Critical Concepts*, vol. I (London: Routledge, 1994), pp. 199–226.

Vincent, David, *Poor Citizens: The State and the Poor in Twentieth-century Britain* (London: Longman, 1991).

Vincent, David, *The Culture of Secrecy: Britain, 1832–1998* (Oxford: Oxford University Press, 1998).

Waddington, Ivan, *The Medical Profession in the Industrial Revolution* (Dublin: Gill and Macmillan, 1984).

Walkowitz, J., *Prostitution and Victorian Society: Women, Class and State* (Cambridge: Cambridge University Press, 1980).

Ward, W. R., *The English Land Tax in the Eighteenth Century* (Oxford: Oxford University Press, 1953).

Warne, Arthur, *Church and Society in Eighteenth-century Devon* (Newton Abbot: David & Charles, 1969).

Warren, W. L., *The Governance of Norman and Angevin England* (London: Edward Arnold, 1987).

Webster, Charles, 'Healthy or hungry thirties', *History Workshop Journal* XIII (1982), pp. 110–29.

Webster, Frank, *Theories of the Information Society* (London: Routledge, 1995).

Westergaard, Harald, *Contributions to the History of Statistics* (London: P. S. King, 1932).

Wettengel, Michael, 'German unification and electronic records', in Edward Higgs (ed.), *History and Electronic Artefacts* (Oxford: Clarendon Press, 1998), pp. 265–76.

Whitehead, Frank, 'The Government Social Survey', in Martin Bulmer (ed.), *Essays in the History of British Sociological Research* (Cambridge: Cambridge University Press, 1985), pp. 83–100.

Whiteside, Noel, 'Private provision and public welfare: health insurance between the wars', in David Gladstone (ed.), *Before Beveridge: Welfare before the Welfare State* (London: IEA Health and Welfare Unit, 1999), pp. 26–42.

Wiener, Martin J., review of A. P. Donajgrodzki (ed.), *Social Control in Nineteenth-Century Britain*, *Journal of Social History*, 12 (1978), pp. 314–20.

Wiener, Martin J., *Reconstructing the Criminal: Culture, Law and Policing in England, 1830–1914* (Cambridge: Cambridge University Press, 1990).

Williams, Naomi, 'The implementation of compulsory health legislation: infant smallpox vaccination in England and Wales, 1840–1890', *Journal of Historical Geography* 20 (1994), pp. 396–412.

Winter, J. M., *The Great War and the British People* (London: Macmillan, 1986).

Woollard, Matthew, 'The natural philosophers' (paper in the author's possession, [2000]).

Wrightson, Keith, 'Two concepts of order: justices, constables and jurymen in seventeenth-century England', in John Brewer and John Styles (eds), *An Ungovernable People: The English and their Law in the Seventeenth and Eighteenth Centuries* (London: Hutchinson, 1980), pp. 21–46.

Wrightson, Keith, *English Society, 1580–1680* (London: Hutchinson, 1982).

Wrightson, Keith, 'The social order of early modern England: three approaches', in Lloyd Bonfield, Richard M. Smith and Keith Wrightson (eds), *The World we have Gained: Histories of Population and Social Structure: Essays Presented to Peter Laslett on His Seventieth Birthday* (Oxford: Blackwell, 1986), pp. 177–202.

Wrightson, Keith, 'The politics of the parish', in P. Griffiths, Adam Fox and Steve Hindle (eds), *The Experience of Authority in Early Modern England* (Basingstoke: Palgrave Macmillan, 1996), pp. 10–46.

Wrightson, Keith and Levine, David, *Poverty and Piety in an English Village: Terling, 1525–1700* (London: Academic Press, 1979).

Wrigley, E. A. and Schofield, R. S., *The Population History of England, 1541–1871* (London: Edward Arnold, 1981).

Yates, JoAnne, *Control through Communication: The Rise of System in American Management* (Baltimore, MD: Johns Hopkins University Press, 1989).

Index